NELSON'S ANNUAL

Children's Ministry Sourcebook

2005 EDITION

NELSON'S ANNUAL

Children's Ministry Sourcebook

2005 EDITION

Vicki Wiley, Editor

NELSON REFERENCE & ELECTRONIC
A Division of Thomas Nelson Publishers
Since 1798

www.thomasnelson.com

Nelson's Annual Children's Ministry Sourcebook, 2005 Edition
Copyright © 2004 by Thomas Nelson, Inc.
Published in Nashville, Tennessee, by Thomas Nelson, Inc.

Unless otherwise indicated, Scripture quotations are from the International Children's
Bible, copyright © 1986, 1988, 1999 by Tommy Nelson™, a division of Thomas Nelson,
Inc., Nashville, Tennessee, 37214. Used by permission.

Weekly alternative versions of the memory verses, and verses marked nkjv, are from the
New King James Version, copyright © 1979, 1980, 1982, 1990 by Thomas Nelson, Inc.,
Publishers.

Book design and composition by Mark McGarry, *Texas Type & Book Works*, Dallas, Texas
Book composition *A&W Publishing Electronic Services, Inc.* Chicago, Illinois

Wiley, Vicki (ed.)
Nelson's annual children's ministry sourcebook, 2005 edition

ISBN 0-7852-5208-8

Printed in the United States of America
1 2 3 4 5 6 7 – 10 09 08 07 06 05 04

Contents

CONTENTS

CONTENTS

Preface

How can we, the children's ministry staff, help facilitate a child's early direction into a life of faith? What can we do in our ministries to be sure that each child not only enjoys their time with us, but goes home with more understanding of God's Word?

The *Children's Ministry Sourcebook* was written with these questions in mind. Using a children's sermon as the foundation of the lesson, various activities, crafts, snacks, memory verses, and enrichment ideas are suggested to help the lesson take root in the child's heart and mind. The child not only hears the story, she experiences it for herself!

Faith develops best in all of us when knowledge and experience combine. Facilitating this for our children at age-appropriate levels is the foundation for this book. Each lesson contains an easy-to-understand story from the Bible, practical applications, activities that engage the senses, crafts that lock in the main point of the lesson, helpful memory verse activities, and stimulating enrichment information.

How to Use This Book:

This book has been designed to provide flexibility for the teacher.

The 52 dated weekly segments include two main parts: The first part may be used for midweek services and *introduces* the subject for the following Sunday. The second part contains the Sunday lesson.

If you do not have a midweek program, the two parts of the lesson can be combined for one extended Children's Church time.

Each lesson contains several components, all of which work together to gently push the point of the lesson into the heart of the child. These are:

Scripture: The Bible text from which the lesson is drawn.

Lesson Aim: The "target" of the lesson, the one thing that we want them to remember and take away with them.

Bible Skill: A specific skill or concept from the Bible for children to practice.

Bible Lesson/Sermon: An age-appropriate sermon, often using everyday objects as illustrations.

Supply List: All items are listed at the beginning of the lesson.

Song Suggestions: Current and traditional songs that enhance the lesson.

Bible Learning Activity for younger children: An activity that will help the younger child remember the point of the lesson.

Bible Learning Activity for older children: An activity designed for grades 3–6 intended to engage the children with the Bible passage.

Enrichment for younger children: Information, conversation, or activity that will help the younger child more accurately grasp the lesson.

Enrichment for older children: Further background information about the passage, such as the culture, archaeology, or life and times of the people and places from the lesson.

Craft for younger children: A simple craft for younger children to create on their own that will remind them of the lesson.

Craft for older children: A take-home project for older elementary children, intended to remind them of the theme of the lesson. These crafts are made from easy-to-find materials and supplies listed at the beginning of each craft.

Snack: A lesson-related food item to make in class.

Memory Verse ICB: The memory verse from the International Children's Bible.

Memory Verse NKJV: The memory verse from the New King James Version.

Memory Verse Activity: An activity to help the children learn the memory verse.

Prayer Focus: A prayer "starter" that guides children to talk with God about the lesson. Consider incorporating children's prayer requests and praises.

Special Holiday Activities: Activities, crafts, and information that coordinate with holidays, when appropriate.

Feature Articles: Special articles written by children's ministers to help and encourage you on your journey. You will find these collected near the back of the book.

It is my prayer that the *Children's Ministry Sourcebook* will equip you with the tools you need to provide a complete year of dynamic children's worship for your congregation. May God bless you in your efforts!

—Vicki Wiley
Director of Children's Ministries
First Presbyterian Church, Honolulu

Contributors

Michael Bonner Michael is currently the Pastor of Children and Families at First Federated Church in Des Moines, Iowa. Michael has a BBA in accounting from Baylor University, an MBA in finance from Dallas Baptist University, and a MACE from Dallas Theological Seminary. He has a heart for kids and families, and has been speaking and writing on those topics for a number of years. (May 29, August 10,)

Karl Bastian has been entertaining and ministering to children around the country and around the world through puppets, magic, balloons, and other creative means since he was a kid! Karl has a bachelor's degree in Bible theology from Moody Bible Institute, is near completing a masters in children's ministry at the Trinity Evangelical Divinity School, and is on staff at the Village Church of Barrington, Illinois, as their Children's Pastor. You can find Karl at kidology.org. (March 13, March 27, April 24, May 22)

Ivy Beckwith is the Minister to Children and Families at Colonial Church of Edina, Minnesota. Ivy has served churches in Boston, Chicago, and Minnesota and holds a Ph.D. in education from Trinity International University. Ivy also has worked for two curriculum publishers as a consultant and editor. She is the author of *Postmodern Children's Ministry: Ministry to Children in the 21st Century*. (July 24, September 18, December 11, December 25)

Vic Copeland is a math and science teacher at Punaho School in Honolulu, Hawaii. He is a graduate of UCLA. Vic enjoys the outdoor life Hawaii has to offer and spends much of his time enjoying God's creation through hiking, camping, and boating. A science teacher at heart, Vic likes to use his expertise in the sciences to find interesting ways to share theological concepts with children.

Susan Harper is the founder of Caring Hands Ministries, with over 25 years' experience teaching kids and their teachers. With a rich background in teaching public school, Christian elementary school, university teacher education, and Christian conference classes, she conveys a dynamic way of learning God's Word by writing inspirational curriculum. (February 6, June 15, June 19, September 21)

Tina Houser Tina is the Minister of Children at First Church of God in Kokomo, Indiana, and has worked in children's ministry for over 20 years. She has her degree in elementary education from Indiana University and is ordained by the Church of God, Anderson, IN. For the past 14 years she has written Sunday school curriculum for Warner Press and also writes two Bible school programs each year for use by First Church. (May 11, May 18, June 8, June 29, July 3, August 7, August 31, September 7, October 5, October 12, October 19, November 16, November 23, November 30)

Mary Rice Hopkins is a singer and entertainer with a wonderful way of communicating gospel truth through songs. She is a pioneer in the field of children's Christian music and has planted seeds that will last a lifetime with her upbeat style of music. You can learn more about Mary at maryricehopkins.com (January 9, February 13, April 17)

Becky Howell has a background in Bible school and nursing. She had always planned to return to the nursing field, but children's ministry is in her heart and soul. She's a preacher's kid and has been involved with children's ministries all her life. For the last 14 years she has been the Director of Children's Ministries at Sierra Bible Church in Sonora, California. (June 22, June 26)

Arlen Nagata is Children's & Administrative Pastor at Christ's Church at Kapolei in Hawaii. He loves to connect people (both young and old) with the life-changing truths of the Bible. He especially enjoys creating and tweaking games to teach God's truth. Arlen is a graduate of Simpson College and has an M.A. from International College and Graduate School. He is married to Melissa. (September 14)

Susan Rutledge is a 26-year veteran of children's ministries and is the Children's Pastor of Hillcrest Church in Dallas, Texas. Susan is a graduate of Oklahoma State University, a writer, a teacher, a public speaker, and an inspirational "teacher of teachers," committed to sharing her years of ministry knowledge with the next generation of children's leaders. Susan was awarded the Year 2000 "Ministry of Excellence" award by the International Network of Children's Ministries. (Feature articles)

Rev. Eric J. Titus serves as pastor at the First Reformed Church in Fishkill, New York. He has a great heart for kids and enjoys finding ways to communicate

Bible stories to them so that they will understand. He holds B.A. and M.A. degrees in biblical literature from Oral Roberts University and an M.Div. from Yale University Divinity School. (January 16, February 20, April 10, July 27, July 31, October 30, November 2, November 20, December 18)

Pat Verbal is the founder of Ministry to Today's Child and an inspirational guest speaker in churches, conferences, and the media. Pat holds a master's degree in pastoral studies and is a best-selling author who served 20 years as Pastor of Children and Christian Education. (January 23, March 6, April 3, June 1, June 5, June 12, July 10, July 17, October 2, November 13)

Gordon and Becki West are popular conference speakers and writers known especially for their work in the areas of preschool ministry, preteens, and volunteer team-building. They are frequent contributors to *Children's Ministry Magazine* and *Evangelizing Today's Child*, as well as regular workshop speakers for Group's Children's Ministry Magazine Live! Workshops and the International Network of Children's Ministry's Children's Pastors' Conferences. (Feature articles)

Vicki Wiley is the Director of Children's Ministries at First Presbyterian Church in Honolulu, Hawaii. Vicki has a master's degree in theology from Fuller Seminary and has been in children's ministries for over 20 years. She loves to speak, study, and write about the faith and spiritual development of children and is on the faculty of the Bible Institute of Hawaii. (January 2, 5, 12, 19, 26, 30, February 9, 16, 23, 27, March 2, 9, 16, 23, 30, April 6, 13, 20, 27, May 5, 8, 25, July 6, 13, 20, August 3 17, 24, 28, September 4, 11, 28, October 9, 16, 23, November 2, 9, 27, December 4, 14, 21)

2005 Calendar

January 1	New Year's Day
January 2	
January 6	Epiphany
January 9	
January 16	**Sanctity of Human Life Sunday**
January 17	Martin Luther King Jr. Day
January 23	
January 26	Australia Day
January 30	
February 1–28	Black History Month
February 1	National Freedom Day
February 2	Groundhog Day
February 6	**Super Bowl Sunday**
February 9	Ash Wednesday
February 12	Lincoln's Birthday
February 13	**First Sunday of Lent**
February 14	Valentine's Day
February 20	**Second Sunday of Lent**
February 21	Presidents' Day
February 22	Washington's Birthday
February 27	**Third Sunday of Lent**
March 6	**Fourth Sunday of Lent**
March 13	**Fifth Sunday of Lent**
March 17	St. Patrick's Day
March 20	**Passion/Palm Sunday; Spring begins**

March 24	Holy Thursday
March 25	Good Friday; Purim
March 27	**Easter Sunday**
April 3	**Daylight Savings Time Begins**
April 10	
April 13	Jefferson's Birthday
April 17	
April 22	Earth Day
April 24	**Passover**
April 27	Administrative Professionals' Day
May 1	
May 5	National Day of Prayer; Ascension Day; Holocaust Remembrance Day
May 8	**Mother's Day**
May 15	**Pentecost**
May 21	Armed Forces Day
May 22	**Trinity Sunday**
May 29	
May 30	Memorial Day
June 5	
June 12	
June 14	Flag Day
June 19	**Father's Day**
June 21	Summer begins
June 26	
July 1	Canada Day
July 3	
July 4	Independence Day

July 10	
July 17	
July 24	**Parent's Day**
July 31	
August 6	Transfiguration Day
August 7	**Friendship Day**
August 14	
August 21	
August 28	
September 4	
September 5	Labor Day
September 11	**Grandparent's Day**
September 18	
September 22	Autumn begins
September 23	Native American Day
September 25	
October 1–31	Pastor Appreciation Month
October 2	
October 4	Rosh Hashanah begins
October 9	**Clergy Appreciation Day; Children's Day**
October 10	Columbus Day
October 13	Yom Kippur begins
October 16	**Bosses' Day**
October 23	
October 26	Mother-in-Law Day
October 27	Reformation Day
October 30	**Reformation Sunday; Daylight Savings Time ends**

October 31	Halloween
November 1	All Saints' Day
November 6	
November 8	Election Day
November 11	Veterans Day
November 13	**International Day of Prayer for the Persecuted Church**
November 20	
November 24	Thanksgiving Day
November 27	**First Sunday of Advent**
December 4	**Second Sunday of Advent**
December 7	Pearl Harbor Remembrance Day
December 11	**Third Sunday of Advent**
December 18	**Fourth Sunday of Advent**
December 21	Winter begins
December 24	Christmas Eve
December 25	**Christmas Day**
December 26	Hanukkah begins; Kwanzaa begins
December 31	New Year's Eve

WEEKLY SUGGESTIONS FOR 52 WEEKS

January 2, 2005

God's Mind
By Vicki Wiley

Scripture
Romans 11:33, 34

Lesson Aim
Children will realize that while we can't explain or understand God's wisdom we can know it is there.

Life Skill
Children will learn that we can trust our wise God

Bible Learning Activity for Younger Children: God Is Wise!
Needed: The following Scriptures on wisdom, copied onto strips of paper. Hide the strips throughout the classroom and let children search for them with a simple game of "you're getting hotter/colder."

While they are searching, remind them that we are searching for "wisdom" and that when we search for wisdom we can know God better. When they find the Scriptures, read them together.

"Listen to my teaching, and you will be wise" (Proverbs 8:33 ICB).

"Now I truly realize wisdom comes from God" (Job 32:7 CEV).

"Let wisdom be your sister and make common sense your closest friend" (Proverbs 7:4 CEV).

"Listen to wisdom. Try with all your heart to gain understanding" (Proverbs 2:2 ICB).

"By his wisdom and knowledge the LORD created heaven and earth" (Proverbs 3:19 CEV).

Ask: What is wisdom? What does it mean to be wise? Where does wisdom come from? These verses tell us about the wisdom of God.

Even though people may be smart or well educated, true wisdom comes only from God. How can we get true wisdom? Easy! Ask God for it!

Bible Learning Activity for Older Children: Brainy Zanie

Ask the following questions:

What's faster than any computer that has ever been invented?

What fills the top part of your head?

What part of your body looks like a soft, wrinkly, gray sponge?

What is in your head and will weigh three pounds by the time you are grown up?

It's your brain! Your brain is the organ inside your head that gives you the ability to think. It can also be called "your mind." When you think with your mind, you know what you are thinking, but other people don't know unless you tell them. So your thoughts are private, and no one else can know what they are.

It's the same with God. We can know some of God's thoughts because he tells us what they are. But we cannot know everything God is thinking, and we cannot understand everything God does.

We do know that God wants us to think like Jesus did. Philippians 2:4–5 CEV tells us to "Care about them as much as you care about yourselves and think the same way that Christ Jesus thought." Then the Bible tells us how kind and humble Jesus was.

What does the Bible teach about how your thoughts can be more like Jesus? How can you use your mind to be more like God?

Enrichment for Younger Children

Needed: A small stuffed animal.

Let children sit in a circle.

Say: We are going to play a game. One person needs to leave the room. When you come back, you will try to guess who has the hidden doggy.

Choose one child to leave the room. Give the stuffed animal to a child in the room to hide or sit on it. Tell all the children that when the "finder child" comes back in the room, they will try to help him or her find the doggy. They may not talk or point, but they may use their eyes or head movements to show where it is.

After a few rounds have been played say: Was figuring out where the dog was easy or hard? If you could know what everyone was thinking, would it be easier? But would it be fun? No! You would know where it was, and there would be no game!

God knows everything that is going to happen in your whole life, but God is not going to let you know everything that is going to happen. You have to live your life and find out each day what great plans that God has for you!

Enrichment for Older Children: Short–Term and Long–Term Memory
Needed: Poster board or heavy paper, felt-tip marker, paper, and pencil. Cut the paper into thirty rectangles. Use the felt-tip pen to mark numbers from 1 to 30 on the rectangles.

Purpose: To understand that certain parts of the brain have different functions.

Say: Did you know that the human brain contains billions of nerve cells? The brain has three parts: the cerebrum, the cerebellum, and the brain stem. Today we are going to learn how our memory works and how information stays in our short-term memory.

Have the students work in pairs. One will be the tester; the other will take the test. The tester will show a number to the test taker and then turn it upside down. The person taking the test says the number out loud. As each number is shown, the person taking the test must repeat all the numbers that came before and then add the new number.

The tester should record the number the test taker gets correct. Continue until the test taker makes a mistake. This number is the number of items the person can put into his short-term memory. Reverse roles, changing the order of numbers before you begin.

Short-term memory is important. When do we use it? To remember instructions, directions, for example. When do we use long-term memory? To remember people, things that we have learned, and other information that we will need many times.

Both of these types of memory are important to us. Wisdom that comes from God can be found in both types of memory. When we first learn something, it is in our short-term memory; but if we use that knowledge, we will remember it, and it will go to our long-term memory.

Bible Lesson: God's Mind
Pass out small pieces of paper to several children who can write.

Say: I am thinking of a number between 1 and 10. Write down what you think the number is. Let children show their answers and tell them what the number was.

Say: Did anyone guess right? (Several will have guessed right.) Great! Now, everyone write down what animal I am thinking of. (Think of an unusual animal that the children will not guess such as an aardvark or a tapir.)

Say: I was thinking of a(n) _____. Did anyone guess that? (They will all say no.) No one can read someone else's mind, but sometimes it's easy to know what someone else is thinking and what he or she wants us to do. If I pass out some cookies, you would know that I was giving you a snack and that I wanted you to eat it. If I held my finger over my lips, you would know that I wanted you to be quiet, wouldn't you?

But sometimes it isn't so easy. If I knew what was best for you, I would help you do what was best. I would help you make good decisions and good choices, but you would have to listen to me.

God's mind is like that too. God knows everything that is going to happen in the whole world, but that doesn't mean that God will tell us what is going to happen. God knows what we should know and what we shouldn't know. God is wiser than anyone on earth could ever be! No matter what, though, we do know one thing: God always wants the best for us!

The Bible talks about how wise God is. God doesn't need to try to guess anything because He knows everything. Someday you might pray for something that you really think would be good for you, but God might not give it to you. That's because God knows what is best for you. God is wise, and God makes the best decisions.

God is wise, and God will give you the right instructions. God will help you make good choices. Sometimes God speaks through your conscience, and sometimes you know what God wants by reading the Bible. God has many ways to speak to us; we just need to learn to listen to our very wise God.

♪ Song Suggestions

Believin' On by Jana Alayra from "Believin' On" (Montjoy Music 2002)

Little Is Much by Mary Rice Hopkins from "15 Singable Songs" (Big Steps 4 U 1988)

Faith Will Do by Dean-o from "You Got It All" (FKO Music, Inc. 1997)

God's Power Songsheets published by CEF Press, P.O. Box 348, Warrenton, Mo. 63383

Craft for Younger Children: Wise Choices

Needed: Paper plates, paste, magazine pictures of foods including good healthy foods and junk foods.

Say: One of the choices you can make is what you are going to eat. Let's look at these pictures and choose good foods. Paste the good foods on your plates.

Let children decide which foods are healthy. Make gentle comments about their choices and let them paste the pictures onto their plates.

 Craft for Older Children: Wisdom of God

Needed: One sheet of construction paper per child, markers. Write across the top of the paper "God's Wisdom and Riches."

Ask: How does God show that he is wise? (He made us. He made beautiful flowers.) What are the "riches" of God? (beautiful sunsets, everything in the whole world!)

Let's draw a picture of the wisdom and riches of God.

Draw whatever you think it would look like. God has more wisdom and riches than any person can ever have!

Snack: Brainy Food

Needed: Two platters—one with cookies on it and one with fruits and vegetables on it. Show both platters to the children.

Ask: Which one of these platters has the healthiest food on it? Which snacks would you like to choose? Which snacks would help your brain? Which foods would be wise to eat?

Discuss and let children eat the foods that they choose.

Memory Verse: Romans 11:33 ICB

Yes, God's riches are very great! God's wisdom and knowledge have no end! No one can explain the things God decides. No one can understand God's ways.

Alternate Version (New King James)
Oh, the depth of the riches both of the wisdom and knowledge of God! How unsearchable are His judgments and His ways past finding out!

Memory Verse Activity
Write the verse on a white board. Have children say the verse together. Erase the following words and let the children help to draw a picture to represent the word:

         riches   wisdom   no one   God   understand   ways

   Say the verse again together and repeat it until children can say it without reading it.

Prayer Focus
Dear God, you are a wise God, and you have so much knowledge! No one can ever know how much! We love you, and we praise you, for you alone understand everything about yourself. Amen.

January 5, 2005

Everybody Has a Body, Midweek
By Vicki Wiley

Scripture
Psalm 133

Lesson Aim
Children will learn that God desires that all his people love one another.

Life Skill
We are all needed and important in the body of Christ.

Bible Learning Activity for Younger Children: Flower Power
Needed: Flower with stem and leaves attached.

Show flower to children.

Say: This is a beautiful flower. Which is the most important part of the flower? (Let children discuss.)

All the parts of the flower are important. The pretty petals would not even be here without the stem; the leaves bring the sun to the plant. All parts are equally important.

It's the same with the church. All of us have an important job to do, and when we do it, the church will be healthy, just like this flower. This flower will grow when all the parts of it are healthy. When God's people live together in peace, the Bible tells us that "it is good and pleasant" (Ps. 133:1 ICB).

Bible Learning Activity for Older Children: It's What's Inside
Needed: One ballpoint pen (Before class, take the pen apart and remove the spring. Put the pen back together and keep the spring available.)

Show the pen to the children and say: This is a pen. Which part of the pen is the most important? (Children will probably say the ink.) What would you do without the ink? (Let children answer.)

OK, here is a pen with the ink. Samuel, can you show us how it works? (Let him try, but it probably will not work. Let other children try. Take their comments on why it is not working.)

Actually, the reason this pen is not working is because it is missing a part. It may seem like very small part, but as you can see, the pen can't work without it. Does anyone know what it might be? The spring!

Insert the spring back into the pen, and let a few children try the pen.

This kind of pen needs all of its parts to be able to write. Some parts may seem important, like the ink, while others may seem unimportant, like the spring, but all of the parts are needed.

The Bible tells us that everyone in the church is important, too. Some people or some jobs may seem unimportant, but the church would not be complete without them. For us to all work together in unity, we must understand that we all have a job to do and that all the jobs are important.

Enrichment for Younger Children: Heads, Shoulders, Knees, and Toes
Have children stand up and lead them in the song "Heads, Shoulders, Knees, and Toes" while they perform the actions.

The second time through, skip the shoulders. Let the children tell you that you missed something. Pretend to be surprised.

The third time skip the toes. Again act surprised. Say: What difference would it make it we didn't have shoulders? Why do we need our toes? Let children respond.

We need all the parts of the body, don't we? It's the same with the body of Christ, or the church. The church needs everyone to be a complete body of Christ!

Enrichment for Older Children: Missing Body Pieces!

Needed: Posterboard with body shape drawn on it. (Simple shape is great!)

Cut the posterboard into puzzle type pieces, with a body part in each piece (Eyes are one piece, ears one piece, arms one piece, etc.)

Hand one piece to each child.

Say: Which one of these pieces of the body is most important? (Let children discuss.)

Let children put the puzzle together and discuss what would happen without each piece. The body would not be complete!

Say: Each piece of our body is important, isn't it? It's the same with the body of Christ. We need each piece of the body or each person in the church to have a complete body.

Memory Verse: Psalm 133:1 ICB

It is good and pleasant when God's people live together in peace!

Alternate Version (New King James)
Behold, how good and how pleasant it is for brethren to dwell together in unity!

Everybody Has a Body
By Mary Rice Hopkins

Scripture
Psalm 133

Lesson Aim
Children will learn that God wants all his people to love one another.

Life Skill
We are all needed and important in the body of Christ.

Bible Lesson: Everybody Has a Body
Needed: Chenille wire people (bend chenille wire to form several human shapes) or people shapes cut from paper.

Did you know that you are part of a very big family? (Show many people shapes.) Your family has more people in it than this! (Kids will object!)

What, you don't have this many in your family? You only have one brother? You only have one sister? What? No, really, your family is this big!

The family I am talking about is the family of God. Your mom and dad, sisters, cousins, brothers, and aunts and uncles are part of your family. But in God's family your friends who know the Lord are your family too. Those who know Jesus, even people you have never met, are part of the family of God. In fact, all of you (point to all the kids) are in the same family, the family of God!

In your family, do you all have chores to do? Who takes out the trash? Who makes the bed? Who cooks the dinner?

In God's family each person has a job to do too. The Bible says that some of you might be a foot in the body of Christ; maybe you will be a missionary and carry the gospel to another country. Or maybe you are a hand who helps your neighbor. Maybe you are a mouth that has the gift of singing or preaching in the family of God.

Even though we do different things, we are all important, and we all work together. You all have eyes, don't you? Well, the eye can see, but it can't think. The eyes can see, but they cannot hear. We need our ears, our eyes, and our brains—every single part of us!

The Bible says, "All of you together are the body of Christ. Each one of you is a part of that body" (1 Cor. 12:27 ICB). God made us each different so that the family of God would be complete. Now each time you do something in the church, you will know that you are helping the family of God and the body of Christ!

Pass out the chenille or paper people so that each child can have one.

 Song Suggestions

The Family of God by Kurt Johnson, a.k.a. MrJ from "Kid Possible" (Kurt Johnson 1995)

No One Else I Know by Mary Rice Hopkins from "15 Singable Songs" (Big Steps 4 U 1988)

This Is Love by Dean-o from "God City" (BibleBeat Music, 2001)

What a Mighty God We Serve Songsheets published by CEF, P.O. Box 348, Warrenton, Mo. 63383

 Craft for Younger Children: Life-size Me!
Needed: Butcher paper, fabric scraps, markers, yarn for hair.

Let children lie down on butcher paper while you trace around them. Let children decorate "themselves" with fabric, markers, and other items.

Say: God made you just the way you are! Look, she has blond hair, and he has black hair. She has blue eyes, and he has brown eyes. Aren't you glad God made you just the way you are?

Craft for Older Children: Silhouettes
Needed: White and black paper, flashlight, pen, scissors.

Tape a large piece of paper to the wall. Have the child stand or sit sideways next to the paper. In a darkened room shine the flashlight on the child so the child's profile is shadowed on the paper. Trace around the shadow. Cut out the profile and mount it on black piece of paper.

Say: A silhouette is a different kind of picture of you. It's a picture without the details. You can't tell what color your hair is or what color your eyes are in a silhouette. But you might be able to tell who it is.

Let children guess who the silhouettes are. It's kind of hard to tell, isn't it? Aren't you glad that God made us with special details—our eyes, hair, smiles, and everything else that makes us special in God's family!

Snack: People Cookies!

 Needed: People-shaped cookies.

Pass out cookies to children.

Ask: How many of you look just like these cookies? That's right! None of you do! What do these cookies really look like? Yes, you're right (cartoon people, gingerbread men, for example). No one looks like these cookies, and you know what else? No one in this class looks like anybody else in this class, either! (Unless you have twins, and even they are not exactly alike.)

That's how it is in the church. Even though none of us look alike, we are alike because we all love God and we love Jesus. Even though we are different from one another, we all work together because we want the same thing: we all want to go to heaven and take other people with us!

Memory Verse: Psalm 133:1 ICB
It is good and pleasant when God's people live together in peace!

Alternate Version (New King James)
Behold, how good and how pleasant it is for brethren to dwell together in unity!

Memory Verse Activity: Rhyme and Chant
Lead children in this rhyme and chant.
  It is good. (Children echo, It is good.)
  It is pleasant. (It is pleasant.)
  When God's people (When God's people)
  Live together in peace! (Live together in peace!)
  Psalm 133:1 (Psalm 133:1)

Prayer Focus
Dear God, we thank you, and we praise you for making us who we are. We want to learn to work together in peace just as you want us to do. Help us love one another and become a loving family of God. Amen.

January 12, 2005

Sharing "Good News," Midweek
By Vicki Wiley

Scripture
2 Kings 6:24—7:11, especially 7:9

Lesson Aim
To help children understand that good news (especially about God) is to be shared.

Life Skill
Children will know how to share good news.

Bible Learning Activity for Younger Children: Good News Relay
Divide children into two teams,

Say: What do you do when you get good news? (I tell my mom. I tell my friends. I e-mail grandpa.)

We like to share good news because we are so excited about it. We are going to play a game about sharing good news.

Place half the team on each side of the room. Give this message to the first child in each line: The Bible says for us to share the good news.

Have them run down to their team on the opposite side of the room and tell the next child the news. Continue this game until all children have had a turn.

Ask: What is the good news? Let children answer. Correct any wrong information. Sometimes good news gets mixed up, doesn't it? Good news is supposed to be shared, and when we get good news, we should share it!

Bible Learning Activity for Older Children: Can You Hear Me Now?
Play a typical game of telephone with the children. Line the children up and

tell them that you are going to give a telephone message to the first child. Then each child will in turn tell the next child until all children have the message. Let the child at the end tell the message and compare what he or she says to the original message.

The message will be, "The Bible says for us to share the good news."

Say: What is the good news that the Bible talks about? Let children answer any way that they like, but direct them to the answer: Jesus is born.

How was the good news shared when Jesus was born? (Angels announced it. A star appeared.) How do we tell good news that happens to us? (Let children discuss answers.)

We should always share good news. It's another way to tell people what God is doing in our lives!

Enrichment for Younger Children: Telephone!

Needed: Two empty cans, string, something to punch a hole.

String two cans together by punching a hole in the bottom of each can and threading string through the holes. Let children stand about twenty feet apart and try to talk to each other.

Say: Our real telephones are much better than this, aren't they? It's hard to hear what someone is saying through a phone like this.

What if you had just received some really good news and you wanted to share it with your friend. Would you want to use a phone like this? No! You would want to be able to talk in person or use a real phone.

Whenever we have good news to share, we want to be sure people hear what we have to say. Sharing our good news is very important!

Enrichment for Older Children: Leprosy

Leprosy is talked about in the Bible. What is it? It is an incurable skin disease.

There are several types of leprosy. Biblical leprosy was most likely a severe type of psoriasis or a rash that is rare in modern times. It is an infectious disease characterized by sores, scabs, and white shining spots beneath the skin. The people did not have a medicine to treat this disease.

If the symptoms of leprosy showed up on a person, the priest was to decide if this was leprosy or some other disease. Because of the need to control the spread of a disease for which there was no cure, the law required that a leper be isolated from the rest of society (Lev. 13:45–46). People who had leprosy were called lepers, and they were required to wear mourning clothes, leave their hair in disorder, and cry, "Unclean! Unclean!" so everyone could avoid them.

When people were healed from leprosy, they were so excited that they told everyone the good news! When God heals people, they can be so excited that they want to share their good news, which is what these people wanted to do. Good news, especially about what God has done for us, is meant to be shared!

Memory Verse: 2 Kings 7:9 ICB
Then they said to each other, "We're doing wrong. Today we have good news, but we are silent. If we wait until the sun comes up, we'll be punished. Let's go now and tell the people in the king's palace."

Alternate Version (New King James)
Then they said to one another, "We are not doing right. This day is a day of good news, and we remain silent. If we wait until morning light, some punishment will come upon us. Now therefore, come, let us go and tell the king's household."

January 16, 2005

(Special activity: Martin Luther King Day)

Sharing "Good News"
By Eric Titus

Scripture
2 Kings 7:9

Lesson Aim
To help children understand that good news (especially about God) is to be shared.

Life Skill
Children will know how to share good news.

Bible Lesson: Sharing Good News
Needed: Two security envelopes, money (play or real), and a letter opener. You are going to make a "gimmicked" envelope so that it can be shown empty first and then full a moment later. To do this, take one envelope and cut away the front and both sides leaving only the back leaf of the envelope (the leaf with the sealing flap). From the leaf you will need to trim the slightest amount from the sides of the lower portion and perhaps a bit from the bottom side. What you want here is for this leaf of the first envelope to fit snuggly inside the second envelope to create a false back. Place your money inside and use the sealed flap from the full envelope to secure the false insert. Now when you show the envelope, it will appear empty.

The book of 2 Kings tells some of the history of God and the people of Israel, especially about Israel's kings. One story in 2 Kings starts sad and ends happy. The people of Israel were poor. They had nothing—no money, no food. Their lives were as empty as this envelope. (Show the envelope to be empty. Let the children look inside, and then seal the flap to the front of the envelope, and keep the envelope in their sight the entire time.) Think for just a minute about what it would be like to have no money, not much food, and on top of that to be cold. The people of Israel had to do some sad things just to stay alive. This made the king of Israel sad too.

What the people needed was for someone to tell them some good news. When you're feeling sad, doesn't it make you feel better to hear some good news? A messenger of God named Elisha brought the king good news. He told the king that there would be plenty of money and food the very next day! If you were the king, would you have believed Elisha? Maybe it would have been hard to believe the good news, and the king didn't.

Then four men who had a bad disease called leprosy walked out of the city into a camp where Israel's enemies were staying and waiting to attack Israel. All sorts of strange things started happening. The enemies thought they heard a whole army coming, when it was just four sick men! The enemies ran out of the camp and left food and money, lots of it! There was enough for everyone.

The men talked back and forth about what to do. They finally decided to tell the king. (Ask a child to come up and stand by you, open the envelope with the letter opener, this will open up the "secret compartment" of your envelope revealing the money. Allow only child to see it.) Do you think the king believed their good news? (Ask the child to share with the others what he or she saw in the envelope). Do you believe _____'s good news? Do you believe there is money in this empty envelope? The king didn't believe, but the people of Israel did. Was it important for the sick men to share their message of good news even though some wouldn't believe it? Of course it was.

When something good happens to you or you learn something wonderful, you want to share it like Elisha did, and like these four men did, and like _____ did. You want to know something. (Show the full envelope to the children.) The envelope was full!

One of the best things we know about as Christians is the good news that God loves us and sent Jesus to give us lives that are full of hope and love because he died for all the wrong we have done. We should share the message of God's love with everyone. Some won't believe, like the king; some will, like the people of Israel. Either way we should share our good news with everyone.

Prayer Focus
Dear God, thank you for good news. Thank you especially for the good news that Jesus loves us. Help us to share the good news of your love with everyone we know. Amen.

Song Suggestions

He Is Really God! by Dean-o from "You Got It All" (FKO Music, Inc. 1997)

Superman by Mary Rice Hopkins from "15 Singable Songs" (Big Steps 4 U 1988)

My Very Best Friend by Cindy Rethmeier from "I Want 2 Be Like Jesus" (Mercy/Vineyard Publishing 1995)

Holy, Holy, Holy traditional hymn (words included in activity)

 Craft for Younger Children: Good News Sharing

Needed: Construction paper, markers.

Say: What is the best way to share good news? (by phone, talking, e-mailing, newspapers, television)

Let children draw a picture of how they get good news.

 Craft for Older Children: Good Newspaper!

Needed: Newspapers, construction paper, glue, pens.

Say: Good news is so important! The best news in the whole world is that Jesus is our Savior. What other good news has your family had recently? (We moved. We have a new car. I have a baby sister.)

Let's look at these newspapers and find some good news. Let children find news stories and cut them out.

Let's make our own newspapers. Show children how to put the news stories that they cut out along with stories of the good news that they can write themselves. Create a "good news paper."

Snack: Shouting the Good News!

Needed: Bugle-shaped corn snacks, juice.

Say: Sometimes we want everyone to know our good news, and the news is shouted through megaphones that look something like this. Let children eat the snacks as you discuss ways to tell really good news to other people.

Memory Verse: 2 Kings 7:9 ICB

Then they said to each other, "We're doing wrong. Today we have good news, but we are silent. If we wait until the sun comes up, we'll be punished. Let's go now and tell the people in the king's palace."

Alternate Version (New King James)

Then they said to one another, "We are not doing right. This day is a day of good news, and we remain silent. If we wait until morning light, some punishment will come upon us. Now therefore, come, let us go and tell the king's household."

Memory Verse Activity: Erase the Verse!

Needed: Whiteboard and markers.

Write the verse on the board and read it to the kids. Have them say the verse with you. Erase a section of the verse and say it again. Erase another section and repeat the verse over and over again.

Prayer Focus

Dear God, thank you for the best news of all: that you sent your Son to be the Savior to the world! Please help us to know how to share that good news with everyone we know. Amen.

Martin Luther King Junior Day Craft: Unity Wreath
Needed: Construction paper in different skin-tone colors, paper plate cut into wreath. (Cut two-inch border from edge of paper plate forming a two-inch circle.) Let children choose which paper color is closest to their own. Cut out their handprints from the paper. Cut one handprint for each child in the room.

Let children pass out their handprints and paste them onto the wreath, forming a wreath of different colored handprints.

Say: Tomorrow is Martin Luther King Jr. Day. Martin Luther King Jr. tried to help people. He wanted people to feel that they were free, and he wanted people to love one another, no matter what race they were or what color their skin was. We will make this wreath to remember him today.

January 19, 2005

Switching Places, Midweek
By Vicki Wiley

Scripture
Ephesians 4:32

Lesson Aim
Children will discover that others deserve to be forgiven simply because Jesus forgives them.

Life Skill
Children will put themselves in another person's place and feel his or her hurt.

Bible Learning Activity for Younger Children
Ask children to stand up and show you what these movements mean:
   What does *deep* mean?
   What does *wide* mean"
   What about *high*?
   What about *long*?
   If something was deep and wide, high and long, it would be huge, wouldn't it? That's what the Bible says about God. Ephesians 3:18 says that God's love is so great that God always forgives us when we do something wrong. "And I pray that you and all God's holy people will have the power to understand the greatness of Christ's love... how wide and how long and how high and how deep that love is" (Eph. 3:18 ICB).

Bible Learning Activity for Older Children
Needed: Whiteboard or large paper.
   Make two columns. At the top of the board, write: God forgives. We forgive.

Let children fill in the lists with things we do that God forgives us and the things we forgive others for doing. After writing the lists, say: Is it easier for God to forgive us or for us to forgive others? What kinds of things are hard for us to forgive? Is anything hard for God to forgive?

God forgives us for whatever we do. We need to learn to forgive others for whatever they do to us too!

Enrichment for Younger Children:
Needed: A large wrapped package that is empty except for a piece of paper with *forgiveness* written on it.

Show the present to children. Ask: What do you think is in this present? After a few guesses let children unwrap while you are saying:

It is something God gives us.

It is something we give others.

It is always free!

When children unwrap the present, let everyone see what is inside. Yes! It's forgiveness!

Enrichment for Older Children
Needed: Six two-liter bottles, rings to throw at them that are large enough to circle the top easily. Set up a game of ring toss.

Say: We are going to play ring toss. If you are able to throw the ring around the bottle, you will get a piece of candy (or a nickel).

As the children participate, reward them regardless of whether they circle the bottle or not. Wait for reactions from the kids.

Ask: What was it like to get rewarded? Was it fair? How did you feel when you received a gift you did not deserve?

Forgiveness is like that. God gives us forgiveness whether or not we deserve it!

Optional Activity: Save Nathan from the Doghouse

Write a note back to Nathan. Tell him what he should do about his problem. Will running away help him? Have you ever felt like Nathan? What did you do?

Most children feel like running away at some time or another. The fact is every day more than three thousand kids do leave home. Many of them live on the streets and get involved in drugs and gangs. Pride and unforgiveness are often the reasons kids feel they can't go home again.

Memory Verse: Ephesians 4:32 ICB

Be kind and loving to each other. Forgive each other just as God forgave you in Christ.

Alternate Version (New King James)

And be kind to one another, tenderhearted, forgiving one another, even as God in Christ forgave you.

January 23, 2005

Switching Places
By Pat Verbal

Scripture
Ephesians 4:32

Lesson Aim
Children will discover that others deserve to be forgiven simply because Jesus forgives them.

Life Skill
Children will put themselves in someone else's place and feel his or her hurt.

Bible Lesson
Needed: Bring a book on dog training to class. Ask students ahead of time to bring pictures of their pets.

Open with these questions: What do you like best about your pet? Has your pet ever done anything wrong? Like chewing up a favorite shoe or CD? Or messing up the carpet with muddy paws? It's easy for people to get mad at a dog or cat, but it is hard to stay mad. Why? Because we assume our pets really want to please us, and they don't understand everything. They are only animals.

It's a different story when it comes to forgiving someone who has hurt us. When that someone is a parent, life can get confusing. Nathan wrote the following letter to his youth pastor.

> Dear Pastor Sam,
> I'm moving out of my room and moving in with my dog. I would rather sleep in a doghouse than keep fighting with my mom and dad. They are always mad and I'm sick of the yelling. You can visit me in the little green house behind our garage.
> Nathan

What advice would you give Nathan?

Maybe you've seen the movie *Freaky Friday*. It's a funny story of a mother and daughter who magically change places. In doing so, they discover a lot about one another's lives. They get a whole new picture of why each one acts the way she does, and as a result the two grew to be good friends. A "Freaky Friday" might help at Nathan's house. A big part of getting along as a family is trying to understand where each person is coming from and why they feel the way they do. Most parents are trying to do their best. After all, they are only human!

If you were your mom or dad for one day, what kind of things would you do? Let's write a time schedule on the whiteboard. (Let children call out parental chores from sunup to sundown.) Looking at this list helps us see why parents can sometimes get tired and grouchy.

When that happens, Ephesians 4:32 reminds us how important forgiveness is, but it's not easy. We can only do what this verse says with God's help.

The best example we have of a "Freaky Friday" is in the story of Jesus. God came to earth in a human body through his Son, Jesus (Luke 1:35; John 1:12). Jesus was a baby, a child, and a man. He even died in our place on what we call Good Friday (1 Cor. 15:3). He knows everything we think and feel. He knows why parents do the things they do. Because he forgives us, he can ask us to forgive others. Because God is kind to us, he can ask us to be kind to others.

 Song Suggestions

Did You Ever Talk to God Above Songsheets published by CEF Press, P.O. Box 348, Warrenton, Mo. 63383

Purest of Gold by Kurt Johnson, a.k.a. MrJ from "Pure Gold" (Mr. J Music 1995)

Believe His Promises by Dean-o from "Soul Surfin" (FKO Music, Inc. 1999)

Do Not Fear by John J. D. Modica from "Ablaze with Praise" (Revelation Generation Music 2000)

Craft for Younger Children: My Heart
Needed: Small heart for each child out of craft foam with hole punched in top of each heart, cord for necklace.

Show children how to make a heart necklace. Let them add beads if desired.

Say: God wants us to have a loving and forgiving heart. What do you think that means? Let children respond. God treats us that way too. God forgives and loves us. We can remember how much God loves us by looking at our heart necklaces.

 Craft for Older Children: Forgiving Heart
Needed: One poster board heart (at least six inches) and piece of clear contact type sticky paper for each child, dry-erase markers.

Show children how to cut out hearts from poster board and how to carefully put sticky, clear contact type paper on top of the heart. Trim edges.

Wrong things that we do are called sins. Let's write the wrong things that we do on our hearts. Let children write them on their heats with the dry-erase markers.

Say: When you ask God to forgive you for the wrong things you do, he wipes them away. Show children how to wipe away what they have written.

Whenever you have done something wrong, you can write it on this heart. Then pray and ask God to forgive you before you wipe it away!

Snack: White as Snow

 Needed: Vanilla ice cream and marshmallow topping, whipped cream, bowls, spoons, and napkins.

Say: The Bible says that when God forgives us, he makes us clean. God says that when we're forgiven, we're so clean that we're as white as snow. Let's eat a white snack that will remind us how clean we are when God forgives us.

Let children make ice cream sundaes with the white toppings and ice cream.

Memory Verse: Ephesians 4:32 ICB

Be kind and loving to each other. Forgive each other just as God forgave you in Christ.

Alternate Version (New King James)
And be kind to one another, tenderhearted, forgiving one another, even as God in Christ forgave you.

Memory Verse Activity

Needed: Craft sticks (8 sticks for each set).

For each set of memory verse sticks, write the following phrases on the sticks, one phrase on each stick:

Be kind	to each other	just as God	forgave you
and loving	Forgive	each other	in Christ.

Pass out one set of sticks to each group of four children. Place the sticks face down on the table. Let them turn sticks over and place the sticks in the right order. Say the verse together.

Prayer Focus

Dear God, thank you for forgiving us. Please help us to learn to forgive other people. Amen.

January 26, 2005

The Lord Stretches Us Through Difficulty, Midweek
By Vicki Wiley

Scripture
Deuteronomy 32:4

Lesson Aim
Children will learn that God is fair and gives us security.

Life Skill
Children will understand that God is always fair even when life is not.

Bible Learning Activity for Younger Children: God Is Fair!
Needed: Jelly beans or other candy that comes in several colors.

Ask: What is "fair"? When is something "not fair"? We are going to play a game, and you can tell me if it is fair or not fair.

Randomly pass out six candies to each child. Pay no attention to the color of the candy. When you are finished, do the following actions:

Say: Everyone give back their red candy.

Everyone give the person on their right all their green candy.

Everyone can eat their blue candy.

Ask: Is this game fair? (You will get many reasons why it is not fair. Listen to all the reasons.)

This game wasn't fair at all. Many things that happen to us don't seem fair either. But there is One who is fair. He is always fair, and at the same time he wants the very best for us. Who is it? You guessed it. The answer is God!

Hebrews 6:10 ICB says that God is fair: "God is fair. He will not forget the work you did and the love you showed for him by helping his people. And he will remember that you are still helping them."

Bible Learning Activity for Older Children: God Is Like a Rock
Needed: Rocks of many different sizes and shapes.

Show children the rocks and talk about each one. Which is largest, smallest, prettiest? Ask: What do you think of when you look at these rocks? Why do you think the Bible says that God is like a rock? How could God be like a rock?

On a white board, make two lists: one with the heading "God" and one with the heading "Rock." Let children make lists of the characteristics of each. Compare the lists to try to find how God is like a rock. Ideas might include: God is strong. God is everywhere. God is close to us like these rocks we can hold and far away like cliffs. We can touch God like we can touch these rocks, but rocks can also be huge like God is.

Enrichment for Younger Children: Rocks! Rocks!
Needed: A variety of rocks for children to examine.
Show children the rocks and let them comment on them.
Ask: Which is the prettiest? Biggest? Smallest? Hardest?
Say: I wonder why the Bible says that God is like a rock? Let children discuss their ideas.

Enrichment for Older Children: Rocks and Science
Needed: Rocks of many different sizes and shapes, a copper penny, a steel file, a piece of glass, a magnifying glass, and a notebook or piece of paper.

To understand how rocks are an important part of God's creation, begin by having children observe the rocks. Choose four rocks and write down a description of each including color, texture, and other qualities. Test rocks for hardness. Give it the following point values:
If you can scratch it with your finger, 2.5 points.
If you can scratch it with the penny, 3.5 points.
If you can scratch it with the steel file, 7.5 points.
If you can scratch it with the piece of glass, 5.5 points.
With this data conclude which rock is the hardest. Rocks are strong; diamonds are the strongest rocks.

Discuss: What did you learn about rocks to help you understand why the Scripture says, "God is like a rock"? What else did you learn about rocks? What can science teach us about rocks and God?

Memory Verse: Deuteronomy 32:4 ICB

He is like a rock. What he does is perfect. He is always fair. He is a faithful God who does no wrong. He is right and fair.

Alternate Version (New King James)
He is the Rock, His work is perfect; for all His ways are justice, a God of truth and without injustice; righteous and upright is He.

January 30, 2005

The Lord Stretches Us Through Difficulty
By Vicki Wiley

Scripture
Deuteronomy 32:4

Lesson Aim
Children will learn that God is fair and gives us security.

Life Skill
Children will understand that God is always fair even when life is not.

Bible Lesson: From Bad to Good
Needed: Striped towel with several colors on it, Silly Putty.

Show the towel to kids and say: Do you know what this towel reminds me of? There is a story in the Bible about a boy named Joseph. Do you remember hearing about him? What do you remember?

Joseph had some things happen to him that weren't fair at all. Have you ever had something happen to you that wasn't fair? The Bible tells us that one day Joseph's brothers threw him into a pit in the ground and then pretended that he was dead. Then they sold him to some people looking for some slaves. He became a slave, which is bad enough, but that wasn't all!

Next, Joseph was falsely accused of doing something wrong and put into jail when he was innocent! He was in jail for a long time. But God never forgot about Joseph. God knew that Joseph was good, and God changed all the bad that happened to good. Because Joseph believed in God and did what was right, God took all the bad things that happened and turned them all into good things.

Because Joseph was in Egypt and because he was in charge of all the food in Egypt, he was able to save his entire family from starvation. God used the fact that Joseph was right there at the right time to save the nation of Israel.

God does the same thing in our lives today. Whenever bad things happen—whenever we go through bad times, make bad decisions, have bad things happen to us—God is there. God cares and God changes the bad to good.

Show Silly Putty. This is play putty. Right now it fits nicely inside this egg, doesn't it? But we can also stretch it out. When we stretch it out, it doesn't fit anymore, does it? But it is still play putty, and if we mold it again, it will go back into the egg. It isn't quite the same as it was before, but it goes back in.

When bad things happen, we have to be stretched out. That means we might not feel the same for a while (like the play putty didn't look the same), but we really are the same. The difference is that when we are stretched by God, we become better!

 Song Suggestions

He's Got Plans by Dean-o from "Soul Surfin'" (FKO Music, Inc. 1999)

I Do Believe by Jana Alayra from "Dig Down Deep" (Montjoy Music 1997)

Grow Me Up Like You by Mary Rice Hopkins from "Come on Home" (Big Steps 4 U 2002)

More Precious than Silver Songsheets published by CEF Press, P.O. Box 348, Warrenton, Mo. 63383

 Craft for Younger Children: Stretchy Slime

Needed: Borax, white glue, paper cup, food coloring. Make the following slime for the children. Put 2 tablespoons of plain white glue into a paper cup. Add 1 or 2 drops of food coloring if desired. Stir in about 2 teaspoons of borax (found in laundry aisle of supermarket). Mix together until slime has formed. Knead the slime to make it a consistent texture. If the slime is too sticky, you can add a little more borax. If it is way too slippery, you can add more 50/50 glue.

Craft for Older Children: Stretchy Slime!
Using the above recipe, let children make the slime and experiment with stretching it. Ask: How do you know that this is stretchy? What else is sretchy? If something is called stretchy, what does that mean?

Sometimes we say that "God stretches us." What could that mean? Does God really pull our arms and stretch us? No, of course not! When God stretches us, it means that he wants us to do things we have never done before. Just as the slime is small now (roll it into ball) and long now (pull it into long rope), we are stretching it into shapes that it hasn't been in before. God does that to us too.

Maybe God wants you to be friends with someone you didn't like before; that's one way to be stretched. Maybe God wants you to tell someone about him, and you don't think you are good at that; that is another way to stretch you. God will stretch you in many ways all your life; and it will always help you!

Snack: Stretchy Snack

Needed: One fruit roll snack per two children.

Let each pair of children have one fruit roll snack. Let children hold each end and stretch it until it breaks.

Say: Did this break in half? (No. Let children show their pieces.) If each of you had the part that you got when it broke, would it be fair? If we divided it equally, would it be more fair?

When God stretches us, it might not seem fair or good. But God always turns the bad to good. When things in your life seems unfair, you can remember that the Bible teaches us that God is fair.

Let children redivide the fruit roll so that each has an equal portion, and then they can eat it!

Memory Verse: Deuteronomy 32:4 ICB

He is like a rock. What he does is perfect. He is always fair. He is a faithful God who does no wrong. He is right and fair.

Alternate Version (New King James)
He is the Rock, His work is perfect; for all His ways are justice, a God of truth and without injustice; righteous and upright is He.

Memory Verse Activity
Write the verse on a whiteboard so that all children can see the words. Divide kids into six groups and assign words to say as follows:

Group 1   He is like a rock.
Group 2   What he does is perfect.
Group 3   He is always fair.
Group 4   He is a faithful God
Group 5   who does no wrong.
Group 6   He is right and fair.

Let groups stand, say their part of the verse, and sit down before the next group stands to say their part. Continue until the verse is memorized.

Prayer Focus
God, we thank you because we know that you are fair. We know that you do everything with love for us. Amen.

February 2, 2005

Let Me Help You! Midweek
By Susan Harper

Scripture
Matthew 20:29–34

Lesson Aim
Children will understand what compassion is.

Life Skill
Children will realize that God is full of compassion and will always help us.

Bible Learning Activity for Younger Children
Needed: An 11-inch x 17-inch piece of paper and markers for each child. Before class cut each sheet of paper in the shape of a heart.

Ask: When do you feel that you need lots of help? When do you feel that you are helpless? (When I am sick. When something is too hard for me.)

Have each child draw a picture of how God helps them when they feel helpless.

Bible Learning Activity for Older Children: Blind Man's Touch
Choose one player to be "it." Have all players except "it" roam around the room with their eyes shut. "It" will walk around the room with his eyes open. Have him or her touch each of the other players one at a time saying, "He touched their eyes, and at once they could see." Have the player touched open his eyes and say, "Then they followed Jesus," and follow "it" as he or she touches another player. Continue this until all of the players have been touched.

Alternate Idea: Let Me Help Relay

Needed: Gauze squares, ointment, tape, icepacks, scarves, and blankets.

Divide the class in two to four teams. Have one player on each team be the patient and lie down on the other side of the room. Have all of the players except the patient line up on one side of the room.

Give the first player in line the ointment, the second player the gauze, the third the tape, the fourth a scarf to put around the patient's head, the fifth an icepack, the sixth a scarf to make a sling, and the seventh a blanket.

On "go," the first player on each team runs to the patient and puts ointment on his arm. He runs back to his team and tags the second player who runs to the patient and applies the gauze square over the ointment. She runs back to her team and tags the third player who applies the tape to the gauze square. Continue the relay until all of the players have helped the patient with the item in their hand. The team to complete the relay first wins.

Enrichment for Younger Children: Handprints of Compassion

Needed: One piece of construction paper and markers for each child.

Show children how to trace their hand on a sheet of paper and cut it out. Help them think of five ways they can help others (show compassion) and draw a picture about it on each finger.

Alternate Idea

Have them write the names of five people they can help on the fingers of their paper hand. (Mommy, Daddy, sister, brother, friend)

Memory Verse: Matthew 20:34 ICB

He touched their eyes, and at once they were able to see. Then the men followed Jesus.

Alternate Version (New King James)

So Jesus had compassion and touched their eyes. And immediately their eyes received sight, and they followed Him.

February 6, 2005

Let Me Help You!
By Susan Harper

Scripture
Matthew 20:29–34

Lesson Aim
Children will understand what compassion is.

Life Skill
Children will realize that God is full of compassion and will always help us.

Bible Lesson: Let Me Help You!
Needed: A large basket with a towel covering up what you have in the basket. In the basket place bandages, ointment, and tape; a container of soup, crackers, and a bottle of water; and a small game. Gather the children together as if you are in a hurry.

Say: I am sorry I am in such a hurry! I am on my way to help someone who is hurt. Maybe you can help make sure I have everything I need to help him feel better! (Show the children your basket.) His mommy said he fell and skinned his knee. What do you think I can do to help him? (Get suggestions from the class, and whatever they say pull it out of the basket.)

Wow! You had a lot of good ideas! His mommy also said he was hungry. I have some good soup I just made and some crackers in here that I think he will like. I bet he is thirsty, too. (Pull out the food and water.) I bet there is one more thing I can do that he would like. (Pull out the game.) We can play this game together. I bet he would like to spend some time playing a game to help him not think about his knee hurting. All these things are hard for him to do by himself, but I am going over to his house to help him.

You know, I really like helping people. Do you know what it means to help people when they cannot help themselves? It is called *compassion*. That means we are to show others we care about them. Jesus showed compassion to the people he met. Would you like to hear a story about Jesus showing compassion?

A long time ago when Jesus and his followers were leaving Jericho, a great many people followed him. Two blind men sitting by the road heard that Jesus was going by, so they shouted, "Lord, Son of David, please help us!" (Matt. 20:30 ICB). The people warned the blind men to be quiet, but they shouted even more, "Lord, Son of David, please help us!" (v. 31 ICB).

"Jesus stopped and said to the blind men, 'What do you want me to do for you?' They answered, 'Lord, we want to be able to see.' Jesus felt sorry for the blind men. He touched their eyes, and at once they were able to see. Then the men followed Jesus" (vv. 32–34).

Can you imagine being hurt so badly that you could not see at all? Can you imagine trying to put on your clothes or tying your shoes without being able to see? Can you imagine trying to walk from your bedroom to the kitchen to get a glass of water without being able to see? Can you imagine trying to read the Bible without being able to see? Well, Jesus knew that doing all the things the men needed to do each day was very hard, and he felt sorry for them. He did what he could to help them. Think about someone you know who feels helpless and think what you can do to show compassion to them.

 Song Suggestions

Lord I Give My Heart by Mark Thompson from "Yes Yes Yes!" (Markarts 2000)

Say Thank You by Mary Rice Hopkins from "Miracle Mud" (Big Steps 4 U 1995)

Outta Sight by Dean-o from *Soul Surfin'* (FKO Music, Inc. 1997)

God's Power Songsheets published by CEF Press, P.O. Box 348, Warrenton, Mo. 63383

Craft for Younger Children: Helping Collage
Needed: Large piece of paper (2-feet x 4-feet), old magazines, scissors, and glue.

Tape the large piece of paper on the wall. Give each child a magazine and scissors. Have them look through the magazine and find pictures of someone showing compassion to someone else. Have them cut them out and glue them to the paper on the wall to make a large collage of people helping one another.

 Craft for Older Children: C Is for Compassion
Needed: An 11-inch x 17-inch piece of paper and markers for each child.

Give each child a piece of paper. Have children place the paper on the table lengthwise. Instruct them to write the word COMPASSION down the length of the paper in one color of marker. Then, using a different color marker, beside each letter write a word that starts with that letter and means "to have compassion" (for example: Caring, Only you can help, Many ways to help).

Snack: Compassion Cupcakes

 Needed: Two cupcakes per child plus icing and decorations.

Say: Today we are going to decorate cupcakes for ourselves to eat, but we are also going to decorate them for another group or class.

Let children decorate cupcakes and deliver them to another class or group to show love and compassion.

Memory Verse: Matthew 20:34 ICB

He touched their eyes, and at once they were able to see. Then the men followed Jesus.

Alternate Version (New King James)
So Jesus had compassion and touched their eyes. And immediately their eyes received sight, and they followed Him.

Memory Verse Activity: Eraser Game
Needed: Whiteboard, dry-erase markers.

Write the Bible verse on the board. Have all of the players stand and recite the verse with the Scripture reference. Have all the players sit down.

Choose one player to erase one word of the verse. Then ask all of the girls to stand and recite the verse inserting the missing word.

Choose another player to erase another word of the verse. Ask all of the boys to stand and recite the verse inserting the missing words.

Continue the game by erasing each word one at a time and having different groups of players (all of them who have a birthday in February stand and recite the verse, all those with blond hair). When all of the verse has been erased, have a contest between the boys and the girls to see who can say it with the fewest mistakes.

Prayer Focus
Dear God, thank you for showing us your heart by helping us when we are hurt and feeling lonely! Help us to show compassion to others. Amen.

February 9, 2005

(Special activity: Valentine's Day)

Down in the Mouth (the Story of Jonah and Redemption), Midweek
By Vicki Wiley

Scripture
Jonah 2

Lesson Aim
Children will learn that if you talk to God, God will listen.

Life Skill
When we make wrong decisions and when we ask for forgiveness, God answers and forgives.

Bible Learning Activity for Younger Children:
Let children play a simple game of hide-and-seek for several minutes. When they are finished ask: What was it like to hide and have someone find you? Can you hide forever? Does someone always find you?

The Bible tells us that God can find you wherever you go or hide. God always knows where you are!

Bible Learning Activity for Older Children: Treasure Hunt
On strips of paper, write out the following instructions:

Go 10 steps to the left.

Turn around and clap three times.

Go outside and go 25 steps straight ahead.

Turn around and come back 25 steps.

Come back into the classroom.

Get in a circle and sit down!

Let children read strips one at a time while they do the activity. Change the instructions to meet your needs.

When children are finished, say: What was it like to follow instructions? Was it easy or hard? What would have happened if we had not followed the instructions?

Today we are going to learn about God's instructions. The Bible tells us about Jonah. God gave Jonah instructions, but Jonah did not follow them. Even though he did not follow the instructions, God still loved Jonah and gave him a second chance.

Enrichment for Older and Younger Children: Fish Printing
Needed: Some small fish (from grocery store or self-caught), newspaper, paper towels, newsprint paper, water-based paint, wide and stiff-bristled brush, modeling clay. (Some extra time may be necessary for this "fish encounter," but after this enrichment, children will never forget the story of Jonah!)

1. Gently wash fish to remove mucus. Be careful not to damage scales. Dry thoroughly.
2. Lay fish on a newspaper-covered table. Spread the fins and put modeling clay under them for support.
3. Paint the fish, brushing from head to tail. Be careful not to use too much paint. Do not paint the eye.
4. Carefully lay a piece of newsprint over the fish. Use your hand to press the paper to the fish. Use your fingers on the fins and tails.
5. Peel the paper off and let it dry.

Fish and whales are vertebrates. Both have backbones, and they both live in water. They are *different* because fish breath in the water with their gills, and whales breath air as other mammals do.

The Bible says that a *giant fish* swallowed Jonah. Could that be a fish like the one you printed (except much larger), or do you think it was a whale? We really don't know the answer to that; we just know that God took care of Jonah the whole time.

Memory Verse: Jonah 2:9 ICB

Lord, I will praise and thank you while I give sacrifices to you. I will make promises to you. And I will do what I promise. Salvation comes from the Lord!

Alternate Version (New King James)
But I will sacrifice to You with the voice of thanksgiving; I will pay what I have vowed. Salvation is of the LORD.

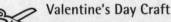 **Valentine's Day Craft**
To prepare for the Valentine's Day craft, make the following clay and have children make hearts. The heart project can be finished on Sunday.

Needed: 1 cup salt, 1/3 cup water, 1/2 cup cornstarch, 1/4 cup water, food coloring or paints, heart cookie cutter, magnets or pin backings

1. Make the clay: Heat salt and 1/3 cup of water over medium high heat for 4 minutes, stirring occasionally. Remove from the heat and add cornstarch and 1/4 cup of cold water. The mixture should look like thick mashed potatoes, stir until it thickens, then let cool for a few minutes before kneading. If the dough seems too sticky at first, work in extra cornstarch as you knead. Add red or pink food coloring so that painting will not be necessary.
2. Using a rolling pin or hands, flatten the dough to 1/2 inch to 1/4 inch thickness depending on your preference. Use cookie cutter to cut out hearts. Let dry for 1–4 days.
3. Decorate the hearts with lace, stickers, glitter, or other items and attach magnet or pin back.

February 13, 2005

(Special activity: Valentine's Day)

Down in the Mouth (the Story of Jonah and Redemption)
By Mary Rice Hopkins

Scripture
Jonah 2

Lesson Aim
Children will learn that if you talk to God, God will listen.

Life Skill
When we make wrong decisions and when we ask for forgiveness, God answers and forgives.

Bible Lesson: Down in the Mouth
Needed: Make seven cardboard signs with the words or sayings from below. Make sure they are big block letters that everyone can see from the back of the room.

1. APPLAUSE
2. HUH?
3. CHEER
4. BOO
5. HISS
6. MOAN
7. OH NO!
8. YUCK!
9. APPLAUSE AND CHEER

On the back of each sign you have written the script so that the children holding the signs can follow along and know when to enlist participation. Choose nine people to hold the signs. When the appropriate word comes up, the person with that word raises the sign in the air. The audience is informed to respond to the sign. This activity can be used for a family service, for older kids, or with teenagers. Make sure you practice with the audience with the appropriate responses before you begin reading the story. This is a fun, interactive way to teach the story and at the same time have audience participation.

Ask children: Have you ever done something you knew was wrong? Did you admit your wrong, or did you try to cover it up and hide what you did wrong? Did God know what you did? Of course he did! The Bible tells us a story about a man named Jonah who did not do what God said. Who wants to help me tell the story?

Tell children that they will do what the sign says as you tell the story.

God choose Jonah to be a messenger for him. (Applause) God had asked him to go to a city called Nineveh. (Huh?) The people in Nineveh at the time were very wicked. (Boo) He knew that Jonah was a special guy and could warn them to turn back to God. (Applause) But instead Jonah disobeyed God and went the other way to Joppa and got on a ship. (Boo)

God sent a big wind that whipped up the water into a storm, and they were all afraid. (Oh no!) The terrified sailors threw everything they had overboard to lighten the load. (Oh no!) The captain found Jonah fast asleep below deck and asked Jonah to pray and ask his God to save them. (Applause) Meanwhile the sailors on deck were drawing lots to discover who among them was the cause of the storm. The name that was drawn was Jonah's. (Hiss and Boo)

"Yes," he said, "I am the cause of the trouble." (Hiss) "Throw me overboard and the storm will die down." (Boo and Applause)

As soon as the sailors threw Jonah into the water, the wind dropped and the water grew calm. (Cheer) But then a giant fish came along and swallowed Jonah. (Oh No! and Hiss)

For three days and nights, he remained in the belly of the whale. (Huh?) And he thanked God for keeping him alive. (Cheer) Finally the whale vomited Jonah onto dry land. (Yuck! and Applause)

Again the Lord told Jonah to go to Nineveh to warn the people to change their ways. This time Jonah was smart and went when he was asked! (Applause and Cheer)

So remember, it's best to do the right thing in the beginning. Otherwise you might feel really down in the mouth.

Song Suggestions

Whale of a Tale by Mary Rice Hopkins from "Lighthouse" (Big Steps 4 U 1988)

He Is Really God! by Dean-o from "You Got It All" (FKO Music, Inc. 1997)

Superman by Mary Rice Hopkins from "15 Singable Songs" (Big Steps 4 U 1988)

My Very Best Friend by Cindy Rethmeier from "I Want 2 Be Like Jesus" (Mercy/Vineyard Publishing 1995)

Holy, Holy, Holy traditional hymn

 Craft for Younger Children: Paper Bag Whale

Needed: One medium-sized paper bag for each child, newspapers for stuffing, and markers.

Make a whale from the paper bag. Stuff the bag with newspapers and draw eyes on the end of the bag. Add details such as a blowhole to the bag whale.

Say: What kind of fish is this? A big fish! Or we might call it a whale! God used a big fish to keep Jonah safe in the middle of the sea. What are some things God uses to keep us safe every day?

 Craft for Older Children: Big Fish!

Needed: For each child one two-liter bottle, sponge shaped "Jonah," markers or paint pens. Cut a simple person figure out of the sponge. Give each child a two-liter bottle, and let them draw a whale on the bottle with the markers.

Insert the Jonah into the bottle, and discuss with the children what it must have been like for Jonah to be in the belly of the giant fish.

Snack: Fishy Jell-O

Needed: Blue Jell-O and fruity fish

Make gelatin as directed on the box. Add fruity fish.

This snack can remind us of an ocean. What looks like the ocean? What is in the ocean? Yep, the fish! What do you think it would have been like for Jonah when he was in the belly of the big fish?

Memory Verse: Jonah 2:9 ICB

Lord, I will praise and thank you while I give sacrifices to you. I will make promises to you. And I will do what I promise. Salvation comes from the Lord!

Alternate Version (New King James)
But I will sacrifice to You with the voice of thanksgiving; I will pay what I have vowed. Salvation is of the LORD.

Memory Verse Activity
Ask: What do these words mean?
  Sacrifices (something you want but you give up)
  Salvation (something that saves you)
  Promise (something that you say you will do and then you do it)
Read the verse together and ask the children what they think it means.
  Say: It is sometimes hard to praise and thank while you are also making a sacrifice, but sometimes that is what God wants us to do. God can see our heart, and God wants us to love him and thank him for what he does for us.
  Say the verse together several times until children know the verse.

Prayer Focus

Dear God, thank you for the directions you give us and thank you for caring so much about us. Please help us do what you tell us to do. Amen.

February 16, 2005

(Special activity: President's Day)

You Can Come Back! Midweek
By Vicki Wiley

Scripture
James 5:19, 20

Lesson Aim
Children will understand that God always forgives when asked and they should too.

Life Skill
We can help others who have sinned.

Bible Learning Activity for Younger Children
Ask: What are some of the sins or wrong things that kids your age can do? Take answers and write them on a whiteboard.

God can forgive all these things. When we ask God to forgive us, he wipes them away like this. (Wipe the sins off the board.) The Bible tells us that God is always waiting for us to talk to him. We can tell God everything!

Bible Learning Activity for Older Children: Soapy Forgiveness
Needed: A bar of white soap and a plastic knife for each child.

Ask: What do you do with a bar of soap? Yes, we wash with it. When God forgives our sins, it's as though he has washed them away. They are gone, just like when you have dirty hands and you use the soap to wash your hands and the dirt is gone.

The reason God can forgive our sins is because Jesus died on the cross. (Begin to carve your bar of soap into a cross.) When Jesus died on the cross, he died without having sinned. He never sinned. But he did a wonderful thing for us; he took away our sins when he died.

We are all going to make a cross now. Since this cross is made out of soap, you can use it to wash with too. When you wash the dirt away, you can remember that God can wash your sins away. All you have to do is ask God to forgive you!

Enrichment for Younger Children: Praying Hands

Needed: Construction paper, pens.

Trace children's hands and cut out the shapes. Let them glue the hands onto a piece of construction paper with hands together as in prayer.

Write, "I can pray for forgiveness," on top of the paper.

Ask: Why do you pray for forgiveness? God always forgives us when we ask him, no matter what we do!

Enrichment for Older Children: Clean Forgiveness

Needed: White handkerchief or cloth and a bottle of disappearing ink from a magic store. Before class, test how long you have to wait for the ink to disappear.

Option: Magic markers that come with the magic erasing marker. You will need to do this option on a sheet of paper instead of the fabric.

Gather kids in an open area and sit down.

Say: Pretend you're this handkerchief. You're all nice and clean, just like this handkerchief is. But sometimes you do things that are wrong. What are some of the wrong things that children your age do? Each time a wrong thing is mentioned, put a drop of ink on the handkerchief.

Say: Each time we do something wrong, we make ourselves dirty, just like this ink makes the handkerchief messy and dirty.

Put the handkerchief aside where kids can't see it. Ask questions to keep the discussion going long enough to give the ink time to disappear. Ask: How do you feel when you do something wrong? How do you feel when you get caught? What do your parents do when you do something wrong? What do you think God does? God did something very special for us. He let Jesus come to Earth so that we can be forgiven for all the wrong things that we do.

When enough time has passed for the ink to disappear, show the handkerchief and say: When we do something wrong and we're sorry we did it, all we have to do is ask God to forgive us. He promises that he will.

Memory Verse: James 5:19 ICB
My brothers, one of you may wander away from the truth. And someone may help him come back.

Alternate Version (New King James): James 5:19, 20
Brethren, if anyone among you wanders from the truth, and someone turns him back, let him know that he who turns a sinner from the error of his way will save a soul from death and cover a multitude of sins.

February 20, 2005

(Special activity: President's Day)

You Can Come Back!
By Eric Titus

Scripture
James 5:19, 20

Lesson Aim
Children will understand that God always forgives when asked and they should too.

Life Skill
We can help others that have sinned.

Bible Lesson: You Can Come Back!
Needed: A shepherd's staff (a good long walking stick will do fine here).

I know that most of you have never been in trouble with your parents, but do you know anyone who has? Please don't say any names, but just think for a moment. Why do children sometimes get in trouble with their parents? (Pause for answers. Most will respond, "Because they did something wrong.") Sometimes parents correct or discipline their children because they don't want their children to be hurt. Can you think of a time that might happen? Maybe riding a bike into the street without looking or playing with matches?

Parents are kind of like shepherds. Jesus says that he is our shepherd. But we are all shepherds to one another in the church. Did you know that? (Bring out the shepherd's staff.) Does anyone know what this is? I bet you think it's a stick. But it's more than that. Shepherds use sticks like these with their flocks. What do you suppose they use them for? No, they don't use them for hitting the sheep. They use them to guide the sheep if they start wandering away from the rest of the flock.

What could happen to a sheep if it went away from the flock and the shepherd? That's right, it could get hurt really badly. (Call a child to come up to help you.) Do you think you could help me for a minute? I want you to start walking, and I'm going to follow behind you. (Gently tap the staff on the child's arm to guide them where you want them to go.) Thank you, you can go back to your seat. That's how shepherds use their staff, to guide the sheep so that it won't go off and hurt itself.

James says (read the passage if you haven't already) that if we see another Christian sinning, doing something that is wrong, we are to correct them. If we are sinning against God or another person, we and maybe someone else will get hurt. If we know this, we are supposed to lead them back to God, to help them do what is right. This doesn't mean we always have to carry a stick with us; it means that we can gently use words to guide our Christian friends to do what is right before God. James says that if we do this, we will help our Christian friends so that they won't do things to hurt themselves spiritually.

Let's pray that God will help us all be good shepherds to one another.

 Song Suggestions

Free Inside by Dean-o from "Soul Surfin'" (FKO Music, Inc. 1999)

Turn It Over by Dean-o from "God City" (BibleBeat Music 2001)

Walk Like Jesus by Mary Rice Hopkins from "15 Singable Songs" (Big Steps 4 U 1988)

I Believe the Bible Songsheets published by CEF Press, P.O. Box 348, Warrenton, Mo. 63383

 Craft for Younger Children: Forgiveness Hands
Needed: Construction paper, pens.

Trace children's hands and cut out. Let them glue onto a piece of construction paper with hands together as in prayer.

Write "I can pray for forgiveness" on top of paper.

Craft for Older Children: Crosses of forgiveness
Needed: For each child, 4 nails, small amount of wire, cord to use as a necklace.

Show children how to wire nails together to form a cross. Wrap wire around two nails with heads facing opposite ways. When they are attached together, add the cross pieces in the same manner. When the cross is made, tie the cord onto the cross to make a necklace.

Snack: Prayer Pretzels

Needed: Ready-made breadstick dough in a can. Roll the dough into 12–15-inch ropes.

Say: Pretzels are shaped to resemble crossed arms in prayer. Lets try to make a pretzel with our arms. (Let children try to form a pretzel with their arms so they get the idea of the shape.) Let children shape their dough into a prayer shape. Sprinkle with coarse grained salt (or sugar). Bake dough according to directions.

Memory Verse: James 5:19 ICB

My brothers, one of you may wander away from the truth. And someone may help him come back.

Alternate Version (New King James): James 5:19, 20
Brethren, if anyone among you wanders from the truth, and someone turns him back, let him know that he who turns a sinner from the error of his way will save a soul from death and cover a multitude of sins.

Memory Verse Activity

Needed: White board and markers

Write the verse on the board, but use a different color for the following words: sinner, wrong, sinner's, sins, forgiven.

Ask: Why do you think these words are in a different color from the rest? I wrote them in a different color because they all have to do with wrong things that we do. Wrong things are called sins. When we sin, we are a sinner. When we are a sinner, we need to be forgiven.

This verse teaches us that we can help people who sin. We can tell them how to be forgiven. How would you teach your friends that they can be forgiven. (Ask God to forgive them.)

Let's read the verse together.

Prayer Focus

Dear Lord Jesus, we thank you that you are our good shepherd, and we ask that you will help us to be shepherds to one another. Help us to use our words gently to guide our Christian friends back to you when they are doing wrong. Guide us back to you when we do wrong too. Amen.

President's Day Activity: Coin Rubbings

Needed: Assortment of coins, aluminum foil or paper, pencil.

Show children how to rub a pencil over aluminum foil over a coin to obtain a rubbing.

Which president is this? Can you tell me what you know about him? We celebrate President's Day because men who have been president deserve to be honored. Some of them were honored by putting their face on coins. How else have presidents been honored? Sometimes we build monuments to them; sometimes books are written about them.

Our presidents are important. They lead a powerful nation! Always remember to pray for our presidents.

To learn more about our presidents look at the White House through the Internet. Go to www.whitehouse.gov.

February 23, 2005

Time for God, Midweek
By Vicki Wiley

Scripture
Psalm 25:4, 5

Lesson Aim
Children will learn to devote time each day to God.

Life Skill
Children will learn ways to study the Bible.

Bible Learning Activity for Younger Children: God's Book
Show children a Bible. Do you know what this book is? That's right! It's a Bible! What is in the Bible? (Let children discuss.)

This is God's book! This book has stories about God's people, God's Son, and everything else that God wants you to know. No other book is like the Bible. It is the only one that God told men what to write. There is no other Word of God. Just the Bible!

Bible Learning Activity for Older Children: Read the Bible!
Needed: A Bible for each student.

Ask: How many of you read the Bible? How do you read it? (Let children tell you what their habits are.) One way to read the Bible is to read a whole book at a time. Let's look at the book of Luke. (Show children how to find the book of Luke is.) Many people choose this book if they want to read about Jesus.

Let's look at the book of Genesis. This is the very first book in the Bible. Turn to it. Many people choose this book if they want to read about God's people and how the world began.

This week, will you read one of these books? Which one will you read? (Let children discuss which one interests them. Encourage them to read the book this week.)

Enrichment for Younger Children: My Bible

Needed: White paper stapled into books. Pass out the "books" to the children.

Say: Does everyone have a Bible? What is your favorite story in the Bible? We are going to make our own Bibles. You are going to draw pictures of your favorite Bible stories. Let children draw their own Bibles.

We should read the Bible every day. Now you can look at your favorite Bible stories everyday!

Enrichment for Older Children

Needed: Envelope for each child addressed to them, and the memory verse written on paper.

Say: The Bible is God's Word for us. The Bible is like a letter that God wrote just to us! Have you ever gotten a letter? What did it say? Today we are going to decorate our envelopes and send a letter to ourselves. When you get the letter in the mail, you can read God's Word!

Help the children put the memory verse in the envelope and stamp it. Encourage them to watch for the letter in their home mailboxes in about three days. Mail the letters to children.

Craft for Older Children: Box on the Wall

Needed: A small box, brown paper bags torn into pieces about 4 inches by 6 inches.

Say: Back in Bible times, people had a way to remember the words of God. It was a container called a *mezuzah*. A mezuzah was a little box in which they put pieces of paper or parchment with Scripture verses written on them. They could open it up any time they wanted to read the word of God. Today we are going to make a mezuzah.

Sometimes the people attached the mezuzah to the frame around their door. That way they saw it when they left home and when they returned. It reminded them how important God and God's Word were to them.

Color the box so that it looks pretty.

Next take the paper bag paper and write this part of the memory verse on it: "Lord, tell me your ways. Show me how to live. Guide me in your truth. Teach me, my God, my Savior. I trust you all day long" (Psalm 25:4, 5 ICB).

Put the verse into the phylactery and attach it to the wall near the door with tape that will not damage the wall. Walk by and touch it. Say the verse as you touch it.

Say: In Bible times the children put their verses inside wooden mezuzahs and attached them to the wall. Every time they walked by they touched it and said their verse.

Memory Verse: Psalm 25:4, 5 ICB

Lord, tell me your ways. Show me how to live. Guide me in your truth. Teach me, my God, my Savior. I trust you all day long.

Alternate Version (New King James)

Show me Your ways, O LORD; teach me Your paths. Lead me in Your truth and teach me, for You are the God of my salvation; on You I wait all the day.

February 27, 2005

Time for God
By Vicki Wiley

Scripture
Psalm 25:4, 5

Lesson Aim
Children will learn to devote time each day to God.

Life Skill
Children will learn ways to study the Bible.

Bible Lesson: Time for God
Needed: A clock, a pillow, a Bible, a towel, cookies or fruit.

Say: I just don't have time to do everything that I have to do! I am just too busy. What about you? Are you too busy too?

Show the clock. Say: When will I have time for everything I need to do?

Show the food. Say: I need to eat.

Show the towel. Say: I need to take a shower.

Show the pillow. Say: I need to sleep! I am so busy!

What's this? Oh, it's a Bible. What am I supposed to do with this? (Let children respond.) Oh, I'm supposed to read it? When will I have time?

The Bible says: "LORD, tell me your ways. Show me how to live. Guide me in your truth. Teach me, my God, my Savior. I trust you all day long" (Ps. 25:4, 5 ICB).

How can God tell us his ways and show us how to live? Right! By reading the Bible! How can God guide us in truth? How can God teach us? How can we learn to trust God? Right! By reading the Bible!

When we read the Bible, we learn more about God. We learn how God thinks. We learn how God cares about us. We learn how God wants us to live.

Reading the Bible is so important; it's just as important as the other things that take up my time.

How can you read the Bible more? What can you do to be sure that you will read it everyday?

Show clock again. When can we read the Bible? (Allow for response.) That's a good idea. We can read the Bible anytime!

 Song Suggestions

G-Mail! By Dean-o from "Soul Surfin'" (1999 FKO Music / ASCAP)

God's Holy Book from "God's Big Picture" (Gospel Light)

The B.I.B.L.E. traditional chorus

God Wrote Us a Letter by Mary Rice Hopkins from "Come Meet Jesus" (Big Steps 4 U)

I Believe the Bible Songsheets published by CEF Press, P.O. Box 348, Warrenton, Mo. 63383

 Craft for Younger Children: Time for God
Needed: Round piece of cardboard or heavy paper for each child.

Say: The Bible is God's Word. We should read God's Word each day. How can we have time to do this? Take ideas from the children.

Let's make a clock. Show children how to draw numbers around the edge of their paper. Circle the times that you would like to make time for God. Letter "Time for God" at the top of the clock.

Craft for Older Children: Take Time for God
Needed: Clay or modeling compound.

Have children mold a piece of clay into a clock shape. With a pencil or sharp instrument, have them make a clock by "engraving" the numbers into the clay. Write "Time for God" at the top of the clock.

Say: We need to take time to be with God each day. How do we do that?

(Read the Bible. Spend time in prayer.)

Use this clock to remind you to spend time with God.

Snack: Bible Verse Snack

 Needed: Alphabet cereal, milk, and bowls.

Wash table and hands. Put cereal out on the table. Have some words written out on a piece of paper such as: God, Jesus, Bible, Savior, love, show, guide, truth. Let children spell out their own words from the Bible before eating "God's words."

Memory Verse: Psalm 25:4, 5 ICB

Lord, tell me your ways. Show me how to live. Guide me in your truth. Teach me, my God, my Savior. I trust you all day long.

Alternate Version (New King James)
Show me Your ways, O LORD; teach me Your paths. Lead me in Your truth and teach me, for You are the God of my salvation; on You I wait all the day.

Memory Verse Activity: Remember! Remember!

Needed: The verse written out on paper strips, one for each child.

Say: Back in Bible times people had a way to remember the words of God. They did something a little different. They placed Scripture verses in small leather pouches called phylacteries and tied the pouches to their heads or to their arms! They valued God's Word so much that they wanted always to have it with them.

One way we can always have God's Word with us is to memorize our verse each week. Then we'll have more and more of God's Word with us wherever we go. You may want to place this verse in your pocket on a book or on your mirror to remind you to read and remember it this week.

Prayer Focus

Dear God, thank you for the Bible, your holy Word. Please help us to learn to take time to read it each day. Amen.

March 2, 2005

Passing the Test of Faith, Midweek
By Pat Verbal

Scripture
1 Kings 17:7–24

Lesson Aim
Children learn that tests and hardships are part of God's plan to help believers grow stronger.

Life Skill
Children will recognize when God is testing their faith and trust him to bring them through any difficulty.

Bible Learning Activity for Younger Children: Nature Walk
Needed: Pillowcase and several common nature items such as pinecones, stones, leaves, sticks, shells.

Today we are going to play a game. I want you to try to guess what you are touching. Put your hand into the pillowcase without looking. Can you guess what you are touching? How can you tell what it is? Is it soft or hard? Flat or round? Smooth or rough?

Whenever we want to know if something is what we think it is, we find evidence. The evidence that an object is an apple might be that it is round, smooth, has a stem, and feels cool. Evidence that you have just touched a stuffed animal might be that it is soft, furry, squishy, and has plastic eyes. What did you feel on these objects that led you to believe what you guessed they were?

How do you know God is real? What can we see that shows us something about God? (sunsets, trees, flowers, people) What happens that we cannot see that shows us that God is real? (answered prayer, wind, people who love us).

When we have faith, we believe in God even though we cannot see him. We believe that God exists, and we believe that what the Bible says about him is true because we have faith in God.

Bible Learning Activity for Older Children: Feeling Your Faith

Needed: One portable electric fan, pieces of ribbon.

What is faith? Do you have faith? How do you know you have faith? Faith is something you get by learning more about God and then trusting God whenever you can.

Have you ever needed to trust God when something bad was happening to you? What was that like? How did you know God was there?

Tie ribbons to fan. Say: When I turn this fan on, what will happen to the ribbons? (Let kids brainstorm.) How do you know that will happen? (Let kids discuss.) How do you know that there is wind if you can't see the wind? (We can see the ribbons blowing.)

We can't see the wind, but we know it's there because we see the ribbons blowing. We can't see God, but we have faith that he is there because we know God answers our prayers and God makes beautiful things all around us!

Enrichment for Younger Children: Faith Grows!

Needed: Strips of paper 4 feet tall for each child.

Say: Have you grown very much this year? Yes, you have! You are always growing and getting bigger.

Did you know your faith is growing too? When you get bigger, you believe more about God, and your faith grows at the same time.

Measure each child and mark their height on their strip of paper. Say: This strip will measure how tall you are. Let's also write on the strip what you think about God so that you can also remember how much your faith has grown.

Help children write their thoughts about God on the strip. Let them take this home as a reminder of their growth.

Enrichment for Older Children: Faith Grows!

Needed: A picture of the teacher as a baby or young child.

Show the picture to the children. Ask: Do you know who this baby is? Believe it or not, it's me! I used to be small, but now I am grown up!

There are stories in the Bible about people with great faith. When they were young like you, they learned to trust God, and their faith grew and grew. When I was little (as I am in this picture), I didn't have much faith. But now my faith has grown, and I have great, great faith!

Has anything happened that has helped your faith in God to grow? (Let children discuss.)

Let's pray and ask God to help our faith to grow.

Memory Verse: 1 Kings 17:24 ICB

The woman said to Elijah, "Now I know you really are a man from God. I know that the Lord truly speaks through you!"

Alternate Version (New King James)

Then the woman said to Elijah, "Now by this I know that you are a man of God, and that the word of the LORD in your mouth is the truth."

March 6, 2005

Passing the Test of Faith
By Pat Verbal

Scripture
1 Kings 17:7–24

Lesson Aim
Children learn that tests and hardships are part of God's plan to help believers grow stronger.

Life Skill
Children will recognize when God is testing their faith and trust him to bring them through any difficulty.

Bible Lesson
Needed: Objects that will help tell the story including a picture of a snowy mountain, first-aid tips for frostbite, and a match.

Ask: Have you ever been lost? (Ask for a show of hands.) Have you been so hungry your stomach hurt? Have you ever been really cold? (Ask for a response from several children.)

In our Bible lesson today, God's prophet Elijah ran for his life and hid from King Ahab. There was a drought in the land, but Elijah didn't worry about how he would get food. He trusted God to provide all his needs. God sent the ravens to feed Elijah.

Later God knew there was a woman and her son who needed help. God used Elijah to perform another miracle. God still does that today too! Listen to this story about how God worked a miracle in a boy's life.

Boy Believes in Miracles After His Mountain Rescue
Ryan's hand shook as he put down the phone. He couldn't believe that a real reporter asked him for an interview. His frostbitten feet were wrapped in

gauze the next day when Ms. James from the Los Angeles Times stopped by. She wanted details on Ryan's amazing rescue from Mount Baldy.

"From what I hear," said Ms. James, "you're lucky to be alive. Not many sixth graders could have survived forty-three hours at thirteen-degree temperatures." Ryan shivered at her description of the worst nightmare of his life. But he knew luck had nothing to do with it.

"How did you get lost, Ryan?"

"Some of the high-school kids from our church planned a hike and let me tag along. That morning we climbed higher and higher up the mountain. After lunch on the trip down hill, Cindy, one of the sponsors, and I got separated from the group.

"When we looked back and no one was there, I yelled at my brother, Sam, to stop messing around. Cindy and I laughed, but Sam didn't answer. We stood motionless, listening for voices or footsteps. We tried to get down the mountain, but we lost the trail. Then the wind started howling, and a heavy snowstorm moved it."

Ryan described the V-shaped shelter they built out of fallen trees to wait out the storm. They gathered twigs for a fire and huddled on the ground. His back and neck ached as he recalled his mom's last words, *Ryan, don't forget your heavy jacket. You might need it.*

"I cried a lot," said Ryan. "I wanted to see my family. Cindy said people were looking for us. Our stomachs growled as we talked about warm beds, hot baths, and French toast with lots of syrup."

On Saturday they heard a helicopter. Cindy tried to signal by catching the sun's rays in a mirror, but hours passed, and no one came. By the second night the numbness in their feet moved up their legs. "Lord, please help us!" Ryan prayed. "I need my legs for baseball. I'm the only short stop on our team."

At their lowest point the fire started to go out. Ryan knew they couldn't live without it. They had already used their last two matches. Cindy and Ryan clasped hands and prayed. When they opened their eyes, the flames leaped up brightly.

"We could believe it!" Ryan said. "I thought, *Wow, this is a miracle!* Later that night, when the fire died way down, we prayed again. The same thing happened. The flame shot right up! It brightened the whole area and our spirits too."

Ms. James looked doubtful. She asked Ryan if he really thought that his prayers kept that fire burning.

Ryan thought of all the people who had prayed for them and how they could have died up there.

"My parents always tell me that God is in control," Ryan said, "and now I believe it! God could have sent help the first day. He could have kept us from being hungry or getting frostbite. Why did God wait? I think he waited because it was only after we were out of matches and firewood that I got to see a real miracle. I saw the flames leaping up twice with my own eyes! I know it wasn't just luck, Ms. James!"

Two days later Ryan's picture with his bandage feet appeared in *the Los Angles Times*. The headline read: "Boy Believes in Miracles After His Mountain Rescue." Maybe Ms. James believed him after all!

 Song Suggestions

Believin' On by Jana Alayra from "Believin' On" (Montjoy Music 2002)

Little Is Much by Mary Rice Hopkins from "15 Singable Songs" (Big Steps 4 U 1988)

Faith Will Do by Dean-o from "You Got It All" (FKO Music, Inc. 1997)

God's Power Songsheets published by CEF Press, P.O. Box 348, Warrenton, Mo. 63383

 Craft for Younger Children: Baggie Greenhouse
Needed: One sandwich-size zipper bag for each child, beans or seeds, one greenhouse frame cut from card stock or cardboard the size of the bag.

Have children place seeds into the zipper bag. Attach the top of the zipper bag to the greenhouse frame so that you can see the entire bag through the frame. Let children color the frame.

After a few days you will see the seed sprout. Say: This is how seeds grow. What is happening to the seed? Is it becoming a plant? Yes, it is! This is how seeds grow into plants!

Our faith grows just as these seeds do. These seeds grow when they get sunlight, water, and food. Our faith grows when we pray, read the Bible, and know God better. God gives us our faith; we need to help it grow.

Craft for Older Children: God's Word Is the Seed
Needed: Pillowcase and several common items, paper, markers or watercolors.

Today we are going to play a game and then draw a picture. I want you to try to guess what you are touching. Put your hand into the pillowcase without looking. Can you guess what you are touching? How can you tell what it is? Is it soft or hard? Flat or round? Smooth or rough?

Whenever we want to know if something is what we think it is, we find evidence. The evidence that an object is an apple might be that it is round, smooth, has a stem, and feels cool. Evidence that you have just touched a stuffed animal might be that it is soft, furry, squishy, and has plastic eyes. What did you feel on these objects that led you to believe what you guessed that they were?

How do you know God is real? What can we see that shows us something about God? (sunsets, trees, flowers, people) What happens that we cannot see that shows us that God is real? (answered prayer, wind, people who love us). When we have faith, we believe in God even though we can not see him.

Let's draw a picture of our faith. Help children think of ways they can picture their faith—sunset, picture of God, trees, or flowers.

Say: We can see God in many things. They all show God's power.

Snack: Enough, Enough!

 Needed: Sprouts of any kind and sprout seeds, pita bread, cheese.

Show children the seeds and then the sprouts. Discuss how the seeds grew from tiny seeds into sprout. Our faith can grow from being very small to getting bigger and bigger.

Let children put cheese and sprouts into pita bread, eat, and enjoy!

Memory Verse: 1 Kings 17:24 ICB

The woman said to Elijah, "Now I know you really are a man from God. I know that the Lord truly speaks through you!"

Alternate Version (New King James)
Then the woman said to Elijah, "Now by this I know that you are a man of God, and that the word of the LORD in your mouth is the truth."

Memory Verse Activity: Popup Verse

Write the verse on a whiteboard where all the kids can see it. Go around the room and assign one or two words to each child, depending upon the number of children. Say the verse all together and then, going around the room, have the children pop up and say their word in turn.

This game gets a little silly, but it is a fun way to memorize a verse.

Prayer Focus

Dear God, I trust you to provide all my needs. I want my faith to grow as you test me. Teach me how to believe in you better and show others your wonderful love. Amen.

March 9, 2005

Our Plans or God's Plans? Midweek
By Karl Bastian

Scripture
Matthew 7:24–27

Lesson Aim
Children will know that God has great plans which include faith.

Life Skill
Children will learn how to build a faith foundation for their lives.

Bible Learning Activity for Younger Children: Building a Tower
Needed: Blocks or boxes.

Tell children that you are going to build a tall, tall tower. Let them experiment with the blocks until they seem to understand that the foundation of the building needs to be big enough to hold the rest of the blocks.

Say: The bottom part of this building is called the foundation. When the foundation is big, the building can be tall. It's the same with our lives; when we build our lives on God, we can have a strong life! The Bible teaches us that God should be the foundation of our life.

Bible Learning Activity for Older Children: Alternate Houses
In Bible times people who built houses were called builders, just as they are today. In fact, in many ways the art of building has not changed much. Builders knew that the most important part of the building was the foundation. Once the builders finished the foundation, the rest of the house would be strong.

Houses were not always built of stone or brick or made from mud. Many people in the Bible, such as Abraham and Moses, spent much of their lives in tents. Many people who took care of sheep and goats moved their livestock from place to place to take advantage of the available pastureland, so it was easier to live in a tent, which they could move with them.

Some people in all periods of Bible history lived in caves. In Israel a cave had several advantages over a house. Maintenance and upkeep were low. A cave is also cool in the summer and warm in the winter. Caves also often served as stables for livestock. According to early Christian tradition, the stable in Bethlehem that became the place of Jesus' birth was located in such a cave.

Enrichment for Younger Children: Standing Sandy

Needed: Cake pan filled with sand, small people toys. Stand the people up in the sand.

Say: Do you think these people can stand up in this sand? (Yes!) Show children how the toy people can stand up in the sand. Then shake the pan until the toys fall down.

These people could stand up in the sand until something went wrong. But when I shook the pan, the toy people fell over! Our lives are like that. If we just have a "sandy" life, we will fall down when something bad happens. Our faith will be shaken!

But if we have a strong foundation with faith in God, we will not be shaken when bad things happen. We will grow firm in our faith, and our faith will grow stronger and stronger.

Enrichment for Older Children: Cup Stacking

Needed: Many paper or foam cups.

Invite two teams of three kids each to come up on stage and compete. Tell them that the goal is to build the tallest pyramid of paper cups in two minutes. The only cups to count will be the ones that are under and connected to the highest cup.

Let kids build the pyramids. When they are finished, point out that the bigger the base, the higher it can go!

Say: In this pyramid, the bigger the foundation, the taller our towers could get. In our lives, the bigger foundation, the deeper our faith can get. How can we have a big foundation? (Read the Bible, pray, come to church.) Having a good foundation in our life of faith is important.

Memory Verse: Matthew 7:24 ICB
Everyone who hears these things I say and obeys them is like a wise man. The wise man built his house on rock.

Alternate Version (New King James)
Therefore whoever hears these sayings of Mine, and does them, I will liken him to a wise man who built his house on the rock.

March 13, 2005

Our Plans or God's Plans?
By Karl Bastian

Scripture
Matthew 7:24–27

Lesson Aim
Children will know that God has great plans for them that include faith.

Life Skill
Children will learn how to build a faith foundation for their lives.

Bible Lesson: Our Plans or God's Plans?
Needed: A pan of Jell-O, a brick, and some playing cards.

Say: I have a story to tell you. Raise your hand if you think you know which story from the Bible this is. This brick (show brick) will represent solid ground (the rock), and this Jell-O (show Jell-O) will represent the sand.

(Teach the lesson using the word *Jell-O* instead of *sand*. The kids who know the story will laugh.)

As the kids are watching, build two card houses, one on the brick and one on the pan of gelatin to represent the wise and the foolish builder. When you are done with this, lift each one up and shake them to simulate an earthquake. The card house on the gelatin will fall, but the card house on the brick will amazingly stay.

The secret is the card house is taped together so it will not fall apart. When you set up this house, do it discretely so the kids don't notice the cards are connected together. You may want to build the houses from the other side of the table with your back facing them so they cannot see how you are setting up the houses.

Say: What story from the Bible do you think I was talking about? Yes, you're right! The Bible tells us a story about two builders. One was wise and made good decisions; the other was foolish and made bad decisions.

Both were building houses. One build his house on sand, and one build his house on a rock. Everything was great. The houses were beautiful and strong until one day when it started to rain. It rained and rained and rained!

The house that was built on the rock was fine. It stayed beautiful and strong just like our house on the brick did. But the house that was built on the sand just fell down! It crashed! Just like the Jell-O house did.

Jesus taught us this story so that we would know that building our lives on a good foundation is important. God's plan is that our foundation is Jesus Christ! When we follow God's plan, we will build our lives on Jesus Christ.

 Song Suggestions

Believin' On by Jana Alayra from "Believin' On" (Montjoy Music 2002)

Little Is Much by Mary Rice Hopkins from "15 Singable Songs" (Big Steps 4 U 1988)

Faith Will Do by Dean-o from "You Got It All" (FKO Music, Inc. 1997)

God's Power Songsheets published by CEF Press, P.O. Box 348, Warrenton, Mo. 63383

 Craft for Younger Children: Wise Houses
Needed: Construction paper cut into rectangles and square shapes, whole piece of construction paper for each child, glue.

Let children "build" a house with the shapes. Glue the shapes onto the whole piece of paper. Write at the top of the paper, "Building a Wise House."

Say: It is important to build a house that will stay for a long time. It is also important to have a life that follows God's plan, and God's plan is for you to have a strong foundation in your life.

Craft for Older Children: Rock Reminder
Needed: Smooth rock for each child, paint pens

Have children write "Foolish" on one side of the rock and "Wise" on the other side. Let them decorate the rest of the rock as they desire.

Say: All of our decisions help us. When we make a bad or foolish decision, we can learn from it and make a better decision the next time. When we make a good decision, we can remember what we did and how it turned out.

This week, when you make a good decision, turn your rock so that you can see "Wise." When you make a bad decision, turn your rock so that you can see "Foolish." When you make a foolish decision, remember to ask God to help you make a better decision next time!

Snack: Building Houses

 Needed: Cookies of different shapes: square, rectangle, round; and icing.

Have children wash hands and put a clean paper or plastic tablecloth beneath their work.

Say: The people in our story today were going to build houses. Today we are going to build houses too.

Let children build a cookie house using the cookies as the walls and the ceilings and the icing as mortar.

Eat and enjoy when you are finished

Memory Verse: Matthew 7:24 ICB

Everyone who hears these things I say and obeys them is like a wise man. The wise man built his house on rock.

Alternate Version (New King James)
Therefore whoever hears these sayings of Mine, and does them, I will liken him to a wise man who built his house on the rock.

Memory Verse Activity: Cup Stack!
Needed: 15 cups and felt-tip marker.
  Write one long word or two short words on each cup with the felt-tip marker. Let kids stack them pyramid style as they say the words. Knock down and stack again!

Prayer Focus
Dear God, thank you for the plans that you have for our lives. Please help us to follow them so that we will have a good foundation of faith. Amen.

March 16, 2005

(Special Activity, St. Patrick's Day)
Submission of Jesus—Challenge to Us, Midweek
By Karl Bastian

Scripture
Matthew 26:39–46

Lesson Aim
Children will learn what it means to be submissive.

Life Skill
Using Jesus as an example, children will learn that the Bible teaches us to be submissive.

Bible Learning Activity for Younger Children: Freeze!
Needed: One stop sign, CD or cassette player, CD or cassette.

Show children how to play freeze tag using the stop sign. Children will move as they please to the music. Hold up the stop sign when it is time to freeze, and at the same time stop the music. Children will stop and freeze their position.

Continue playing using the stop sign to signal the time to stop and freeze.

Say: Why did you stop? How did you know when to stop? You stopped when you saw the sign telling you to stop. That is called "submission." Submission is when you do what someone else wants you to do, even if you didn't want to do it.

God wants us to learn how to use our self-control to submit and be submissive so that we will live a more obedient life. The Bible tells us that Jesus was submissive to God. Can you be submissive to God too?

Bible Learning Activity for Older Children: Freeze Factor
Needed: Deep buckets, ice, and timers.

Fill several deep buckets with crushed ice. Challenge kids to put their arm into the ice up to their elbow or their foot up to their ankle.

Time each child to see how long they can stand the cold before they pull out their arm or foot. When they have had their foot or arm in the bucket for ninety seconds, say, "Freeze," and make them take it out.

Ask: How did you feel when I made you take your arm (or foot) out? Why do you think I did that? I made you take your arm out so that you wouldn't really freeze! I did it for your own good. You may not have wanted to do what I said, but it was better for you to listen to me. That is called submission.

Enrichment for Younger Children: Stop!

Needed: Stop signs from craft time, round cardboard circles for each child.

Say: Have you ever seen a stop sign? Why do we have stop signs? What do you do when you drive up to a stop sign? Let's play a stop sign game!

Explain to the children that one child will be the leader and carry their stop sign. Other children will follow holding their circles as "steering wheels." When the leader holds up the stop sign, all children put on their "brakes" and stop!

Have you ever had a "timeout"? When you did, it was a way for your teacher or mom to tell you that you did not use self-control!

What can you do when you:

Want something someone else has?

Want your mom to get off the phone?

Want lots of candy?

Learning submission will help you become the person that God wants you to be!

Enrichment for Older Children: Who Was Saint Patrick?

Saint Patrick was a man who was submissive to God. He lived in Ireland and was born about A.D. 385.

Patrick studied religion in Europe to become a priest and bishop. He then brought Christianity to the Irish by teaching in Ireland for twenty-nine years. According to early Irish tradition, he died on March 17, 461. The anniversary of his death is celebrated as Saint Patrick's Day.

An Irish tale explains how Patrick used the three-leafed shamrock to explain the Trinity. He used it in his sermons to represent how the Father, the Son, and the Holy Spirit could all exist as separate elements of the same entity. His followers adopted the custom of wearing a shamrock on his feast day. Green is associated with Saint Patrick's Day because it is the color of spring, Ireland, and the shamrock.

Memory Verse: Matthew 26:42 ICB

Then Jesus went away a second time. He prayed, "My Father, if it is not possible for this painful thing to be taken from me, and if I must do it, I pray that what you want will be done."

Alternate Translation (New King James)

Again, a second time, He went away and prayed, saying, "O My Father, if this cup cannot pass away from Me unless I drink it, Your will be done."

March 20, 2005

Submission of Jesus—Challenge to Us
By Karl Bastian

Scripture
Matthew 26:39–46

Lesson Aim
Children will learn what it means to be submissive.

Life Skill
Using Jesus as an example, children will learn that the Bible teaches us to be submissive.

Bible Lesson: Listen to Instructions!
This lesson teaches the importance of following instructions and submitting to what we should do. Enlist two volunteers who are outgoing and willing to look a little silly. Mention that they must be good at reading and following directions. When they come up, give each an envelope with the following instructions inside. Be sure the first line is included.

Read these instructions all the way through and then do what they say.

1. Jump up and down ten times.
2. Run and touch the back wall, come back and yell, "I'm Back!"
3. Say the alphabet standing backwards.
4. Pat the teacher on the head.
5. Go play one note on the piano.
6. Sing "Row, Row, Row Your Boat" all the way through fast.
7. Turn around three times.
8. Sit on the ground and yell, "I'm so silly!"
9. Say, "Supercalifragelisticexpealidosious."
10. Only do number 4 and yell, "I'm all done!"

Most kids will start out doing everything on the sheet and fail to notice the top line. Let them go for awhile; they may even finish. Then announce that nobody won, because they did something wrong. Choose another group of children. After awhile you can start interrupting the game sooner, announcing that a mistake has been made. Eventually a kid will get it and read all the instructions first and then only do number 10 and win.

Say: How did it feel to know that you only had to do one thing? How did it feel to know that if you paid attention to all the instructions, it would have been easier? Life is like that too. A lot of people try to follow God but don't listen to all the instructions. We need to be submissive to Jesus and live life His way!

 Song Suggestions

He's the One by Dean-o from "Soul Surfin'" (FKO Music, Inc. 1999)

He Can Do by Mary Rice Hopkins from "Kids Kamp" (Big Steps 4 U 1999)

No Other God by Kurt Johnson, a.k.a. MrJ from "Kid Possible" (Kurt Johnson 1995)

God's Power Songsheets published by CEF Press, P.O. Box 348, Warrenton, Mo. 63383

 Craft for Younger Children: Stop and Go
Needed: Red construction paper, cardboard, markers, wide craft stick.

Help each child make a stop sign using the red paper. Glue onto cardboard and attach a stick for a handle. Use this craft in the Enrichment Activity.

Craft for Older Children: Saint Patrick's Day Shamrocks
Needed: Construction paper, glue, tissue paper, crayons, green glitter.

Cut a shamrock shape from construction paper. Glue pieces of green tissue paper or scraps of green paper on shamrock.

If you have more time, decorate with crayons or coat shamrock with glue. Sprinkle with green glitter, then remove excess.

Shamrock Prints
Needed: Bell peppers cleaned out and cut into halves.

Dip the pepper into green paint and press onto the paper to make a shamrock.

Snack: Stop and Go!

 Needed: Graham crackers, red icing, and green icing.

Break the crackers into squares and let children ice them with either red or green icing.

Say: We are going to play a game with our snack. If you iced your cracker with green, you will eat when I say, "Go," and if you iced your cracker red, you will eat when I say, "Stop."

Play the game a few times until children have finished their crackers. Give them all one more cracker at the end of the game.

Say: How did you feel when you played that game? It's easier to eat whenever we want to isn't it? But sometimes we need to listen to someone else tell us what to do. In our lives we need to listen to God. The reward in this game was another cracker; the reward in life is eternal life!

Snack: Pot o' Gold Rainbows for St. Patrick's Day

Needed: 1 graham cracker, blue frosting, 1 mini Reese's cup, 1 pack Skittles for each child.

Students spread frosting over graham cracker and place Skittles in the shape of a rainbow. Then place the Reese's cup at the end of the rainbow

Say: Sometimes we associate Saint Patrick's Day with rainbows. Let's make one to eat right now!

Memory Verse: Matthew 26:42 ICB

Then Jesus went away a second time. He prayed, "My Father, if it is not possible for this painful thing to be taken from me, and if I must do it, I pray that what you want will be done."

Alternate Translation (New King James)
Again, a second time, He went away and prayed, saying, "O My Father, if this cup cannot pass away from Me unless I drink it, Your will be done."

Memory Verse Activity
Needed: Poster board.
Write the verse on a poster board, covering most of the board. Cut the board into a giant puzzle shape. Let children say the verse together, then try to work the puzzle.
Repeat the verse several times.

Prayer Focus
Dear God, thank you for your Son. Thank you for his total submission to you, which is an example to us. Help us to follow his example. Amen.

March 23, 2005

Easter, Midweek
By Karl Bastian

Scripture
1 Corinthians 15:1–20

Lesson Aim
Children will learn the meaning of Easter.

Life Skill
Children will know that Jesus died for them.

Bible Learning Activity for Younger Children: Empty Eggs
Needed: Plastic eggs.

Put the following words inside the eggs, one word in each egg: We celebrate Easter because Jesus died for you.

Have the children open the eggs and take out the words. Let them try to put them together in a sentence.

Say: Today we are going to learn all about the real meaning of Easter, which is that Jesus died for you and that's why we celebrate Easter!

Bible Learning Activity for Older Children: Egg Relay
Needed: One egg and one spoon per team or small group. Play outside if possible.

This is a classic replay where each team is provided with a spoon and an egg. They race (perhaps blindfolded) trying to get across the room and back one at a time holding their egg on the end of a spoon. If they drop the egg and it breaks, they are disqualified. (Hint: have extra eggs on hand!)

During the weeks around Easter, we see lots of special eggs everywhere we go. But Easter is more than eggs. Easter is about Jesus! The Bible tells us about Jesus' resurrection. That is why we celebrate Easter.

Enrichment for All Children: Giant Egg

Needed: Make a giant Easter egg puzzle by cutting shapes out of poster board.

Make one piece a cross but at an unusual angle so it isn't obvious. Let the children complete the puzzle.

Ask: What is this shape? Yes, an Easter egg! This is the time of year we celebrate Easter. Some people celebrate it with lots and lots of Easter eggs, and others celebrate it as we do by praising God. We remember that Jesus died for us, but he didn't stay dead. No, he rose from the dead to fix the problem of death once and for all. We can try to "put our lives back together" when we mess up, but only God can save us from the ultimate puzzle, providing salvation for all the "eggs we've broken" and the mess we sometimes make of life.

Memory Verse: 1 Corinthians 15:3 ICB

I passed on to you what I received. And this was the most important: that Christ died for our sins, as the Scriptures say.

Alternate Version (New King James)
For I delivered to you first of all that which I also received: that Christ died for our sins according to the Scriptures.

March 27, 2005

Easter Sunday

Easter

By Karl Bastian

Scripture
1 Corinthians 15:1–20

Lesson Aim
Children will learn the meaning of Easter.

Life Skill
Children will know that Jesus died for them.

Bible Lesson: The Meaning of Easter
Needed: Six plastic eggs, each labeled with the letters of the word EASTER. Each egg should be filled with candy except one of the Es. It is ideal if the eggs can be clear, although it is not necessary. This presentation is done with a puppet, although that too is an optional presentation method.

Overview the meaning of Easter, concluding with an explanation of the gospel message and an invitation.

Hide all of the eggs that have candy in them around the room. The empty E egg should be in the puppet's possession or held by another leader who can say the same line as the puppet below. Write the word EASTER on the whiteboard or prominently display it some other way.

Begin by talking about Easter. Say: Who knows what today is? What do you like about Easter? Have you ever been on an Easter egg hunt? Today we are going to learn about the meaning of Easter, and to do so I'd like to introduce you to a friend of mine.

Get out puppet and introduce the puppet. Ask the puppet if he has prepared the lesson for the boys and girls. After he says yes, have him tell the kids what he did. He will say he hid just a few eggs with letters on them that spell

Easter. Explain that when you say *go*, they can look for them. When they find one, then can come back to their seat and hold it above their head so you can see it.

After the kids hunt and find the eggs, have them all sit down. Ask them if they know how to spell the word *Easter*. (Point to where you wrote it.) Say that you are going to use the letters of the word *Easter* to explain what it means. Your puppet is going to help.

Ask what each letter is and then talk about what that letter means. (See chart below.) When you get to the second E, say that it is missing. Before the kids start to look again (they may jump up to look), have the puppet admit that he has it. Ask why. Because he thought something was wrong with it. You ask, What's wrong with it? He replies, "It is empty." But you go on to explain that it is empty for a reason. Because the tomb was empty too.

Easter is for Everybody because everybody has sinned and everybody will someday die and everybody will stand before God and have to be punished for the bad things they have done.

But A is for the word *Agape*. *Agape* means "love." God loved us so much that he sent Jesus to die for us so that we can live forever in heaven with him!

Jesus had to die because of our Sins. Sin is anything we do that God does not want us to do, and we all have sinned.

After Jesus died, he was buried in a Tomb. That is where they put dead people. Dead people don't come back; their life on Earth is over.

The second E egg is Empty because three days later the tomb was empty because Jesus did come back to life! God raised him from the dead! (See note above about the missing egg.)

Resurrection is a big word that means "to rise again from the dead." Since God raises Jesus from the dead, we know that he can someday take us to heaven to live with him there. Jesus' resurrection proved that he was God because only God has power over death!

Song Suggestions

Little Is Much by Mary Rice Hopkins from "15 Singable Songs" (Big Steps 4 U 1988)

You Got Game (It's in the Name) by Dean-o from "Game Face" (BibleBeat Music, 2003)

We Will Shout for Joy by Cindy Rethmeier from "I Want to Be Like Jesus" (Mercy Vineyard 1995)

Take My Heart by Kurt Johnson, a.k.a. MrJ, from "Kid Possible" (Kurt Johnson Music 1995)

Good News Songsheets published by CEF Press, P.O. Box 348, Warrenton, Mo. 63383

 Craft for All Children: Cross Necklace
Needed: Craft foam cut into cross shapes, cord, and beads.

Say: The cross is a symbol Christians use to remind them that Jesus died on the cross. Sometimes people wear a cross around their necks so that they can always remember that Jesus loves them.

Show children how to punch a hole in the top of the cross and string it on the cord. Add beads and tie a knot to form a necklace.

Snack: He Is Alive!

 Needed: One snowball snack cake, one round cookie, icing, and a small sign that reads "He is not here. He is alive!"

Say: Today we are going to make an "empty tomb" to remind us that Jesus not only died on the cross but that he also came back to live and still lives today!

Put the snack cake on a paper plate. Cut off a small end of the snack cake. Using the snack cake for the tomb, place it on a paper plate with the sign in front of the part that has been cut. Use the round cookie for the stone in front of the tomb. You now have an empty tomb!

Memory Verse: 1 Corinthians 15:3 ICB
I passed on to you what I received. And this was the most important: that Christ died for our sins, as the Scriptures say.

Alternate Version (New King James)
For I delivered to you first of all that which I also received: that Christ died for our sins according to the Scriptures.

Memory Verse Activity: For Our Sins
Needed: Whiteboard with verse written on it.

Say: What can you do when you know there is something you should do, and you want to do it, but it's really hard to do? What if you knew you had a difficult report to do, you knew you would learn so much from doing the report, and you wanted to please your teacher. But at the same time, you wanted to play instead? What would you do?

Jesus had a difficult decision to make too, much harder than that. He wanted to please his Father, knew what he had to do, but it was hard to do. It meant that he would die.

When Jesus had this hard decision to make, he prayed to God for strength. He told God exactly how he felt. Let's read what he said. (Read the verse.) These words are good for us to memorize. Let's try to make up a song with the words of this verse. Let children brainstorm some tunes to use and put the verse to music. Sing a few times together.

Prayer Focus
Dear God, our spirit is often willing, but we are weak. Help us to do what is right and what you want us to do. Amen.

March 30, 2005

Pray, Pray, Pray! Midweek
By Vicki Wiley

Scripture
Daniel 6:6–11; 1 Thessalonians 5:16–18; Matthew 15:36; 26:39

Lesson Aim
Children will learn how powerful prayer is.

Life Skill
Children will begin to make prayer a lifelong habit.

Bible Learning Activity for Younger Children: My Bible Says to Pray!
The Bible is full of stories of people who prayed.

> David prayed for his own protection.
> Hannah prayed to have a child.
> Jesus prayed for people to be healed.
> Moses prayed for the Hebrew people.
> David told God how wonderful he is.

Ask: What do you pray for? We should pray for others and for ourselves and what we need. We should thank God for everything he does. We should pray to ask for forgiveness. What can you pray for now?

Bible Learning Activity for Older Children: God's Protection
Needed: A Bible turned to Psalm 18. Read it with the children.
List as many situations as you can find where God protected David. Does God protect us like he protected David? Yes, he does!

Enrichment for Younger Children: I Can Pray!

Needed: CD player, ball or similar object, CD.

Play hot potato with the children. Have children sit in a circle. Put a CD on and play music. While music is playing, pass a ball or similar object around the circle. When the music stops, the person holding the ball will say, "I can pray for _____!"

Be sure that every child gets a turn.

Pray together for the different things the children named.

Enrichment for Older Children: Were There Really Giants?

What are giants? Did they really exist? The Bible tells us that there were beings of abnormal size and strength. Races of giants are first mentioned in the Old Testament in Genesis 6:4, where giant godlike beings were produced by the union of "the sons of God" and "the daughters of men." The giants were called "mighty men" (NKJV), perhaps a reference to their tremendous height.

When Moses sent twelve men to spy out the land of Canaan, they returned with a report that they saw "giants" who made them feel like "grasshoppers" (Num. 13:33). These giants were descendants of Anak, "a people great and tall" (Deut. 9:2 NKJV).

Goliath is the most famous giant in the Bible (1 Sam. 17:4), measuring six cubits and a span, which is more than nine feet tall. Goliath taunted the Israelites and demanded that a warrior meet him in combat. David, the shepherd boy, with his sling and stone, dared to accept the challenge of the Philistine giant in full armor because he knew that God would direct him in the battle (1 Sam. 17:45). David's stone struck Goliath in the forehead, and Goliath fell facedown and died.

Memory Verse: 1 Thessalonians 5:16–18 ICB

Always be happy. Never stop praying. Give thanks whatever happens. That is what God wants for you in Christ Jesus.

Alternate Version (New King James)

Rejoice always, pray without ceasing, in everything give thanks; for this is the will of God in Christ Jesus for you.

April 3, 2005

Pray, Pray, Pray!
By Pat Verbal

Scripture
Daniel 6:6–11; 1 Thessalonians 5:16–18; Matthew 15:36; 26:39

Lesson Aim
Children will learn how powerful prayer is.

Life Skill
Children will begin to make prayer a lifelong habit.

Bible Lesson: Pray! Pray! Pray!
Needed: Small stones.

Show stones to the children.

Say: What Bible story do these stones remind you of? (David and Goliath) Did you know that this same David battled against another giant? Well, he did. Listen to what the Bible says about it.

David's hands shook as he wiped the sweat from his head and replaced his heavy metal helmet. He glanced at the afternoon sun beating down on Israel's weary troops that were in battle with their dreaded enemy, the Philistines.

They were no ordinary soldiers. They were giants! This one was named Ishbi-Benob, and he was a descendant of Goliath's cousin. He carried a bronze spearhead that weighed about twenty pounds. He bragged to everyone that he would kill David with his new sword.

"Will these ugly, godless giants ever give up and go home?" David said to his officer.

"Please sir, let me escort you back up the hill where you can observe the battle," begged his first officer. "You are too tired to fight any longer."

David grabbed the horn of his saddle and tried to sit up straighter. "I've killed a giant, and with God's help Ishbi-Benob will be the next," David yelled as his horse charged forward into the thick of the battle.

His head throbbed with pain as he tried to remember when he was a fearless, young boy who killed a giant with faith in his God and a slingshot. Suddenly he saw the blinding glare of a silver blade. Clutching his shield tightly to his chest, David whispered a prayer and said, "I will call to the Lord. He is worthy of praise. And I will be saved from my enemies" (2 Sam. 22:4 ICB).

Those words were the last thing he remembered. David's nephew, Abishai, had been watching David's back all day. When he saw David fall from his horse, Abishai rode in to rescue him. He quickly struck down the Philistine and killed him. David's army cheered their victory but was worried about David. "You are not going out to battle again!" Abishai declared to David. "Why should we risk God's anointed king?"

They all agreed and kept David safe in future battles. Four other descendants of the giant were killed by David's men, including one who had six fingers on each hand and six toes on each foot!

David praised God, this time not for strength to kill another giant but for God's protection in every situation.

What do you do when you need protection? God wants us to pray like David did and he will protect us!

 Song Suggestions

No Need to Worry by Jana Alayra from "Jump into the Light" (Montjoy Music 1995)

Pray, Pray, Pray by Mary Rice Hopkins from "Good Buddies" (Big Steps 4 U 1994)

Let the Lord Have His Way Songsheets published by CEF Press, P.O. Box 348, Warrenton, Mo. 63383

Craft for Older and Younger Children: Prayer Chain
Needed: White, black, blue, red, and green construction paper.
Cut into 3-inch x 1-inch pieces. Each child should have one strip of each color.

Say: We are going to make a prayer chain to help us remember how to pray. Make a circle with the white strip. The white will remind us of praise and worship. We praise and worship God who is in heaven. The white will remind us of the purity of heaven.

Now we will add a black strip. The black will remind us to tell God about our sins, the things that we have done wrong.

The next color will be blue. The blue will stand for thanks. We thank God for everything that God does for us. Blue is like the sky that never ends; that's how much God does for us. His loving-kindness never ends!

Now we will add a green ring to remind us of the needs of others. We always want to pray for other people, and green will remind us of this. Green is the color of growing plants, and we will grow when we think of others.

We also need to pray for our own needs and ourselves. We will use red for this. Red is the color of love, and we should love ourselves as God loves us. Whenever we pray, we should pray for all these things

Snack: Talking to God

Needed: Bananas and peanut butter (be careful of allergies).
Using a banana as a phone, pretend to call someone and have a little conversation.
Say: Oh, hi kids, I just talked to my friend. Now I'm going to talk to God.

Pretend to dial the banana phone. Wait for responses from the kids. They will tell you that you can't talk to God that way. Act surprised and then ask children, Well, how can we talk to God?

Let children tell you.

Say: You're right! We don't need a phone to talk to God! We can always talk to God. He is always listening. We can close our eyes when we pray; we can also pray with our eyes open. We can pray anytime and anywhere!

Eat the snack!

Memory Verse: 1 Thessalonians 5:16–18 ICB
Always be happy. Never stop praying. Give thanks whatever happens. That is what God wants for you in Christ Jesus.

Alternate Version (New King James)
Rejoice always, pray without ceasing, in everything give thanks; for this is the will of God in Christ Jesus for you.

Memory Verse Activity: Say It Again!
Say the verse together. Then say the verse a section at a time, while leading the children to echo the section back to you.
Always be happy.
Never stop praying.
Give thanks whatever happens.
That is what God wants
For you in Christ Jesus.

Prayer Focus
Dear God, thank you for giving us a way to talk directly to you through prayer! Help us to remember to pray every day. Amen.

April 6, 2005

Rewards of Faithfulness, Midweek
By Vicki Wiley

Scripture
1 Corinthians 3:14, 15

Lesson Aim
Children will learn that God gives instructions for our lives.

Life Skill
Children will learn that God provides a "blueprint" for our lives and for everything in creation.

Bible Learning Activity for Younger Children: Building a Foundation
Needed: Blocks.

Let children build a building with the blocks in this manner.

Ask: What is important to remember when we think of God? (Place a block on the foundation for each thing they mention.)

Ask: What is important to remember when we think of our family? (Add the second layer of the building.)

Continue in this manner until a tall building is completed. Continue asking questions as they build: What is important to remember when we think of Jesus? Our friends? People who don't know Jesus?

Say: The Bible says that we can build a strong house with a strong foundation when we remember God first!

Bible Learning Activity for Older Children: Life Building!
Needed: Real blueprints, paper, and blue markers for each child.

Show children the blueprints and talk about them.

Ask: What is interesting about these blueprints? Did the builders follow the blueprints when they built the building?

We need to live our lives by God's blueprints too. What are some of the things that God wants us to include in building our life? (kindness, love, faith)

Let's draw a blueprint of our *life building*! Show children how to draw pictures of the important things and people in their lives.

Enrichment for Younger Children: Being Faithful

Needed: Fruits and vegetables, a knife.

God is always faithful to us. What does it mean to "be faithful"? God is faithful, and that means we can trust him always to be there for us, always to love us, always to help us.

Let's try a little experiment. Let's guess what is in these fruits and vegetables.

Bring them out one at a time and let children guess what is inside. They will, of course, always be right.

God is faithful with our food. The same thing is always in the vegetables. You will never buy an orange that is filled with peas, will you? It's the same with God. You can always trust him to be the same, every time you talk to him!

Enrichment for Older Children: Celery Surprise!

Needed: Celery, food coloring, glass, water.

Add food coloring to water in glass. Stick celery stalk into water. Tell children that in a few hours you can look at this again and see what has happened.

When you return, you will see that the celery has absorbed the colored water and that it has begun to color the celery, too.

God made the vegetables so they could grow. This shows how they "drink" water and grow. This is God's "blueprint" for plants. God is faithful to us. God always has a fun way to find out things!

Memory Verse: 1 Corinthians 3:14 ICB

If the building that a man puts on the foundation still stands, he will get his reward.

Alternate Version (New King James)
If anyone's work which he has built on it endures, he will receive a reward.

April 10, 2005

Rewards of Faithfulness
By Eric Titus

Scripture
1 Corinthians 3:14, 15

Lesson Aim
Children will learn that God gives instructions for our lives.

Life Skill
Children will learn that God provides a "blueprint" for our lives and for everything in creation.

Bible Lesson: The Rewards of Faithfulness
Needed: A set of blueprints (or a floor plan for a house), a tape measure, and a Bible.

How many of you children have ever seen a building or a house being built? What did you think when you saw it? Do you think it's easy or hard to build a house? I think that it might be hard because I don't know a lot about building buildings! But people who build houses and buildings have tools to help them to build in the right way.

The first and most important thing they have is a plan of how to put the building together, like this one. (Show the children the blueprint or floor plan.) Sometimes these plans are called blueprints. This shows the builders how long boards should be cut, how big a room is, where to put the plumbing, how large each room is and where every room will be when it is finished and many other important things about the building.

A tape measure helps to show how long, high, or thick boards and other kinds of materials need to be. (Have a child come and help you with the tape measure). Let's pretend the blueprint tells us we need a board to be 8 feet long. (Pull out the tape measure until it reads 8 feet.) What if the builder decided not to be faithful to the blueprint? By the way does anyone know what *faithful* means? Those are good answers.

Faithful means "loyal," and it also means to be true and to keep close to that which we know is right and to try not to do what is wrong. If the builder decided to make the board only 6 feet long (change the tape measure to 6 feet), would the builder be faithful to the blueprint? If the builder makes a lot of changes and is not faithful to the blueprint, what do you think will happen to the building he or she is building? So you think that it might be a real big mess? What do you think would happen if the builder followed the plans? Do you think the house or building might be beautiful? Nice? Useful? Do you think the builder would be rewarded for following the blueprint? The first reward the builder would get is knowing that he or she built a good strong building or house. Then somebody might want to buy the house. The builder's boss would reward the builders with more work because they were faithful in following the plans.

God has a blueprint that he would like you to follow. One of Jesus' followers, Paul, wrote to a church in a city called Corinth a long time ago. He told the church at Corinth that Jesus was the blueprint and that we should build everything in our lives to be exactly like the blueprint God gave to us. We need to be faithful to live our lives like Jesus lived his.

Sometimes we don't live our lives like Jesus did (change the measuring tape again), and if we do that a lot, what do you think our lives will look like? They might be a real big mess! But if we are faithful to live our lives like Jesus lived his and taught us how to live ours, then what do you think our lives would look like? Beautiful? Strong? Useful, Full of Love? Full of Kindness?

When we are faithful to live like Jesus, Paul tells us that there is a special reward for us. The building of our lives will look like we have built them by God's plans, and that means our lives will be beautiful, loving, kind, full of joy. Those are things that last forever.

Song Suggestions

He's Got Plans by Dean-o from "Soul Surfin'" (FKO Music, Inc., 1999)

You're in My Heart to Stay by Jana Alayra from "Dig Down Deep" (Montjoy Music 1997)

Good News Songsheets published by CEF Press, P.O. Box 348, Warrenton, Mo. 63383

It Started with an Egg by Mary Rice Hopkins from "In My Garden" (Big Steps 4 U 1995)

 Craft for Younger Children: Building a House
Needed: Construction paper sheet and construction paper shapes such as triangles, squares, and rectangles.

Say: We are going to build a house. You get to choose what your house will look like. Show children how to combine the shapes to form a house.

You had a plan in your mind when you build this house. Look how well your house turned out! God has a plan in his mind for your life. Your life will turn out well too!

 Craft for Older Children: Planning the House!
Needed: Scraps of wood, paper tubes, paper, other scrap materials, and glue.

Say: When a builder wants to build a building, he finds materials to use to help him. Let's try to build a building now using these materials.

Let children build their buildings.

Ask: Was that hard or easy to build? (hard because we didn't have everything we need, easy because it was kind of fun)

When a builder builds a building, he makes sure that he has everything he needs. When God decides what your life will be like, he will also make sure that you have everything that you need!

Snack: Mini Houses

Needed: Square crackers, small squares of cheese, toothpicks, cherry tomatoes, mini marshmallows, any other "building supply" you want to use.

Place all ingredients on a table and let children "build" a house with the food. Remind them of the memory verse as they build and eat their snack.

Memory Verse: 1 Corinthians 3:14 ICB

If the building that a man puts on the foundation still stands, he will get his reward.

Alternate Version (New King James)
If anyone's work which he has built on it endures, he will receive a reward.

Memory Verse Activity: Building the Verse

Write the verse on the whiteboard in this manner: Make "bricks" (rectangles) around each word forming a "building."

> he will get his reward.
> still stands
> on the foundation
> that a man puts
> If the building

Ask: What is the "foundation" of this verse? (the bottom line: if the building) What is the top of this verse? (he will get his reward) This will help us remember that if we follow God's blueprint for our lives, we will be rewarded!

Prayer Focus

Dear God, help us to build lives so that we are faithful to Jesus and follow the ways Jesus taught us to live so that our lives might be filled with your great rewards. Amen.

April 13, 2005

Shhhh … Did You Hear That? Midweek
By Vicki Wiley

Scripture
Psalm 29:2

Lesson Aim
Children will learn what worship is and how to worship God.

Life Skill
Children will learn that worship is more that singing.

Bible Learning Activity for Younger Children: Worship and Praise
Needed: Simple instruments for the children to use such as blocks, bells, something to clang, CD playe and CD

Say: Worship is a way to praise God. The Bible tells us that we can worship with instruments or just by singing and praising. Let's try to make a joyful noise to praise God.

Put on CD and let children play instruments to the music. Congratulate them on the "joyful noise."

Bible Learning Activity for Older Children: Collage of Worship
Needed: Markers, cardstock, assortment of buttons, glitter, other leftover craft supplies.

Say: Let's all make a worship banner. On the top of your banner, write the word *Worship*.

Now you have a worship banner! It's all finished! But how can you make it more meaningful? (Put more on it. Make mine different from the others.) You're right! You can add some glitter, some buttons, anything you want. Your worship banner will still be a worship banner, but now it will really be yours.

Real worship is like that too. You can worship God in many ways: by singing, by thanking and praising God, by telling God how much you love him. No matter what you do to worship God, God loves the worship!

Enrichment for Younger Children:

Needed: Glass vase, spoon, baking soda, food coloring, vinegar.

Place some baking soda into the vase. Add some food coloring; red works great.

Say: Worship is like this. When I begin to worship, I begin to feel good. I enjoy the worship, and it makes me feel close to God. This baking soda will represent God.

After I worship for awhile, my worship overflows like this. (Pour in vinegar.) Worship makes our hearts overflow as we are filled with the Holy Spirit. Worship makes us close to God!

Enrichment for Older Children: Worship Overflows!

Ask the kids what is valuable to them, and list their answers on the whiteboard.

How do you show that it is valuable? (take care of it, protect it, lock it up)

Write *Worth* on the top of the board as you say, "These things are worth a lot to you."

Then ask: What or who is the most valuable thing or person in the universe? They will answer: God.'

Say: Today we are going to talk about worship.

Erase the *th* is *Worth* on the whiteboard, and change it to *Worship*. Say: *Worship* means "to give a show of worth." We do this by:

W   Witnessing or telling others about Jesus

O   Obeying God

R   Reading God's Word

S   Singing praises to God

H   By being holy, as God is holy

I   Receiving Instruction

P   Praying to God

Ask: How do you like to worship?

Memory Verse: Psalm 29:2 ICB

Praise the Lord for the glory of his name; worship the Lord because he is holy.

Alternate Version (New King James)

Give unto the LORD the glory due to His name; worship the LORD in the beauty of holiness.

April 17, 2005

Shhhh ... Did You Hear That?
By Mary Rice Hopkins

Scripture
Psalm 29:2

Lesson Aim
Children will learn what worship is and how to worship God.

Life Skill
Children will learn that worship is more that singing.

Bible Lesson
Needed: Bird whistle or recording from nature.

Shhhhh. Did you hear that? There it is again!

Just stop for a moment and listen to all that God has made.

Listen! Isn't it great to hear the sound of God's creation? Why, it's just like a nonstop creation concert. Every one of God's creatures is adding to the song. Do you hear the hummingbirds, the flutter of their tiny wings? How about the grasshoppers with their steady chirping beat. It's all music played for the Creator.

Did you ever wonder why we sing praises to our heavenly Father? The Bible tells us in the book of Psalms that God takes great pleasure in the praises of his people. The same God who made the delicate hummingbird gave you a voice to sing praises. Whether you are on the playground laughing, leaving for school, cleaning your room, or wherever you find yourself, God wants you to celebrate his creation with the voice he gave you. The God of creation loves you more than you know. He takes pleasure, which means it makes him happy, in the songs that come from your heart. The creation concert has already begun. Sing out!

Song Suggestions

Do You Know About Jesus? Songsheets published by CEF Press P.O. Box 348, Warrenton, Mo. 63383

He Is Really God! by Dean-o from "You Got It All" (For Kids Only, Inc. 1997)

Can You Hear My Heart? by Jana Alayra from "Dig Down Deep" (Montjoy Music 1997)

 Craft for Younger Children: Shake and Praise!
Needed: Heavy plastic disposable plates, chenille sticks, and bells. Before class punch holes around the edges of the plate.
Let the children use chenile sticks to attach bells to the plate through the holes. Shake and praise!

 Craft for Older Children: Shaker Praiser!
Needed: Clean 16-ounce plastic soda bottle with the lid, white glue thinned with water, tissue paper.
Tear several colors of tissue paper into small pieces and place them in the center of the table. Have the children paint a small portion of their bottle with glue. Children will cover the glue with pieces of tissue paper. Continue gluing and covering the bottle with tissue paper. Allow to dry.
Place beans or rice into the bottle and put the lid back on. When it is dry children can shake and praise!

Snack: Children Praising!

Needed: Cubes of cheese, grapes, stick pretzels.

Show children how to make a "praise person." The cube of cheese is the body. The grape is the head. The stick pretzels are arms and legs; stick them into the cube of cheese.

Say: Does this look like a real person? Of course, it doesn't! But can real people praise Jesus? How do they do it? We can praise Jesus because he loves us!

Alternative snack: Using a cookie cutter, cut children out of Jello-O. Let children add features with raisins, coconut, and carrot shavings.

Memory Verse: Psalm 29:2 ICB

Praise the Lord for the glory of his name; worship the Lord because he is holy.

Alternate Version (New King James)
Give unto the LORD the glory due to His name; worship the LORD in the beauty of holiness.

Memory Verse Activity: Praise and Worship

Lead the children in a time of praise and worship. Using the instruments they made, say the verse together many times. Create a tune to sing the verse.

Say: God is pleased whenever we praise and worship!

Prayer Focus

Dear God, thank you for all you do for us. Thank you that we can praise and worship you. Amen.

April 20, 2005

The Image of God, Midweek
By Tina Hauser

Scripture
Acts 9:31

Lesson Aim
Children will learn that they are made in the image of God.

Life Skill
Children will learn to live a life that reflects the image of God.

Bible Learning Activity for Younger Children: Images, Images!
Needed: Handheld mirrors.

Show children the mirrors and say: Whom do you see in this mirror? How do you know who it is? When you look at the mirror, you are seeing an image of that person. It is not the real person, but the image looks so much like the person that we know just who it is!

We are made in the image of God. That means we are like God. We can act like God, and people can know God just by knowing us!

Bible Learning Activity for Older Children: Mirror, Mirror
In a mirror we see a reflection of our self. It is not really us we see, just a reflection. In fact, you may not realize it, but it is a backwards, or inverted image of yourself that you see in a mirror. The Bible says in Genesis 1:26 that God created us in his image. This means that we are not God, but we are a reflection of what God is like. The things that make us different from other creatures is because of this image of God in us. Sometimes that image gets tainted, and we need to clean it up.

Read James 1:23–25. When we look in the Bible, it shows us the stains on the mirror of our life. It shows what is out of place, what we need to clean or cut or remove or adjust. When you get ready in the morning, you look in the mirror to see what needs to be fixed so that you are presentable to the world. God's Word shows us what we need to fix to be presentable to God and to others, what we need to do so that our reflection of God is clear and untainted. These verses say that the person who does not listen to the Word of God and make the changes it shows is like a person who after looking in the mirror in the morning, goes out for the day without changing anything. He will be a disgrace. So will we if we do not read and heed God's Word!

How's your image of God? Are there some things you need to fix? If there are, don't be like that foolish man. Get them fixed today through confession and repentance!

Enrichment for Younger Children: Doh What I Doh

Needed: Play clay, objects to copy.

Choose four kids to compete in this contest. Each is given a tub of play clay. Show an object to each child but not to the audience. Let the children try to create the object with the play clay so the audience can tell what the object is. Show objects and images to the audience. The audience votes by clapping volume.

Say: It is hard to make a perfect image out of play clay. It is hard to make it look just like the real. It is also hard for us to be an image of God since we are not perfect, but we should do the best we can!

Enrichment for Older Children: Silhouettes

Needed: Butcher paper, black paper, flashlight, and a somewhat darkened room.

Show children how to make a silhouette by attaching the butcher paper to the wall at head height. Have child stand next to the paper.

Shine the flashlight at the child standing in front of the butcher paper. Have another child draw around the shadow created by the flashlight. Cut the silhouette out by putting the black paper behind the pattern created by the butcher paper drawing. You now have a silhouette!

After each child has made one, put the silhouettes on a table and try to match the silhouettes with the children.

Say: These silhouettes look like us enough for us to know who they are, but they are not the same as a photograph, are they? They are images of what we really look like, but not an exact copy.

God made us in his image. What do you think that means?

Memory Verse: Acts 9:31 ICB

The church everywhere in Judea, Galilee, and Samaria had a time of peace. With the help of the Holy Spirit, the group became stronger. The believers showed that they respected the Lord by the way they lived. Because of this, the group of believers grew larger and larger.

Alternate Version (New King James)

Then the churches throughout all Judea, Galilee, and Samaria had peace and were edified. And walking in the fear of the Lord and in the comfort of the Holy Spirit, they were multiplied.

April 24, 2005

The Image of God
By Karl Bastian

Scripture
Acts 9:31

Lesson Aim
Teach children that they are made in the image of God

Life Skill
To learn how to live a life that represents that image

Bible Lesson: Image of God
Needed: Several picture frames with glass only in them. (Simply purchase certificate frames and remove paper and backing, secure glass so it won't fall out.) You will also need some markers that can write on glass well, probably whiteboard markers.

Have several adult leaders come up front and give each a frame to hold up in front of their face. Then choose a child (older, good at drawing) for each leader. Their job is to decorate the leaders face by drawing on the glass. They can add beard, glasses, freckles, etc. Encourage them not to over-do it, as you still need to be able to see the leader. The audience will vote the best one. After they are done, have the audience choose the best one by volume of applause. Have fun switching them from leader to leader, and holding them up to yourself, and to the kids who drew them.

Say: The way that each leader looked was changed by what was drawn on the glass. God created us to be a perfect image of him, but too often sin marks us up and changes that image of what God intended. While these altered images were funny, the consequences of a marred image of God in life, can be tragic and difficult to live with.

God wants us to be like him, to act like him and be a part of a church family. God created us and God created the church and wants us to worship together in it with other believers.

OPTIONS:

(1) Have pre-drawn faces that you hold over volunteers faces.

(2) Get a full length mirror(s) and draw on them with black marker board, mustache, glasses, etc. and let the kids take turns looking at their image in the mirror altered.

 Song suggestions:

Lovin' God Is Livin' Great! by Dean-O from <u>You Got it All</u> (FKO Music, Inc. 1999)

He Can Do by Mary Rice Hopkins from <u>Kids Kamp</u> (Big Steps 4 U 1999)

Fix No Other God by Kurt Johnson, a.k.a. MrJ from <u>Kid Possible</u> (Kurt Johnson 1995)

God's Power Songsheets published by CEF Press, P.O. Box 348, Warrenton, Mo. 63383

 Craft For Younger Children: Children in the Image of God
Needed: construction paper

Cut children out using a typical shape of children. Let children glue the "paper doll children" onto another piece of construction paper. Write "Children in the Image of God" across the top of the paper.

Say "Who do you look like? Yes, your mom and dad! Who do you act like? (listen for repsonses)

Do you know who else you are like? You are like God! God is your heavenly father who will always love you. We are God's children, we are all God's children and we are made in the *image* of God.

Craft for Older Children: Tin Foil Mirrors

Needed: For each child: square of tin foil, ruler and construction paper or cardboard, optional: one cardboard frame

Make a frame by cutting one from construction paper or cardboard or use pre-made frame.

Show children how to make a mirror by attaching the tin foil to the frame (by the edges, not underneath) to cardboard and frame it. With the ruler flatten out the tin foil.

On the top of the frame write their name, and along the bottom, "Created in the Image of God." (Genesis 1:26)

Snack: Images, Images

Needed: Crackers or cookies in the shapes of objects, animals or people

Put all cookies and crackers on a tray. Have children guess what each one is.

Talk about the crackers and cookies and how they are "images" of the real thing.

Eat and enjoy!

Memory Verse: Acts 9:31 ICB

The church everywhere in Judea, Galilee, and Samaria had a time of peace. With the help of the Holy Spirit, the group became stronger. The believers showed that they respected the Lord by the way they lived. Because of this, the group of believers grew larger and larger.

Alternate Version (New King James)

Then the churches throughout all Judea, Galilee, and Samaria had peace and were edified. And walking in the fear of the Lord and in the comfort of the Holy Spirit, they were multiplied.

Memory Verse Activity: Practice Makes Perfect!
Write the verse on a tall standing mirror with an erasable marker. Say the verse over and over, each time allowing a child to come up and erase one word. By the time you get to the end, they will know the verse.

Prayer Focus
Dear God, Thank you for creating us in your image. Help us to follow you, love you, and be like you. Amen.

April 27, 2005

Jesus Is the Way! Midweek
By Vicki Wiley

Scripture
John 14:5–8

Lesson Aim
Children will learn that Jesus is the only way to salvation.

Bible Skill
Children will learn that the Bible teaches only one way to heaven.

Bible Learning Activity for Younger Children: Way, Truth, and Life!
Needed: Three signs, each one with one word on it, *Way, Truth, Life*.

Jesus said that he is the way, the truth, and the life. What do you think that means?

Hold up sign with the word *Way*.

Jesus said that he is the way. If you know the way to somewhere, what does that mean? (That is how you get there.) Jesus is the way to heaven!

Hold up sign with the word *Truth*.

Jesus said that he is the truth. If you tell the truth, what does that mean? (What you say is real.) Jesus said that he is the truth because what he says is real.

Hold up sign with the word *Life*.

Jesus said that he is the life. If you have life, what does that mean? Jesus said that he is the life because you will have eternal life in heaven with him and a great life here on earth with him!

Bible Learning Activity for Older Children: One Way to God!
Today many people believe that you can follow any religion and still go to

heaven, but that is not true. Do you know what other religions teach, what their followers believe?

Judaism is the religious culture of the Jewish people and is one of the world's oldest religions. It is the religion in the Bible, especially in the Old Testament. In Judaism, everyone is under God's rule.

Islam is a major world religion founded in Arabia. Based on the teachings of a man named Muhammad, one who practices Islam is called a Muslim. A practicing Muslim follows the teachings from the Koran, which Muslims believe is the written revelation from Allah (their God) to Muhammad.

Buddhism began in northeastern India and is based on the teachings of Siddhartha who became known as Buddha.

Hinduism originated in the area now called India and is still practiced by 80 percent of the people who live there. This religion does not have a holy book or a god to worship.

Although the people who worship in these religions believe that you should be moral and kind, they do not believe the most important truth; they do not believe that Jesus Christ is the Son of God. Without Jesus Christ, we cannot go to heaven. Jesus is the only way to get to God!

Enrichment for Younger Children: One Way to Go!

Needed: Footprints cut from paper.

Spread footprints on the ground. Have them lead from the classroom to a treat.

Say: I have a treat for you today! But where is it? (Let children guess. Some may guess that the footprints lead to the treat.) Yes! You're right! If we follow the footprints, we will get to the treat. Let's go! Let children follow you to the treat, bring the treat back to your room, and give it to the children as they return to their seats.

Say: There was only one way to get to this treat today. What was it? Since you followed the right way, did you get there? What would have happened if you had gone another way? You might not have found the treat. Jesus tells us that there is only one way to get to heaven and that is to follow him!

> **Enrichment for Older Children: Mapping the Way**
>
> Needed: A city map. Choose sites familiar to the children.
>
>   Ask: How do you get to the zoo? How do you get to the park? Yes, there is one way to go. If you follow this map you will get there.
>
>   Jesus also gave us a "map" to tell us how to get to heaven. Jesus' map is the Bible. The Bible tells us that if we follow what Jesus tells us to do, we will follow him to heaven!

Memory Verse: John 14:6 ICB

"I am the way. And I am the truth and the life. The only way to the Father is through me."

Alternate Version (New King James)

Jesus said to him, "I am the way, the truth, and the life. No one comes to the Father except through Me."

May 1, 2005

Jesus Is the Way!
By Vicki Wiley

Scripture
John 14:5–8

Lesson Aim
Children will learn that Jesus is the only way to salvation.

Life Skill
Children will learn that the Bible teaches only one way to heaven.

Bible Lesson
Needed: A road map, a backpack full of things that you would need to travel including a snack, a water bottle, and a Bible.

Say: Hey! Look at what I have in my backpack!

Take things out one at a time and explain them, taking out the map last. Say: I have a snack in case I get hungry. I have a water bottle in case I am thirsty. A map? Why is this in here? Why do I need a map? (Let kids answer.)

This map can show me lots of ways to get where I am going. (Show it to the children.) Look! If I want to go to Disneyland (replace with a location close to your house that would be familiar to the kids), here is one way I can get there, and here is another way for me to get there. There are lots of different ways to get to Disneyland.

But I know another place that I want to go. See if you can guess what I am talking about. To get to this place, there is only one way to get there. The Bible has the directions to this place.

Can you guess? Yes! It's heaven! There is only one way to get to heaven, and that is to believe in Jesus Christ and follow him as Lord of your life. The Bible tells us that Thomas asked Jesus how to get to heaven. This is what Jesus said: "I am the way. And I am the truth and the life. The only way to the Father is through me" (John 14:6 ICB).

Today some people might tell you that there are many ways to have eternal life. Other religions might tell you that all roads lead to heaven. But that is not true; it is a lie. There is only one way to get to heaven, and that is through Jesus Christ!

 Song Suggestions

God's Way Right by Dean-o from "You Got It All" (FKO Music, Inc. 1997)

Let the Lord Have His Way Songsheets published by CEF Press, P.O. Box 348, Warrenton, Mo. 63383

Open the Eyes of My Heart by Norm Hewitt from "Fired Up" (Revelation Generation 2002)

Craft for all Children: One Way Magnet

Needed: One piece of cardstock for each child cut in shape of an arrow or with a pattern for children to cut out, magnet, felt-tip markers.

Say: There are many religions in the world today, but only one leads to heaven. Let's make a magnet to remember this. Write on the arrow: "One Way to Jesus." Color the arrow as you wish with markers and attach the magnet to the back.

Snack: One Way!

Needed: Large stick pretzels, cheese cut into triangles.

Show children how to make an arrow by sticking the pretzel into the cheese triangle.

Say: There is only one way to have eternal life and that is by accepting Jesus Christ into your life as your Savior. This snack will stand for the one way there is to go to heaven (point the arrow up)—straight up through Jesus!

Memory Verse: John 14:6 ICB
"I am the way. And I am the truth and the life. The only way to the Father is through me."

Alternate Version (New King James)
Jesus said to him, "I am the way, the truth, and the life. No one comes to the Father except through Me."

Memory Verse Activity: One Way!
Needed: Whiteboard with verse on it, balloon for each child.
   Say: This is an important verse for us today because it tells us how to get to heaven.
   Show children how to bounce the balloons into the air. Bounce once for each word. Lead the children to chant the verse and bounce the balloons. Then sit and repeat the verse together.

Prayer Focus
Dear God, thank you for all you do for us and especially for giving us a way to have eternal life. Thank you for your Son who came to save us. Amen.

May 4, 2005

(Special Activity, Mother's Day)

Listen to Your Mother! Midweek
By Tina Hauser

Scripture
Psalm 78:6, 7

Lesson Aim
Children will understand that faith can be passed from generation to generation.

Life Skill
Children will learn to cherish the traditions in their faith-filled families.

Bible Learning Activity for Younger Children: Are You My Mother?
Needed: Recording of mothers' voices. Record the voices of some of the children's mothers. Ask each mother to say one sentence that reflects something she would like her child to know about God. Instruct them not to say the child's name.

Play the tape for the children, pausing after each mother's statement. Ask the children to raise their hand if it is their mother.

Say: Was it difficult to recognize your mother's voice? Why was it so easy? Can you remember what your mother said to you on the tape? Ask children to repeat what they heard their mother say. We listen to our mothers because they are important people in our lives. God tells mothers to teach their children about him, and he also tells children to listen to their mothers.

Bible Learning Activity for Older Children: Here She Is!
Needed: For each child, a chocolate bar, a piece of paper cut to 6 inches x 5 1/2 inches (or a size to fit the chocolate bar), tape.

Say: Our mothers teach us many wonderful things. We need to listen to our mothers because God gave them the special job of teaching their children.

Give each child a plain piece of paper (pastels are fine) cut to 6 inches x 5 1/2 inches and a chocolate bar. The children will be making a new wrapper for the candy bar. About halfway down, write "HERE SHE IS" in large capital letters, except push the words together so it appears to be one word "HERESHEIS." The children will write things they have learned from their mothers in smaller writing all over the new label. When they have completed the label, wrap it around the already wrapped candy bar and secure it with a piece of tape.

Enrichment Activity for Younger Children: My Mom Says That!
Needed: Paper party blowout for each child.

Say: Some of the things your mom says to you are to keep you from getting hurt. Some things she says help you learn manners. Some things are to help you make good habits. And some are just because she loves you!

Give each child a paper party blowout. Say: Each time I say a sentence that you have heard your mom say, celebrate our moms loving us by blowing on your party blowout.

Is your room clean?

Don't touch that pot, it's hot.

Have you finished your homework?

Don't forget to put your gloves on.

What did you learn at school today?

This is the last time I'm telling you.

Don't talk back.

We don't want to be late.

This is a great paper.

If it's OK with your father.

I'm so proud of you.

Do you have your permission slip?

When are they coming over?

I love you!

Say: Today is a special day for your mom. What do you do to celebrate Mother's Day? Can you do something special for your mom today?

Enrichment Activity for Older Children: History of Mother's Day

Ask: Has there always been a Mother's Day? Have you ever wondered when people started honoring mothers on a special day?

There was a day in England called Mothering Sunday but no special day in America. Early in the 1900s a woman named Anna Jarvis began wearing a carnation in honor of mothers everywhere. She encouraged other people to wear the carnations and worked hard at getting a special day celebrated all over the country. In 1914, President Woodrow Wilson made Mother's Day a holiday for our whole country. Mothers everywhere would be honored every year on the second Sunday of May.

Were you thinking of giving your mother a flower for Mother's Day? Why not get her a carnation like the one worn by Anna Jarvis! The woman who started Mother's Day would like that.

Memory Verse: Psalm 78:6, 7 ICB

Then their children would know them, even their children not yet born. And they would tell their children. So they would all trust God.

Alternate Version (New King James)

That the generation to come might know them, the children who would be born, that they may arise and declare them to their children, that they may set their hope in God.

May 8, 2005

(Special Activity, Mother's Day)
Listen to Your Mother!
By Tina Hauser

Scripture
Psalm 78:6, 7

Lesson Aim
Children will understand that faith can be passed from generation to generation.

Life Skill
Children will learn to cherish the traditions in their faith-filled families.

Bible lesson: Listen to Your Mother!
Needed: Family photos, baby clothes, other family memorabilia.

Say: What are these? (Show family photos.) Yes, you're right. These are pictures of my family. What are these? (Show baby clothes.) Yes, you're right! These were my daughter's little clothes from when she was a baby. She can't fit into them anymore, what do you think I should do with them? Yes, I'll "pass them down."

"Passing them down" means that I am going to give them to someone else. Maybe there is another little girl who needs these clothes now. The Bible has a story about someone who passed something down too, but it wasn't baby clothes!

It was faith! In Bible times there was a grandmother named Lois. Lois told her daughter, Eunice, all about faith in Jesus. Lois passed down her faith to Eunice. Then one day Eunice had a son named Timothy. Eunice passed down her faith to Timothy. Timothy likely passed down his faith to someone else too!

How does your mom pass down her faith to you? Yes, by reading the Bible to you and taking you to church, by praying with you and telling you all about Jesus. That is how you build your own faith, by learning first and then believing! When you listen to your mother, you can learn all about Jesus!

Can you pass down your faith? You can! Even children can pass on their faith by telling someone else about Jesus!

 Song Suggestions

Believin' On by Jana Alayra from "Believin' On" (Montjoy Music 2002)

Little Is Much by Mary Rice Hopkins from "15 Singable Songs" (Big Steps 4 U 1988)

Faith Will Do by Dean-o from "You Got It All" (FKO Music, Inc. 1997)

God's Power Songsheets published by CEF Press, P.O. Box 348, Warrenton, Mo. 63383

 Craft for Younger Children: Mother's Day Card

Needed: Cardstock, heart shapes, markers, left over lace, ribbons.

Say: Have you ever received a card? It's fun to get a card from someone, especially when it says something that means a lot to us. Let's make a card for our moms.

What should the card say? What can we draw on the card?
After children discuss, let them create their cards.

Craft for Older Children: Generations of Faith Family Tree
Needed: Green, brown, and red or white craft foam. Cut hearts from red or white craft foam. Cut tree shape from green craft foam and truck shape from brown craft foam. Glue trunk to tree prior to class.

Say: Today we are going to make a family tree. Who are the people in your family? Let children tell you the names of the people in their families.

Pass our hearts and write names of family members on the hearts (one name on each heart). Glue the hearts on the tree. Write "Generations of Faith" on the top of the tree.

Snack: Mom Cookies

 Needed: Heart-shaped cookies, frosting, decorations.
Say: Today is Mother's Day. Today is a special day for your moms, isn't it? What do you plan to do to make this a special day?

We are going to make cookies for you to take to your mom. You may decorate two cookies right now, one for you to eat and one to give to your mom!

Memory Verse: Psalm 78:6, 7 ICB

Then their children would know them, even their children not yet born. And they would tell their children. So they would all trust God.

Alternate Version (New King James)
That the generation to come might know them, the children who would be born, that they may arise and declare them to their children, that they may set their hope in God.

Memory Verse Activity: Clothesline Relay

Needed: One clothesline hung across the room, two sets of the words of the verse printed on paper—one word on each sheet, clothespins.

Say: We are going to learn our verse today by "hanging it up" on the line. Divide the group into two teams. Give each team one set of the words in order. Children will run to the clothesline, pin their verse on the line and run back. When the verse is all hung up on the line, kids will read the verse and then sit down. The first team to sit wins!

Prayer Focus

Dear God, thank you for our mothers. Thank you for the love they give us. Help us always to be kind to our mothers. Amen.

May 11, 2005

Dial 777, Midweek
By Tina Hauser

Scripture
Ephesians 5:15

Lesson Aim
Children will understand the work of the third person of the Trinity, the Holy Spirit.

Life Skill
Children will want to seek the Holy Spirit's leading in every area of their lives.

Bible Learning Activity for Younger Children: Be Careful!
Needed: Raw egg and a teaspoon for each child.

Give each child a raw egg and a teaspoon. (You may want to do this activity on a tile floor, just in case.)

Children will walk across the room and back, carrying their raw eggs in their spoons.

Ask: How did you feel when you were carrying your egg across the room? What would've happened if you weren't careful when you were carrying the egg? If you had been carrying a marshmallow, would you have been so careful? What would've happened if your egg had fallen out of your spoon?

Just as we were careful carrying the egg, God wants us to be careful when we make decisions. God sent the Holy Spirit to help us make decisions. The Holy Spirit helps us know what is right and wrong.

What are some decisions you have to make? When someone takes the swing away from you at the park, you have to make a decision about what you are going to do. When you see the kid next door put a scratch in the side of your neighbor's car, you have to decide if you are going to tell anyone. When your teacher tells you to practice more on your spelling, you have to decide whether you are going to watch another television show or spend your time studying.

Ask the Holy Spirit to help you be careful and wise in your decisions.

Bible Learning Activity for Older Children: Caution!

Needed: A piece of plastic caution tape for each child and a black permanent marker like a Sharpie.

Give each child a piece of yellow caution tape about two feet long. This can be purchased in the hardware section of any of the large discount department stores. In large lettering the children will write on their tape with a permanent black marker: "Be careful how you live."

Say: The Bible tells us that we need to be careful when we make decisions. We need to use God's wisdom. That wisdom comes from the Holy Spirit who lives in us and teaches us about God's truth. Name a decision you need to be careful in making. The children will write these decisions in small lettering on their caution tape.

You may want to hang your piece of caution tape in your room to remind you to be careful in making decisions, and to help you remember to ask for the Holy Spirit's help with each one.

Enrichment for Younger Children: Listen, Listen!

Needed: *Finding Nemo* DVD

Most of the children have probably already seen the movie *Finding Nemo*. Show a clip (scene 6, Nemo Lost) from the movie where Nemo breaks the rules and goes beyond where he is supposed to swim. He gets angry with his father for telling him what to do.

Ask: Does Nemo ask for advice from anyone? Does Nemo think about what he's going to do? Why do you think Nemo's father made that rule for Nemo? Disobeying his father was not a wise thing for Nemo to do. He was not being careful when he broke the rules. Are there places your parents don't want you to go? Are there places you can't go alone? How do you feel about the rules?

The Holy Spirit will teach you and help you obey if you ask him.

Enrichment for Older Children: Keeping Safe

Needed: Carpenter with power handsaw, piece of wood.

Ask an experienced carpenter to demonstrate safe use of a power handsaw. Before he begins, ask children if they know of any safety precautions the carpenter should take before starting to cut the wood.

Some safety tips to cover include: Keep the power tool unplugged until you are ready to use it. Keep observers back from where you are using the tool. Wear safety glasses in case something flies through the air. Keep the safety guard down over the blade. Never put your fingers close to the blade.

Ask: What would happen if the carpenter did not follow these safety rules? The children will love seeing how the tool works. You may want to mark a safety line on the floor with a piece of masking tape. The children will not be allowed to get any closer to the carpenter and his tool than that line. After the demonstration, give each child a piece of the wood the carpenter cut to take home.

Say: The carpenter was careful in his work. God tells us to be careful when we make decisions. He tells us to let the Holy Spirit guide us. If we do as God says, we will make the right decisions, and we will be much happier. If we aren't careful in making decisions, then we may not be happy with the results of those decisions.

Memory Verse: Ephesians 5:15 ICB

So be very careful how you live. Do not live like those who are not wise. Live wisely.

Alternate Version (New King James)
See then that you walk circumspectly, not as fools but as wise.

May 15, 2005

Dial 777
By Pat Verbal

Scripture
Ephesians 5:15

Lesson Aim
Children will understand the work of the third person of the Trinity, the Holy Spirit.

Life Skill
Children will want to seek the Holy Spirit's leading in every area of their lives.

Bible Lesson: Dial 777
Needed: Use a walkie-talkie or set up a cell phone to work with a mic off stage to place a phone call to the Holy Spirit.

Hebrew children in Bible times were taught to pray this prayer every morning and evening. "Hear, O Israel: The LORD our God, the LORD is one!" (Deut. 6:4 NKJV). Because people worshiped many different gods, the Hebrews needed to be constantly reminded that Jehovah God was the one true God. Children of the Old Testament also prayed for a Savior who would bring a new covenant (a promise or an agreement with God).

God is a Spirit, but he was also a man through His Son, Jesus, who came to earth. Jesus showed us what God is like and sent the Holy Spirit to live in those who believe in him. God, Jesus, and the Holy Spirit are three parts of God's nature. It may sound confusing, but you have different parts to your nature too.

Ask a child to come to the front of the room. Say: Let's describe the many parts of [child's name] nature. She is a daughter, a sister, a niece, a granddaughter, a cousin, and a friend. Is she six different people? No, she is one special person. If time permits, let children ask her questions about her different roles.

No one understands the Trinity completely, not even your pastor. We do know that when Jesus left his disciples and ascended into heaven, he promised to send the Holy Spirit to live inside of them. Maybe it would help if we talked to the Holy Spirit. Would you like me to call him on my cell phone?

Dial the number for the person set up in another room.

Holy Spirit: Hello, this is the Holy Spirit. How can I help you?

Leader: Hi! My name is [your name], and I'm here with the children at [church name]. We're talking about you, and we were wondering if you would answer a few questions.

Holy Spirit: Sure! I'm always ready to talk to my friends.

Leader: People in the Bible said they saw God in visions. They also saw Jesus, but has anyone ever seen you.

Holy Spirit: No, you can't see me, but you can know that I'm there with you. You can't see the wind, but the trees wave to you while it pushes clouds and kites across the sky. The wind is everywhere and so am I (John 3:5–8).

Leader: We know that God made the world and inspired the Bible. Jesus taught people and did miracles. What do you do?

Holy Spirit: I have many jobs. I help people understand more about Jesus. I comfort you when you feel sad and make you feel happy inside.

Leader: Like a mom and dad, right?

Holy Spirit: Yes! And like a parent, I can teach you the difference between right and wrong and help you pray when you're not sure what to say.

Leader: That happens a lot to me and the kids. The Bible tells us that you like to grow fruit.

Holy Spirit: My fruit is special because it grows inside the human heart. It brings a sweet harvest to you and everyone around you. Maybe you have some of my fruit in your class?

Leader: [Lead children in listing the fruit of the spirit in Galatians 5:22, 23.] Love, joy, peace, longsuffering, kindness, goodness, faithfulness, gentleness, self-control—we're working on it, Sir!

Holy Spirit: Well, don't try to do it all on your own. That's what I'm here for. I'm head of the power department. My power is like armor (Eph. 6:10–17). You don't need to be afraid because I'll stay with you.

Leader: Wow! That's what we need.

Holy Spirit: I've got to go. I'm getting another call. Remember, I'm praying for you (Rom. 8:26, 27).

Leader: Thanks, we won't forget! (Hang up.)

Song Suggestions

It's Gonna Rock! by Dean-o from "God City" (BibleBeat Music 2001)

Little Is Much by Mary Rice Hopkins from "15 Singable Songs" (Big Steps 4 U 1988)

Less of Me by Mister Bill from "When I Grow Up" (Mister Bill Music 1997)

G-O-S-P-E-L means Good News! Songsheets published by CEF Press, P.O. Box 348, Warrenton, Mo. 63383

 Craft for Younger Children: Right Living
Needed: Children's magazines, construction paper, glue sticks.

Say: We are going to make a poster of how to live right. Find some pictures in these magazines of kids who are living right. Show children how to cut them out and paste onto paper. Write "Right Living" at the top of the paper.

Ask: Why did you choose that picture? (Because he is playing kindly, eating the right foods, etc.) We should always live the right way, and the Holy Spirit will help you know the right way to live!

 Craft for Older Children: Come Holy Spirit
Needed: Dove shape, construction paper in different colors, glue sticks, scissors.

Say: In the Bible the Holy Spirit came to earth as a dove. Today we use the dove as a symbol of the Holy Spirit. Show children how to cut a dove shape from one color of construction paper and glue it onto a piece of construction paper in a contrasting shade. Write "Come Holy Spirit" on the paper.

Say: When you get home, hang this on your wall. When you look at it, remember that the Holy Spirit will help you make good decisions.

Snack: Holy Spirit Meringues

 Needed: Buy or make meringue cookies.

Say: Put one of these cookies in your mouth. Wait a minute. What happened? (It melted in my mouth.) What does it taste like now? (It tastes kind of sweet but the cookie is gone.)

That is like the Holy Spirit. Jesus had to leave this earth, but he wanted to leave behind the things people need. So the Holy Spirit came to comfort us and to help us learn.

Even though the cookie is gone, we still taste the sweetness of the cookie. Even though Jesus has gone back to heaven, we still have the sweetness of him through the Holy Spirit.

Memory Verse: Ephesians 5:15 ICB

So be very careful how you live. Do not live like those who are not wise. Live wisely.

Alternate Version (New King James)
See then that you walk circumspectly, not as fools but as wise.

Memory Verse Activity: Living Wisely

Needed: Strips of paper with the verse written on them, a few words on each strip. Hide the strips around the room.

Say: How can you live wisely? What does "living wisely" mean? If we live wisely, we are doing what God wants us to do. Let's try to find a verse that tells us about living wisely. Let children find verse strips and put the verse together.

Say the verse together several times.

Prayer Focus

Dear God, thank you for your wonderful gift of your Holy Spirit. We ask you to come into our lives and fill us up. Please help us to let the Holy Spirit lead us. Amen.

May 18, 2005

Sing All the Time! Midweek
By Tina Hauser

Scripture
Psalm 134:1, 2

Lesson Aim
The children will explore praising God through music.

Life Skill
The children will appreciate that God gave us voices to sing praises to him.

Bible Learning Activity for Younger Children: Sing with Your Mouth Closed!
Needed: Masking tape or painters tape.

Ask: Has anyone ever jokingly said to you that they were going to tape your mouth shut if you didn't stop talking and start listening?

Tear off two pieces of masking tape, each about 3 inches long, and tape your own mouth shut. Then play a song your children know well and ask them to sing along while you sing with your mouth taped shut.

Say: It was fun to try to sing with tape on my mouth, but it wouldn't be fun if I were never able to talk or sing! The music is inside of me, and it couldn't get out.

Let's sing this song again, only this time we can sing as loud as we want, and everyone can understand that we are singing about God.

Bible Learning Activity for Older Children: Horns in Bible Times
Needed: For each child a paper towel roll, a small square of waxed paper, and a rubber band.

Say: In Bible times people often played the trumpet or horn. Today we are going to make a horn to blow. Show children how to make this instrument by placing the waxed paper over the end of the towel roll and securing it with a rubber band.

Say: Can you think of a time that trumpets or horns were used in the Bible? (Joshua and Caleb, the walls of Jericho) Yes! God's people used horns, and they were blessed. Let children blow horns.

Enrichment for Younger Children: Musical Instruments

Needed: Pictures of musical instruments or real instruments.

Say: There are many different kinds of musical instruments. Some instruments make music by blowing into them. Can you name any of those instruments? (trumpet, clarinet, flute, saxophone) Some instruments have strings and make music when you touch the strings with a bow or with your fingers. Can you name any of those instruments? (violin, viola, cello, harp, guitar) Some instruments have keyboards. Name some instruments that have keyboards. (piano, organ, synthesizer, xylophone) Some instruments you hit with a stick. (drums, cymbals, triangle, xylophone)

We all carry a special instrument with us everywhere we go. Do you know what that instrument is? God made our voices into an instrument so that we can sing. He loves to hear our voices when we sing praises to him. When we sing about how much he loves us and how we are his children, it makes God's heart happy. I wonder if he is singing along with us and clapping to the music!

Enrichment for Older Children: Lyre, Lyre!
Needed: Shoebox, rubber bands. Make this lyre in the craft time and use in the lesson.

Make a shoebox lyre beforehand by cutting a hole about 4 inches in diameter in the lid of a shoebox. Place the lid back on the box. Stretch several rubber bands around the length of the box so they pass over the hole. Make sure the rubber bands are small enough to be very tight when they go around the box. Show the children how the rubber bands make a sound when they are plucked.

Say: The only instrument I know of that is the same today as it was in Bible times is the instrument God created. That instrument is our voice. People have created many instruments over the years to play along with our singing. The Bible mentions some of the ones from long ago. One that is mentioned several times is a lyre.

The lyre is an ancient stringed instrument that looked a lot like a small harp. It was held by one hand and strummed or plucked with the other hand. What is the difference between strumming and plucking? The lyre had four to ten strings. People would sing along while the lyre played, or they would recite poetry with the lyre music in the background.

Memory Verse: Psalm 134:1, 2 ICB
Praise the Lord, all you servants of the Lord. You serve at night in the Temple of the Lord. Raise your hands in the Temple and praise the Lord.

Alternate Version (New King James)
Behold, bless the LORD, all you servants of the LORD, who by night stand in the house of the LORD! Lift up your hands in the sanctuary, and bless the LORD.

May 22, 2005

Sing All the Time!
By Karl Bastian

Scripture
Psalm 134:1, 2

Lesson Aim
The children will explore praising God through music.

Life Skill
The children will appreciate that God gave us voices to sing praises to him.

Bible Lesson: Sing All the Time!
Needed: Guitar pick.

Ask: Do you know what this is? Yes! It is a guitar pick! A guitar pick is a pretty inexpensive little thing. In fact, I buy them for about twenty cents each. Guitar picks are pretty worthless little things—until you put them in the hand of a guitar player! Then they help produce the music so it can be heard far and wide! Then they become valuable!

Sometimes you may feel like you are not very important, or very strong, or very good looking, or very useful. The truth is that by ourselves, we aren't! But in the Master's hands, we become valuable and useful! When we allow God to use us, we do the same thing a guitar pick does we amplify God's work in this world! We make his love louder so more people can feel it! We make the world a more beautiful place to be; we are even music to people's ears when we are being used by God!

So put yourself in the Master's hands, in God's hands, and let him make beautiful things of your life!

Song Suggestions

Praise His Holy Name by Norm Hewitt from "Ablaze with Praise!" (Revelation Generation Music 2000)

He Is Really God! by Dean-o from "You Got It All" (FKO Music, Inc. 1997)

Did You Ever Talk to God Above Songsheets published by CEF Press, P.O. Box 348, Warrenton, Mo. 63383

He Is God by Jana Alayra from "Believin' On" (Montjoy Music 2002)

 Craft for Younger Children: Praise with a Drum!
Needed: Empty oatmeal box with cover, yarn, construction paper, crayons.

Say: Today we are going to make a drum to use in praising God. Show the children how to decorate a paper and then wrap it around the box for decoration.

Place the cover on the box. Use a pen to make a hole in the center of the cover and in the center of the bottom of the box. Through these holes, pull a piece of yarn long enough to hang around children's neck and down to their waist.

Let them play their drums along with a favorite song

Craft for Older Children: Lyre, Lyre!
Needed: One shoe box per child (with 4 inch hole cut in the lid) and rubber bands. Let children make this shoebox lyre to use in the enrichment activity.

Place the lid back on the box. Stretch several rubber bands around the length of the box so they pass over the hole. Make sure the rubber bands are small enough to be very tight when they go around the box. Show the children how the rubber bands make a sound when they are plucked. (If you have difficulty finding enough shoeboxes, ask in the shoe department of one of the super discount stores. They take the shoes out of the boxes and display them on racks. The shoes are purchased without the boxes.)

Say: In the Bible, this was one of the instruments that they used to praise God. Let's sing a song to praise him while we play our lyres.

Snack: Notes to Sing!

Needed: Round sandwich cookies, craft sticks.
Show children how to make note cookies by sticking craft sticks inside the icing portion of the sandwich cookie.

Say: Musical notes help us know how a song is supposed to be sung. Today we are going to eat our musical notes!

Memory Verse: Psalm 134:1, 2 ICB
Praise the Lord, all you servants of the Lord. You serve at night in the Temple of the Lord. Raise your hands in the Temple and praise the Lord.

Alternate Version (New King James)
Behold, bless the LORD, all you servants of the LORD, who by night stand in the house of the LORD! Lift up your hands in the sanctuary, and bless the LORD.

Memory Verse Activity: Praise with Your Heart!

Needed: Three paper hearts.

Write the words to Psalm 134:1 in large letters on the board: "Praise the Lord, all you servants of the Lord." If you have a banner program on your computer, make a banner of the verse. Hang the banner where it will be easily seen by all the children.

Cut out three red paper hearts or use doilies. The children will take turns placing one heart over one word in the verse. When the heart has been placed, all the children will say the verse, putting emphasis on the word under the heart. Once they have changed the location of the heart several times, add another heart so two words are covered and are being emphasized. Use as many as three hearts at a time.

May 25, 2005

God's Protection in the Face of Our Greatest Fears, Midweek
By Vicki Wiley

Scripture
2 Kings 6:8–23

Lesson Aim
Children will learn that God is there for them any time they are afraid.

Life Skill
Whenever we are afraid, we can pray to God and ask him for protection and help. He will always be there to hear us.

Bible Learning Activity for Younger Children: Protecting the Army!
Needed: Large boxes, approximately one box for each four children; markers; a picture of chariot (there are some on the Internet).

In Bible times there were many armies. The armies sometimes fought for God. How do you think that they kept safe?

One thing they used was a chariot. The chariot had wheels and carried soldiers in it so that they could fight. We are going to make chariots today. Let children copy the drawings onto their boxes to make a chariot.

The chariot was one way the army was kept safe. God watched over the armies, too.

Bible Learning Activity for Older Children: Bible Times Weapons
Today when our soldiers go into battle, they have many weapons to use. They also had many weapons to use back in Bible times! Here are a few:

The battle-ax was a club-type weapon that people swung and hit other people with. But because they always wore armor, the ax didn't work very well. Body armor was worn by soldiers in many nations of the ancient world. It was made from thick leather or thin metal.

Bows and arrows were used often in the Old Testament times. Simple bows were also used for hunting. Simple bows, composed of a piece of wood and string, were easy to make.

The bow was usually the first weapon fired in a battle because people defending the city could fire at the armies that were attacking them before they could get too close

Chariots came in many different forms. They could have two or four wheels. They could be drawn by two to four horses. Some chariots could carry as many as four warriors.

The dagger and the sword are usually talked about together, as if these two weapons were basically the same. A sword was a piercing or cutting weapon, with which a warrior might stab or slash an enemy. Some swords were designed to pierce, others to slash. All swords had two parts, a handle or hilt and a blade. The blade was usually straight, but one unusual variation was the sickle sword. This weapon featured a curved blade with the sharp edge on the outside. Swords were the basic weapon of a Hebrew soldier.

Daggers were similar to swords and were used to stab. Their advantage over swords was their ability to be hidden.

Enrichment for Older Children: Rock Around the Clock
Design a giant clock on the floor using masking tape or colored theater tape. Place chairs in a circle around the outside of the clock. Several of the chairs should be numbered with times of the day (i.e. 8:00 A.M., noon, 4:00 P.M., midnight, etc.). Play musical chairs. As the kids sit down, those that land in a chair that is labeled with a time should go stand on that part of the floor clock. Ask them a question and follow with some possible responses. The goal is to get them to make good decisions and always include prayer in their action plan.

Enrichment for Younger Children: When Are You Afraid?

Needed: A real clock or one drawn on the whiteboard.

Ask: What makes children afraid? (When I can't find my mom. When I am lost. When I think something is under my bed.)

Let kids answer and then say: Is there anything in the morning that makes you afraid? (Point to 8:00 while talking and let kids answer.) Is there anything in the afternoon that makes you afraid? (Point to 2:00 while they answer.) Now, what about the night? (Most answers will fall here.)

God watches over us in the morning, the afternoon, and the night. God is always watching over us!

Memory Verse: 2 Kings 6:17 ICB
The Elisha prayed, "Lord, open my servant's eyes. Let him see."

Alternate Version (New King James)
And Elisha prayed, and said, "LORD, I pray, open his eyes that he may see."

May 29, 2005

God's Protection in the Face of our Greatest Fears
By Michael Bonner

Scripture
2 Kings 6:8–23

Lesson Aim
Children will learn that God is there for them anytime they are afraid.

Life Skill
Whenever we are afraid, we can pray to God and ask him for protection and help. He will always be there to hear us.

Bible Lesson: Talkin' Round the Clock
Needed: A large wall clock that you can hold and make the hands move. The numbers need to be visible to all the children. Have the clock inside a brown paper bag hidden from the view of the children.

As you begin, have the children raise their hands to guess what is inside the brown paper sack. You may want to give them a few clues as you call upon children to guess.

Say: It is round and has numbers on it. It makes a small sound. It has three hands. Once they have either guessed the item or you have chosen several kids, pull the clock out of the bag.

Say: Today we are going to learn about "talkin' round the clock." Our Bible story in 2 Kings 6 tells us of a time when Elisha and a servant were surrounded by a strong army of men. The king of Aram sent this army to capture Elisha. However, Elisha prayed and asked God to help him. God helped Elisha and his servant stay safe.

Say: Do you think Elisha and his servant were afraid? (Take various responses.) Say: Are you ever afraid? Raise your hand if you have ever been afraid of something. Tell the children about a fear you have or had as a child.

Then, using the clock, talk about different times during the day that we might be afraid. Placing the clock hands to 9:00 A.M.

Say: You may be in school at 9:00 in the morning. What things might you be afraid of then? Take several responses (riding the bus, taking tests, reading aloud to the class).

Continue by moving the clock to lunchtime, dinnertime, bedtime. At each time, ask several children to mention something they might be afraid of at that time. Finally, ask the kids what is the one thing that is available to them during every time of the day. Say: There is one thing we can do no matter where we are, what we are doing, or what time it is. That is praying to God. He is always there just waiting to hear us pray!

Explain how Elisha trusted that God would protect him and answer his prayer when he was dealing with the strong army in our Bible story. Likewise, we can trust that God will take care of us. God may not answer every prayer just the way we would like. However, he always hears us and knows exactly what is best for us. No matter what time it is, day or night, we can pray. Prayer is simply talking to God, thanking him for who he is, what he has done, and sharing our needs with him. When we are afraid, he wants us to share that with him too. So, as we pray throughout the day for anything we are afraid of, we are just talkin' round the clock!

 Song Suggestions

You're in My Heart to Stay by Jana Alayra from "Dig Down Deep" (Montjoy Music 1997)

No Need to Worry by Jana Alayra from "Jump into the Light" (Montjoy Music 1995)

Pray, Pray, Pray by Mary Rice Hopkins from "Good Buddies" (Big Steps 4 U 1994)

Let the Lord Have His Way Songsheets published by CEF Press, P.O. Box 348, Warrenton, Mo. 63383

Craft for Younger Children: God's Care Clock
Needed: Paper circle for each child, magazine pictures of children playing and sleeping, felt-tip markers.

Say: God watches over us all day long. Let's make a clock to remind us of God's care for us. Show children how to make the clock. Let children paste pictures of children playing and sleeping on the clock.

 Craft for Older Children: Clock Magnet Reminder
Needed: Plastic cap from a bottle of juice or water, small clock hands cut from paper or foam, cardboard, and magnet.

Have children make small dots around the bottle cap to represent the time on the clock. Add small clock hands. Glue onto cardboard circle and add magnet on the back.

Say: God watches over us all day long. This magnet will remind us of his care and protection.

Snack: Clock cookies

 Needed: Round cookies, icing, red hots or other small decorations or candies.

Show children how to make a clock cookie by icing the cookie and adding candies to designate the time on the clock.

Say: This will help us remember the lesson today. We need to talk around the clock to God!

Memory Verse: 2 Kings 6:17 ICB
The Elisha prayed, "Lord, open my servant's eyes. Let him see."

Alternate Version (New King James)
And Elisha prayed, and said, "LORD, I pray, open his eyes that he may see."

Memory Verse Activity: Let Me See!
Write the verse on a whiteboard. Have children close their eyes and ask them to say the verse. When they protest that they can't, let them look at the verse and say it together a few times.

Say: Now let's close our eyes and say the verse!

Prayer Focus
Dear God, we are sometimes afraid. Thank you for watching over us all the time. Amen.

June 1, 2005

Living Loyal with No Compromise! Midweek
By Pat Verbal

Scripture
John 8:32

Lesson Aim
Children will realize that life's choices lead to reward or punishment.

Life Skill
Children will desire to obey Jesus' warnings and win his praise.

Bible Learning Activity for Younger Children: Black or White
Needed: Black stones and white stones.

Show children the different colored stones.

Ask: What is the difference between these stones? (Some are white, and some are black.) Right! In Bible times, if someone did something wrong, they would use a black stone to show that there was sin or wrong things. If someone was innocent, they would give that person a white stone. White would mean that the person had no sin or did not do wrong things. Today in our lesson we will learn about how other white stones were used in the Bible.

Bible Learning Activity for Older Children: Black or White
Today we have a system of elections and courts to make decisions on political and legal problems. In biblical times people often used "lots," which were sticks, stones, or even piece of bones. They would throw them on the ground like we might do with dice.

Read Numbers 26:55, 56; Proverbs 18:18; Jonah 1:7; Luke 1:9 (see NKJV); or Acts 1:26. In these stories God used "lots" to let people know what he wanted them to do.

When voting for or against someone, colored stones were used. A white stone meant that a person was innocent. A black stone meant the person was guilty. When God says he will give us a white stone in Revelations 2:17, he reminds us that we are innocent because of what Jesus Christ did on the cross for us.

When we receive a white stone, it can remind us that we are innocent because Jesus died for us!

Enrichment for Younger Children: Peace with God

Spell out PEACE on the whiteboard or on a poster board.

Ask: What is peace? Let's define *peace* using the letters of the word. Write down all answers you receive.

Perfect contentment

Everlasting life

Accomplishing things with God

Ceasing quarreling

Everybody getting along with one another

True peace only comes when we have a relationship with Jesus Christ!

Enrichment for Older Children: Peace Chant

Lead children in a peace chant.

Give me a P.

Give me an E.

Give me an A.

Give me a C.

Give me an E.

What does that spell? Peace! How do you get it? With Jesus!

Memory Verse: Romans 5:1 ICB

We have been made right with God because of our faith. So we have peace with God through our Lord Jesus Christ.

Alternate Version (New King James)
Therefore, having been justified by faith, we have peace with God through our Lord Jesus Christ.

June 5, 2005

Living Loyal with No Compromise!
By Pat Verbal

Scripture
John 8:32

Lesson Aim
Children will realize that life's choices lead to reward or punishment.

Life Skill
Children will desire to obey Jesus' warnings and win his praise.

Bible Lesson
Needed: White and black stones from a garden supply store.

Ask: Who are some of your best friends? What are their character qualities? (kind, honest, good listeners, helpful, loyal) Did you know that God values loyalty? Throughout the Old Testament we read about how the Israelites promised to be faithful to God and then were disloyal. When their great leader Joshua was about to die, he begged them one last time to obey God's commands. Once again the people promised him they would serve God. To help them remember Joshua put up a large stone and said, "See this stone! It will help you remember what we did today. It was here the Lord was speaking to us today. It will help you remember what happened. It will stop you from turning against your God" (Josh. 24:27 ICB).

Have you made God some promises? Have you decided to serve him the rest of your life? Are you learning what he wants you to do as you read his Word? How will you remember to keep your promise?

Do you know what a symbol is? It is an image that stands for something else. In Bible times the people sometimes used stones for symbols. When John wrote the book of Revelations, he was on a rocky island, and he picked up a white stone and said that it is a symbol God will give to those who stayed true to him until the end.

God understands your world and mine. God wants us to stay with him all our lives even if doing so is difficult. Today we will get a stone to remember to stay with God until the end of our lives.

Take your stone home and put it in a place where it can remind you of your decision to win Jesus' praises and to live loyal lives with no compromise!

 Song Suggestions

Praise His Holy Name by Norm Hewitt from "Ablaze with Praise!" (Revelation Generation Music 2000)

He Is Really God! by Dean-o from "You Got It All" (FKO Music, Inc. 1997)

Did You Ever Talk to God Above Songsheets published by CEF Press, P.O. Box 348, Warrenton, Mo. 63383

He Is God by Jana Alayra from "Believin' On" (Montjoy Music 2002)

 Craft for Younger Children: Living Loyal Necklace
Needed: One strip of red paper, one cord, beads, felt-tip marker.

Let children string beads on cord as desired. Turn ends of paper strip so that they form a heart. Staple the cord into strip of paper as shown forming a heart necklace.

Ask: What is this shape? What does a heart mean? What can you do for people to show them that you love them? God loves you so much. Love is part of the character of God. Let's write LOYAL on the heart to remind us to be loyal to God!

Craft for Older Children: Living Loyal Stone
Needed: White stones from lesson.

Say: Today we received a stone to help us remember that we will stick with Jesus until the end of our lives. Let's make our stone a little more personal.

Let children decorate their stones with markers. On the stone write: Living Loyal for Jesus. Say: This will help us remember to live for Jesus!

Say: When we love people, they should know that we love them. Don't hide your love; let it show! How can you let it show? How can you be kind? God's love is always there! As we grow older, we see God's love all the time! But even when you are small, you can know God loves you. God's love will always be with you throughout your whole life!

Snack: Stony Cakes

 Needed: Candy stones, cupcakes.

Say: Today we have learned how symbols can help us remember to love God and to be loyal to him. Let's make one more thing to help us remember to do that.

Show children how to make a "stony cupcake" by pressing candy stones into the cupcakes.

Memory Verse: Romans 5:1 ICB

We have been made right with God because of our faith. So we have peace with God through our Lord Jesus Christ.

Alternate Version (New King James)
Therefore, having been justified by faith, we have peace with God through our Lord Jesus Christ.

Memory Verse Activity: Stone Reminders
Needed: White stones, felt-tip marker.
   Write one word from the memory verse on each stone. Have the children say the verse and then put the verse together in order. Say the verse together several times.

Prayer Focus
Dear God, thank you that we can live for you. Help us to remember always to follow you and do what you want us to do. Amen.

June 8, 2005

Standing Tall in Trouble, Midweek
By Tina Hauser

Scripture
Romans 5:3–5

Lesson Aim
Children will learn that the truth keeps them out of trouble.

Life Skill
Children will appreciate God's provisions when they face hardship.

Bible Learning Activity for Younger Children: Set Free!

Needed: A sheet big enough to drape to the floor over a table.

Finish this sentence: When I opened the door of the cage, the bird was set _____. (free) Instruct the children to get under the table. This will be their little cage. The Bible tells us that the truth of God sets us free. Tell the children that you are going to say something that is true about God with one of their names. When they hear the truth and their name, they can fly free from the cage and go back to their chair.

God loves you, _____.
God promises always to be with you, _____.
Jesus died for you, _____.
God wants to lead you every day, _____.
God will forgive your sins, _____.
God has a special plan for your life, _____.
God cares about your family, _____.
God wants the best for you, _____.
God wants you to believe in him, _____.

Continue calling each child by name, attached to a statement of truth, until everyone has been freed, returned to their seats, and the cage is empty.

Bible Learning Activity for Older Children: Keys of Truth

Needed: A Large piece of construction paper for each child and an assortment of keys.

Give each child a large piece of light-colored construction paper. Lay several different shaped keys in the center of the table. Each child will draw the outline of a key as large as they can on their paper. As they work on their key, they can refer to some of the patterns on the keys you have displayed.

Above the toothing on each key, the children will write the words: The truth is … After the caption is written, encourage the children to write things on the key that they know to be true about God. Make the statements personal by using the words *My* and *me*. You may want to write a few of these on the board as starters.

The truth is God loves me.

The truth is God forgives me.

The truth is Jesus died for me.

The truth is God's Spirit lives inside me.

The truth is God has a special plan for my life.

Enrichment for Younger Children: Truth Sets Us Free!

Needed: A large assortment of keys and something that needs a key to be unlocked.

Collect as many keys as you can before you meet the children. Even if the children are not paying attention, pour the keys out on the table. They will immediately turn to see what you are doing. Frantically rummage through the keys, mumbling to yourself, and trying a key now and then in the lock that you are trying to unlock. Let each child take a turn choosing a key and testing it in the lock. Then find the correct key and use it in the lock so that it will come open. What did we find out about the lock? It will only open with one right key.

Our verse today says that the truth will set us free. Where do we find the truth? The Word of God, the Bible, teaches us about God's truth. Just as there is only one key to unlock the lock, God's truth is the only thing that will set us free. Nothing else will make us happy like God's truth.

Enrichment for Older Children: Locking It Away

Needed: Three combination padlocks.

Show the children three combination padlocks. Call a child forward to choose three numbers for the combination and then see if they can twist the dial to open the lock. Allow several children to have an opportunity to do the same. Why weren't you able to get the padlocks open? You don't know the combinations. I'm the only one who knows the combination to the locks. When I tell you, then you'll be able to open the padlock by using the combination I give you.

Some things keep us from being who God wants us to be. They can keep us locked away from God. There is the fear of being alone. Give the combination to one padlock to a child so they can release the lock. When we walk with God, we don't have to be afraid of being alone because he will always be with us. God's truth sets us free from the fear of being alone. There is the fear of what other people might think. Give the combination to another padlock to a child so they can release the lock. When we live by God's truth, the only thing that's important is what God thinks of us. God's truth sets us free from the fear of what other people might say or think about us. Sin also keeps us from being close to God. Give the combination to the third padlock to a child so they can release the lock. When we do things that go against what God would have us do, that locks us away from him. When we ask for forgiveness, God's truth sets us free to be close to him.

Memory Verse: Romans 5:3–5 ICB

And we also have joy with our troubles because we know that these troubles produce patience. And patience produces character, and character produces hope. And this hope will never disappoint us, because God has poured out his love to fill our hearts. God gave us his love through the Holy Spirit, whom God has given to us.

Alternate Version (New King James)

And not only that, but we also glory in tribulations, knowing that tribulation produces perseverance; and perseverance, character; and character, hope. Now hope does not disappoint, because the love of God has been poured out in our hearts by the Holy Spirit who was given to us.

June 12, 2005

Standing Tall in Trouble
by Pat Verbal

Scripture
Romans 5:3–5

Lesson Aim
Children will learn that the truth keeps them out of trouble.

Life Skill
Children will appreciate God's provisions when they face hardship.

Bible Lesson: Standing Tall in Trouble

Needed: Bring two packages of dominoes to class. Let the children play with them before the session begins. Prepare a set of peal-and-stick labels. On each label write a word that represents the character of God: faithful, just, loving, truth, holy, powerful, long-suffering, all-knowing.

Have you every heard of Murphy's Law? It says, "Whatever can go wrong, will go wrong." Do you have days where you live by Murphy's Law? Days when you have a bad hair day that makes you late for school. Then you forget your homework and get picked last for the team. You get into a fight with your best friend and feel like writing the word *Loser* across your forehead. Or maybe these problems seem small compared to having a grandparent with cancer, a father without a job, or parents who are divorced.

Ask each child to take a domino. Say: Let this domino represent one of your problems.

Encourage a few children to share their problem as they stand their dominoes up on the end in a row. When troubles come, it's natural to ask God why, but he doesn't have to answer us. If he did, we wouldn't need faith. Sometimes our faith gets pretty wobbly like these dominoes.

Knock down the first domino in the row and watch the rest fall.

Say: While God may not explain every difficulty we face, he has given us a glimpse into his greater plan in Romans 5:1–5. First, he asks us to be joyful in times of trouble because problems can help us to grow deeper in character. Second, God assures us that the seeds of trouble, when planted in perseverance and watered with love, can produce a harvest. The crop is hope. What do we hope for? Our hope is to become more like God and daily live in his peace.

In the book *Little Pilgrim's Progress*, author Helen L. Taylor told the classic story of a young boy who lived in the City of Destruction. His name was Little Christian. When he learned about a beautiful city ruled by a good and wise king, Christian sets off on a journey to the Celestial City. The road was long and filled with many adversities. The boy traveled through the Wicked Gate, the Valley of Despair, and Vanity Fair. He met people like Evangelist, Help, Faithful, and Giant Despair, to name of few.

Along the way Christian found an old Book. When he got lost or scared, the Book guided him and his friend, Hopeful. When little Christian was in the house of the Interpreter and saw two boys, Passion and Patience, he learned about making good choices from the Book. A woman named Discretion helped Christian pick out a helmet, breastplate, shield, sword, and shoes so he could stand against the king's enemies. He promised to keep the armor shiny and bright.

When Christian and Hopeful finally crossed the river and arrived in the Celestial City, they discovered that the king had been waiting for them all along. A multitude of the king's servants came quickly to help Christian up the steep path. The little pilgrim was happy to be in the presence of the King.

Ask the children if they recognize any of the people or places in this story.

We too are on a journey to a beautiful city. What is its name? (heaven) We will face many dangers on the way. (Discuss a few.) Murphy's Law may try to overtake us. But like little Christian we can decide to persevere (keep walking) and produce character (grow). On the path God will be with us to strengthen us. His character can be in us through the power of the Holy Spirit. We can stand tall in trouble!

Stand up the dominoes that represented the children's problems. This time put a domino flat on the table between each standing one with a label on it representing God's character. When you try to push down the row by pushing the first domino, the row will not fall.

Song Suggestions

He Is Really God! by Dean-o from "You Got It All" (FKO Music, Inc. 1997)

Did You Ever Talk to God Above Songsheets published by CEF Press, P.O. Box 348, Warrenton, Mo. 63383

Purest of Gold by Kurt Johnson, a.k.a. MrJ from "Pure Gold" (Mr. J Music 1995)

Believe His Promises by Dean-o from "Soul Surfin'" (FKO Music, Inc. 1999)

Do Not Fear by John J.D. Modica from "Ablaze with Praise" (Revelation Generation Music 2000)

 Craft for Younger Children: Keys of Faith
Needed: Key shapes cut from paper or craft foam or real keys, key ring.

Say: We are going to make a key ring today. What do keys do? They open doors! These keys are going to open doors for you too, but these doors help you know God.

Write one word or phrase on each key shape (prayer, read Bible, go to church, and other words and phrases). Show children how to put keys on key ring.

 Craft for Older Children: Keys to Faith
Needed: Key shapes cut from paper or craft foam or real keys, key ring.

Say: Do you know how your faith grows? Your faith grows when you learn more about God and experience a life of faith! What helps your faith to grow? Write them on these keys and put them on the key ring to remind you to let God develop your faith.

Snack: Trouble cookies

Needed: Graham crackers, icing, assorted candies, and decorations. Cover the area with paper or plastic.

Say: We are going to decorate these cookies to remind us of the trouble we can get in if we are not careful. I want you to decorate your cookie with your eyes closed!

That was hard, wasn't it? We would do a much better job if we were looking and trying hard. It's the same with our faith; if we just hope it comes out OK and don't try hard and watch what we are doing, it won't come out very well, like this cookie!

Memory Verse: Romans 5:3–5 ICB

And we also have joy with our troubles because we know that these troubles produce patience. And patience produces character, and character produces hope. And this hope will never disappoint us, because God has poured out his love to fill our hearts. God gave us his love through the Holy Spirit, whom God has given to us.

Alternate Version (New King James)
And not only that, but we also glory in tribulations, knowing that tribulation produces perseverance; and perseverance, character; and character, hope. Now hope does not disappoint, because the love of God has been poured out in our hearts by the Holy Spirit who was given to us.

Memory Verse Activity: What Produces What?

Write the memory verse on a whiteboard. Then ask: What produces what?

Let children figure out that troubles produce patience, patience produces character, character produces hope.

Say: What is so important about hope? It never disappoints us!

Prayer Focus

Dear God, thank you that you give us a way to deal with our troubles. Thank you that we can grow stronger when we have trouble and that our character will grow when we do. Amen.

June 15, 2005

Faithful Father, Midweek
By Susan Harper

Scripture
Joshua 24:15

Lesson Aim
Children will understand that they have a perfect heavenly Father.

Life Skill
Children will learn the importance of fathers.

Bible Learning Activity for Younger Children
Needed: Pairs of similar items for children to choose between.

Set up several pairs of similar objects that the children will have to choose between. As each pair of choices is announced, the children will tap their heads for the one they would choose. Here are some suggestions for pair choices to offer the children: Pepsi and Coke, apple and banana, bubble gum and mint gum, potato chips and corn chips, pen and pencil, peanuts and walnuts, two different videos. We make choices every day about the food and drinks we like, the places we enjoy, the sports we play, and the television shows we watch. It doesn't really matter which cola you like more or whether you like peanuts better than walnuts, but there is a choice that is important. It's the most important choice. The Bible tells fathers that they need to make the choice to lead their families to serve God so that each one in their family will make the choice to serve God.

Bible Learning Activity for Older Children
When Joshua said, "As for me and my family, we will serve the Lord" (Josh. 24:15 ICB), he was declaring that his family and everything he had belonged to God. His family and his land were in God's territory.

When the very first man to walk on the moon, Neil Armstrong, stepped out of the *Apollo 11* onto the moon's surface in 1969, one of the first things he did was to stick a United States flag into the moon. Why did he do that? He was declaring that Americans were there; they were on the moon. He was determined that the world would know they were from the United States when pictures were shown around the world.

Norway sent an explorer, Roald Amundsen, to the South Pole. Amundsen was the first man to get all the way to the South Pole. What do you think he did when he got there? He stuck the flag of Norway into the ground to declare that this was Norway's discovery.

If Joshua had a flag that was God's flag, he may have stuck it into his land to declare that this was God's land. Instead, he just made a firm statement that no matter what anyone else did, he and his family would worship God.

Enrichment for Younger Children

Do your dads ever give you rules? Do you sometimes get mad and not want to follow the rules? Why should you follow them? What is the purpose of most rules? Let's look at our Bible verse again and see what it tells us to do. Basically it says we choose whether we will do what is right or what is wrong. If we obey our dads, which are we choosing to do? Can you say the Bible verse again? Whom did Joshua and his family decide to serve? And whom do you want to serve? Let's pray together for God to help us to do what is right.

Enrichment for Older Children

Do your dads ever give you rules? Do you sometimes get mad and not want to follow the rules? Why should you follow them? What is the purpose of most rules? Let's look at our Bible verse again and see what it tells us to do. Basically it says we choose whether we will do what is right or what is wrong. If we obey our dads, which are we choosing to do? Can you say the Bible verse again? Whom did Joshua and his family decide to serve? And whom do you want to serve? Let's pray together for God to help us to do what is right.

Memory Verse: Joshua 24:15 ICB

As for me and my family, we will serve the Lord.

Alternate Version (New King James)
As for me and my house, we will serve the LORD.

June 19, 2005

(Special Activity, Father's Day)

Faithful Father
By Susan Harper

Scripture
Joshua 24:15

Lesson Aim
Children will understand that they have a perfect heavenly Father.

Life Skill
Children will learn the importance of fathers.

Bible Lesson: Faithful Father
Needed: A picture of your father.

Say: Good morning boys and girls! I am so happy you are here today! This morning I woke up thinking of my dad and what a special day this is. Do you know what today is? That's right. It is Father's Day, a day to remember our dads and what they have done for us.

Here, I brought you a picture of my father so you can see what a handsome man he is. (Show them the picture of your dad.) My dad is very special to me. When I was a little girl, he took good care of me. He only wanted the very best for me and did everything he could to provide what I needed to grow up. I bet your dad takes good care of you, too. Can you think of some of the things your dad has done for you? (Get suggestions from the class. Expand on them by asking others if their dad does the same for them.)

The best memory I have of my dad is when he used to teach me things that would help me handle problems I would face as I grew up. He taught me about God and how important God was to him. He told me how God was a faithful Father who took care of the needs of those who loved and obeyed him. He taught me Bible stories about people who served God and about people who did not serve God and how this choice affected their life.

One story was about Joshua, who became the leader of the Hebrew people, now called the tribes of Israel, after Moses led them out of Egypt. Joshua led the people across the Jordan River and, with God's help, defeated the people of Jericho and claimed this land, the promised land, as their home. When the people of Israel obeyed God, they were blessed. When they chose to not serve him, they had a hard life.

What are you going to do? Who are you going to serve? Let's serve God!

 Song Suggestions

A Dad Like You by Mary Rice Hopkins from "Good Buddies" (Big Steps 4 U 1994)

The Family of God by Kurt Johnson, a.k.a. MrJ from "Kid Possible" (Kurt Johnson 1995)

No One Else I Know by Mary Rice Hopkins from "15 Singable Songs" (Big Steps 4 U 1988)

This Is Love by Dean-o from "God City" (BibleBeat Music, 2001)

What a Mighty God We Serve Songsheets published by CEF Press, P.O. Box 348, Warrenton, Mo. 63383

 Craft for Younger Children: Key Ring for Dad
Needed: Key rings, colorful string, plastic beads that spell D-A-D, and plain beads, card stock, and felt-tip markers. You can purchase the key-ring craft as a kit from Oriental Trading Company.

Give each child a key ring, an 8-inch piece of string, the D-A-D beads, and three plain beads. Instruct them to tie the string on the key ring, making sure the knot is in the center of the string. Have them string the beads over both pieces of string in the following order: a plain bead, D, plain bead, A, plain bead, D. Have them tie a second knot in the bottom of the string to secure the beads in place. Give each child half a sheet of card stock. Instruct them to fold it in half to make a Father's Day card to hold the beaded key-chain gift for their dad.

Craft for Older Children: Pocket Reminder
Needed: Wooden or thick foam circles about the size of a quarter, and fine-tip markers in different colors.

Give each child a wooden (foam) circle. Tell them the circle represents a pocket reminder to remind their dad, whenever he reaches into his pocket, that they love him. Instruct the children to write a message on one side of the coin such as: I (heart) Dad, and then sign their name. They are to decorate the coin on the edge of this side as well as the other side using the markers.

Snack: We Will Serve the Lord Cookies!

Needed: House-shaped cookies or create them with square cookies and icing (cut diagonally for roof).

Serve cookies to one another.

Say: Just like we are serving cookies to one another, we also can serve the Lord. That means we do things that are pleasing to him!

Memory Verse: Joshua 24:15 ICB

As for me and my family, we will serve the Lord.

Alternate Version (New King James)
As for me and my house, we will serve the LORD.

Memory Verse Activity

Needed: For each team: seven small strips of paper with the Bible verse written on each as shown below, seven balloons the same color, and one large trash bag. Before class write out the Bible verse on the strips of paper, roll them up, and place in a balloon—one part of the Bible verse in each balloon of the same color for each team. Blow the balloons up, tie them in a knot, and place all the balloons in one large trash bag.

1. As for me
2. and my
3. family,
4. we will
5. serve
6. the Lord.
7. Joshua 24:15

Divide the class into two or more teams with no more than seven players on each team. If you do not have enough players to make equal number of players on each team, some players can go twice. Assign each team a balloon color. Have them line up on one side of the room and place the large trash bag with the balloons in it on the other side of the room. On the word *go* the first player on each team runs to the trash bag, gets one balloon that matches their team's color, pops it by sitting on it or stomping it, and carries the enclosed piece of paper back to his team. He unrolls his part of the Bible verse as the second player on the team runs to the large trash bag to get his part of the Bible verse. As the player is popping his balloon, the rest of the team is putting the Bible verse together in the correct order. When the team has the whole Bible verse in order, they are to sit down. The first team to sit down wins.

Prayer Focus

Dear God, we know we have a choice of whether we will serve you. We choose to serve you! Amen.

June 22, 2005

Sacrificial Giving, Midweek
By Becky Howell

Scripture
Mark 12:42–44

Lesson Aim
Children will learn about giving.

Life Skill
Children will learn the joy of giving what they have, even if it is not very much.

Bible Learning Activity for Younger Children
Needed: Pennies, a bucket, and masking tape.

The woman Jesus talked about gave everything she had. She gave two of the smallest coins used in that day. The two coins were the most important thing to her because that is what she used to buy food. What is the smallest coin we use?

Place a bucket or deep container on the floor. Put a piece of masking tape on the floor about five feet from the bucket. This will be the line behind which the children stand. Give each child two pennies. On their turn they will try to stand behind the masking tape line and toss the pennies into the bucket. If they get either of the pennies or both of them to go in the bucket, ask the child to tell the group what is most important to them. What do you have that would be the most difficult to give up?

Bible Learning Activity for Older Children
Needed: Twenty-five M&Ms (or pennies) for each child, a small cup, and one number cube. (The foam dice are nice because they aren't as loud when rolled.)

Give each child 25 M&M candies and an small empty cup. The object of the game is to be like the poor widow and give all you have to God. Take turns rolling the dice. If a 6 is rolled, the player will say, "I give 6 to God," and place 6 M&Ms in their cup. The player who gives everything to God first is the winner of the game. You can be the winner real fast if you roll a 2 for the two mites the poor widow gave. If a 2 is rolled, the player will yell, "I give it all to God!" Play as many rounds as you have time.

Enrichment for Younger Children

Needed: Penny, nickel, dime, and quarter for each child to use, a metal bowl.

The coins the woman gave at the temple were called mites. They were called the "thin coins" because they were so little. Of all the coins the Jewish people used, it was the smallest, and it was worth very little. Two little thin mites were everything the woman had to give, and she gave both of them to God's work. What is the smallest coin we use in our country? What can you buy with two pennies? Give one child a handful of coins to drop into a metal bowl. Take the coins out and then give another child two pennies to drop into the bowl. Is there a difference in the sound the coins make? The other people in the temple probably knew that the woman was giving very little just by the sound her two coins made when they were placed in the container. How do you think the woman felt? Even though she may have been embarrassed by being able to give so little, Jesus was touched by her gift because she gave everything she could possibly give.

Give each child a penny, a nickel, a dime and a quarter. Put them in order from largest to the smallest.

Enrichment for Older Children: Bible Times Coins

Needed: Coins (modern) to show the children. Show some from other countries if possible.

Ask: What are these coins? (Let children name them.) What kinds of coins are they? How much are they worth? What country do they come from?

When Jesus lived on Earth, most of the coins were Roman coins. These coins had pictures of the rulers on them. The most common coin was the *silver denarius*, which was made out of silver and usually given to workers after they worked for one day. This denarius had the picture of Caesar on it.

They also used Greek coins, which had religious symbols on them. They may have been minted at pagan temples, which served as business centers for granting loans and receiving estates. Most of the Greek coins were made of silver, and gold coins were less popular among the Greeks. If you worked for a day, you might be given a drachma, the Greek coin for a day's wage.

There was another coin in the Bible too. It was a Jewish coin and called the "widow's mite." These coins were very small copper coins worth only a fraction of a penny by today's standards. When the woman put her widow's mite into the offering, Jesus was pleased. Why do you think that is? Yes, Jesus was pleased that, though she was poor, she gave what she had.

Memory Verse: 2 Corinthians 9:7 ICB

Each one should give, then, what he has decided in his heart to give. He should not give if it makes him sad. And he should not give if he thinks he is forced to give. God loves the person who gives happily.

Alternate Version (New King James)

So let each one give as he purposes in his heart, not grudgingly or of necessity; for God loves a cheerful giver.

June 26, 2005

Sacrificial Giving
By Becky Howell

Scripture
Mark 12:42–44

Lesson Aim
Children will learn about giving.

Life Skill
Children will learn the joy of giving what they have, even if it is not very much.

Bible Lesson: Sacrificial Giving
Let me tell you a story: Danny had just come in from his neighbor's house, and he was so excited! He had five dollars, and he sure had earned it! As he clean up before dinner, Dan thought of all the ways he could use that money, but in his heart he knew what he wanted to do.

Teams of missionaries from Danny's church were going to help a new church in Russia. Danny's pastor had been asking everyone in his church family to consider helping out in any way they could. His pastor had said that the money the kids gave would help buy Bibles and teaching materials, and this would help the children in Russia learn about Jesus. This was the last Sunday before the team was leaving, and Danny was so excited because he would have something to give.

Sunday morning came, and Danny took the five-dollar bill and placed it in his wallet. He joined some of the other fifth-grade kids as they went into class. Everyone was so excited about giving toward the missions project. "Here's my offering," announced Kim, "I'm giving twenty-five dollars." "I brought my gift too," said Jeremy, "my dad wrote me a check for fifty dollars," and he proudly placed his gift in the special mission box. Suddenly Danny felt like his gift was very small, but without saying a word, he took the five dollars out of his wallet and put it with the other gifts. Danny was glad he was able to give what he had earned to Jesus. As the teacher opened the class in prayer, Danny asked Jesus to use his few dollars to help a boy or girl come to know Jesus.

Whose offering pleased our heavenly Father? Let's look at a story from God's Word. In the book of Mark, Jesus tells us about a woman who gave all she had. It was two mites, two small coins, and she gave it as an offering to God. Do you know how much money two mites is? It is less then a penny! As the woman went to give her offering, rich people were bringing large amounts of money and throwing it into the donation box. Then the poor widow came and dropped in her two mites. It was all she had, and she was willing to give it to God. When Jesus saw this, he said, "This woman has given even more then the rich people. They have given a lot because they have a lot, but she has given all that she has."

Do you think giving to Jesus made this lady happy? Yes, she was happy because she gave what she had, just like Danny did!

 Song Suggestions

Free Inside by Dean-o from "Soul Surfin'" (FKO Music, Inc.1999)

Turn It Over by Dean-o from "God City" (BibleBeat Music 2001)

Walk like Jesus by Mary Rice Hopkins from "15 Singable Songs" (Big Steps 4 U 1988)

I Believe the Bible Songsheets published by CEF Press, P.O. Box 348, Warrenton, Mo. 63383

 Craft for Younger Children
Needed: A box for each child.

Give each child a small box. This can be a shoebox, or you can purchase these from a craft supply. Children can decorate the box. On the inside bottom of the box, put a sticker with 2 Corinthians 9:7. When children open their box, they can see these words. For younger children you can put a happy face with the simple words: *God loves a cheerful giver.*

Craft for Older Children
Needed: Three envelopes for each child.

Give each child three envelopes. Instruct them to decorate each envelope: one for giving—decorate with a church, a cross; one for savings—decorate with something they are saving their money to buy; one for things they need—decorate with clothes, food.

Snack: Money, Money, Money!

Needed: Coins (preferably from Bible times) one per child, round sandwich cookies with any type design, plain round cookies, toothpicks.

Show sandwich cookies and say: What design is this on the cookie? Yes! The cookie maker decided that he wanted this particular design on the cookie, and he made a cookie press to make that picture. A coin is sort of like that too. The coin makers decide what the picture should be like on the coins, and then they engrave it on. We are going to "engrave" our cookies into a coin too.

Show children how to copy the picture on the sandwich cookie onto the plain round cookie using the toothpick as an engraving tool.

Memory Verse: 2 Corinthians 9:7 ICB

Each one should give, then, what he has decided in his heart to give. He should not give if it makes him sad. And he should not give if he thinks he is forced to give. God loves the person who gives happily.

Alternate Version (New King James)
So let each one give as he purposes in his heart, not grudgingly or of necessity; for God loves a cheerful giver.

Memory Verse Activity: Happy or Sad

To help children get the phrases in the right order, teach these motions. For the first phrase, lead children to clasp their hands over their hearts. For the second phrase, they will make frowning faces. For the third phrase they will act as if someone is twisting their arm behind their back, forcing them to give. And finally, they will have happy faces. Practice saying the verse in parts. Then make the sign or motion to get them to say the appropriate phrase.

Prayer Focus

Dear God, thank you for all you give us. Help us to be generous. Amen.

June 29, 2005

(Special Activity, Independence Day)
America's Need for Revival, Midweek
By Tina Hauser

Scripture
2 Chronicles 7:14

Lesson Aim
Children will understand the need to pray for our country.

Life Skill
Children will learn to pray for their leaders.

Bible Learning Activity for Younger Children: Five a Day!
If you knew an activity that takes five minutes a day could impact and change America, would you be willing to spend five minutes doing it? Leaders for the National Day of Prayer suggest that if we pray for five minutes each day, we can change the country! They tell us that we should pray for five things:

1. **Government**—Pray for your leaders, the president and other leaders where you live.
2. **Media**—Pray for the people who write our news, TV shows, and movies.
3. **Education**—Pray for the people who decide what you should learn at school. Pray for your teachers.
4. **Church**—Pray for your church and your teachers at church. Pray for your pastor.
5. **Family**—Pray for your family and the families of your friends.

The Bible tells us that prayer is important; and if we pray, God will answer. Let's remember to pray for our country!

Bible Learning Activity for Older Children: Icy Honor
Needed: Ice cube for each child.

Give each child an ice cube to hold in their hands. Rub the ice cube with your warm hands and see what happens.

Say: What two things have changed since you held this ice cube? (Your hands are cold, and the ice cube is melting.) Is the ice cube melting quickly or slowly?

Let's pretend that the ice cube is our country's love for God. The ice cube has slowly changed, and our country has slowly changed also. When our country was brand new and for many years after that, the people had a great respect for God. If we left the ice cube for an hour, what would happen to it? It would gradually become all water and no ice cube at all.

Different things happened in our country, and many people slowly stopped giving God the respect and honor he deserves. One day God might no longer be included in our country at all. That would be very sad. We can stop the ice cube from melting by putting it back where it belongs—in the freezer. The only way for our country to stop moving further from God is for many people to change their hearts and start giving God the most important place in their lives. God deserves all of our honor and respect.

Enrichment for Younger Children: Christians Are Everywhere!

Needed: Pictures of people from different countries. Make these questions appropriate for the pictures you obtain.

Show a picture of someone from China. What are the people who call China their home called? Chinese.

Show a picture of someone from Spain. What are the people who call Spain their home called? Spaniards.

Show a picture of someone from Africa. What are the people who call Africa their home called? Africans.

Show a picture of someone from Peru. What are the people who call Peru their home called? Peruvians.

People from every country have a special name they are called that tells everyone what their country is. People who are called by God's name, Christians, do not belong to a special country. They don't wear the same kind of clothes, speak one particular language, or have the same color of skin. People who are called by God's name are recognized because of the way they live. They have asked God to forgive them; they pray; they obey God; and they have stopped doing things that do not please God. Before anything else I want to be called by God's name.

Enrichment for Older Children: Pray, Pray, Pray!

Prayer has been a part of our country even before our country became a country. Does anyone know who discovered our country? What do you think they did when they got off their ship and stood on the shore? In 1492, when Columbus landed at San Salvador, which by the way means Holy Savior, the first thing he and his men did was to kneel on the beach and pray. Then they put Spain's flag and a cross in the sand. They claimed this land for God and for Spain.

In 1775, the Continental Congress asked the colonies to pray for wisdom and guidance as the new country was formed. Abraham Lincoln asked the nation to observe a whole day of prayer in 1863. Then, in 1952, President Truman actually signed a law that stated there would be a day when the entire nation was asked to pray. With President Reagan's help in 1988, there is now a special day set aside called the National Day of Prayer. It is the first Thursday of May every year.

Ask each child to name one specific part of the country that we need to pray for. We should pray for our president, all of our representatives, the judges who decide how the law is carried out, governors, mayors, and the military. Pray that our leaders would ask God for guidance in the decisions they have to make for our country. Pray that God will give them wisdom. Pray that our leaders will honor God in their work. In prayer time, ask each child to finish the sentence, "Help our country, Lord, by guiding our _____."

Memory Verse: 2 Chronicles 7:14 ICB

"Then my people, who are called by my name, will be sorry for what they have done. They will pray and obey me and stop their evil ways. If they do, I will hear them from heaven. I will forgive their sin, and I will heal their land."

Alternate Version (New King James)

"If My people who are called by My name will humble themselves, and pray and seek My face, and turn from their wicked ways, then I will hear from heaven, and will forgive their sin and heal their land."

July 3, 2005

(Special Activity, Independence Day)
America's Need for Revival, Midweek
By Tina Hauser

Scripture
2 Chronicles 7:14

Lesson Aim
Children will understand the need to pray for our country.

Life Skill
Children will learn to pray for their leaders.

Bible Lesson: America's Need for Revival!

Needed: Large bandage for each child, bandages with words written on them: *sorry, pray, obey,* and *stop.*

Say: Have you ever gotten cut while you were playing? (Let children describe their injuries.) If you got cut while you were playing in the yard, what would your mother do for you? With each response ask why she would do that. (She would wash out the cut to get rid of the dirt, put some medicine on the cut to kill the germs, and then put a bandage on it to protect the cut while it healed.)

Say: If your mom is like most moms, she would also tell you not to do it again. Many people in our country have turned away from God. They have stopped praying, stopped worshiping God, and have stopped honoring God. How do you think that makes God feel? It must hurt him.

God is sad about that, but the Bible tells us that he still wants our country, and every country, to come back to him. He even tells us how to heal our land. Just like when we get hurt and we have to wash away the dirt, God wants us to say we are sorry for the things that we have done against Him. We should pray to get rid of the thoughts of sin that come into our minds just like germs that get into our cut. He wants us to obey him. Obeying God protects us against sin, just as the bandage protects the cut from getting dirty. The last thing God tells us is to stop our evil ways. God is saying, just like our mothers, "Don't do it again."

What are the four ways to heal our country? Show children the bandages with words on them. Let them say the words together: *sorry, pray, obey,* and *stop.* These bandage will remind you of how we can help our country get back to honoring God.

 Song Suggestions

No Need to Worry by Jana Alayra from "Jump into the Light" (Montjoy Music 1995)

Pray, Pray, Pray by Mary Rice Hopkins from "Good Buddies" (Big Steps 4 U 1994)

Let the Lord Have His Way Songsheets published by CEF Press, P.O. Box 348, Warrenton, Mo. 63383

History Makers by Kurt Johnson, a.k.a. MrJ from "Kid Possible" (Kurt Johnson Music 1995)

 Craft for Younger Children: Prayer Flag
Needed: Magnet, blue craft foam, red craft foam, white craft foam, glue.

Cut a 2-inch x 4-inch rectangle of white foam. Cut blue foam squares 1 1/2 inch x 1 1/2 inch. Cut thin red and white pieces to use as stripes. Show children how to glue to form a flag. Glue a magnet on the back.

Say: A flag is the symbol our country uses to show who we are. Let's use this flag to remember that we need to pray. Each time that you see it, remember to pray for our country.

Craft for Older Children: Prayer Reminder
Needed: Red, white, and blue pony beads, large safety pin.

Show children how to put the beads onto the safety pin (in any order). Let children design their own.

Say: The colors of the U.S. are red, white, and blue. When we see the red, white, and blue, we remember our country. Now each time you see the red, white, and blue together, I want you to remember to pray for our country!

Show children how to wear the prayer reminder.

Snack: Flag Cakes

 Needed: Rectangle snack cakes iced white with red string licorice and blueberries. Show children how to make a flag by cutting red licorice into small pieces for the stripes and putting the blueberries where the stars should be.

Say: Our flag is the symbol of our country. It should also remind us of how much God loves our country and protects us.

Memory Verse: 2 Chronicles 7:14 ICB

"Then my people, who are called by my name, will be sorry for what they have done. They will pray and obey me and stop their evil ways. If they do, I will hear them from heaven. I will forgive their sin, and I will heal their land."

Alternate Version (New King James)
"If My people who are called by My name will humble themselves, and pray and seek My face, and turn from their wicked ways, then I will hear from heaven, and will forgive their sin and heal their land."

Memory Verse Activity: Echo, Echo!
Write the verse on a whiteboard. Tell children that they will echo you as you say the verse:
  Then my people, (Then my people,)
  Who are called by my name, (Who are called by my name,)
  Will be sorry for what they have done. (Will be sorry for what they have done.)
  They will pray and obey me (They will pray and obey me)
  And stop their evil ways. (And stop their evil ways.)
  If they do, (If they do,)
  I will hear them from heaven. (I will hear them from heaven).
  I will forgive their sin, (I will forgive their sin,)
  And I will heal their land. (And I will heal their land.)

Prayer Focus
Dear God, thank you for protecting our land and our country. We are sorry for our sins, and we ask you to heal our land. Amen.

July 6, 2005

Faith Glorifies God, Midweek
By Vicki Wiley

Scripture
John 12:1–8

Lesson Aim
To show children examples of people giving to others and bringing glory to God.

Life Skill
Children will learn what compassion is and how to show it.

Bible Learning Activity for Younger Children: Anointing Oil
In the Bible we often learn about special oil that people use for healing or anointing. What is anointing? *Anointing* means to put a small amount of oil on a person's head while praying for that person.

People in Bible times made a type of perfumed oil from a plant called nard. The nard plant had a special oil in its roots and stem. They had to squeeze hard to get the oil out of this plant!

Bible Learning Activity for Older Children: What Is Nard?
People in Bible times sometimes made perfume from the oil of a plant called nard. The spikenard, or nard, plant contained oil in its dried roots and stems. This plant came from Asia and was rare, which made it expensive. The oil was used as a liquid or made into an ointment. The spikenard plant had many spikes growing out of it, which produced clusters of pink flowers.

Spikenard was imported from India in alabaster boxes. These were stored and used only for special occasions. When household guests arrived, they were usually anointed with this oil. Jesus was anointed on two occasions as an honored guest (Mark 14:3; John 12:3). When he was anointed with this oil, it meant that he was very special indeed!

Enrichment for Younger Children: Missions for the Poor

Needed: Pictures of poor people in the United States, a gift-wrapped empty box.

Say: Have you ever tried to help poor people? Many churches adopt a mission project for Vacation Bible School and learn about the poor in other countries. But did you know that we don't need to leave the U.S. to help the poor? In every city there are children who go without food and warm clothes.

Show the pictures and the gift-wrapped box.

Say: Do you believe that you can make a difference in these children's lives? Yes, you can!

Ask a child to open the box.

Say: What could you do to help? When you buy a pair of shoes for yourself, can you also buy a pair for a poor child? Can you give some of the clothes you don't wear anymore to someone who needs them?

Let children brainstorm other ways to help. Talk about how the Salvation Army helps by collecting usable goods and redistributing them.

Enrichment for Older Children: Perfumed Oil

Needed: Baby oil, whole cloves (or fresh potpourri), and small jar for each child.

Say: In Bible times people made perfume by taking the oil out of herbs and adding it to some pure oil. Today we will make some perfume similar to the perfume they made when Jesus was still living on earth.

Show children how to take the clove and add it to a small amount of the baby oil in the jar. Shake the oil with the clove in it for a few minutes until the oil smells like the clove.

Say: Now you have made some perfume! You can use this just like perfume, and it will remind you of our Bible story today.

Memory Verse: John 12:7, 8 ICB

Jesus answered, "Let her alone. It was right for her to save this perfume for to-day—the day for me to be prepared for burial. The poor will always be with you, but you will not always have me."

Alternate Version (New King James)

But Jesus said, "Let her alone; she has kept this for the day of My burial. For the poor you have with you always, but Me you do not have always."

Faith Glorifies God
By Pat Verbal

Scripture
John 12:1–8

Lesson Aim
To show children examples of people giving to others and bringing glory to God.

Life Skill
Children will learn what compassion is and how to show it.

Bible Lesson: Faith Glorifies God
Preparation: Bring pictures of homeless people or invite a mission chaplain to class. Gift-wrap a new pair of children's shoes with a note about God's love tucked inside one of the shoes.

Say: Have you ever visited a homeless shelter or mission? What did you see? How did it smell? In large cities where people live in old cars, cardboard boxes, and dirty hotels, there is a foul odor. People are too poor for bubble baths and perfumes.

We don't talk about it very much, but Jesus was homeless. He was poor by worldly standards. In today's Bible lesson Jesus visited his good friends in Bethany. Find John 12 and follow along as we read verses 1–8.

Mary wanted to show Jesus how much she loved him. She probably thought for a long time about what she could do. Finally, a good idea came to her, but she knew it would be risky. She opened a treasured bottle of perfume and poured it on Jesus feet, wiping his feet with her hair. In those days perfume was like money in the bank, and this bottle was worth a year's wages. It may have been her only savings, but she freely gave it to honor her Lord. Do you think Mary knew people might think she was crazy for pouring her savings on someone's feet? Why did Jesus defend Mary? (Let children respond.)

Not only did Jesus praise Mary, but he also gave a message that day about helping the poor. He said we would always have poor people in our world, and we could help them if we wanted to.

Do poor families live in your town? Ask the Lord to open your eyes to opportunities you've never seen before. Would someone like to give this pair of shoes to a child who needs them?

 Song Suggestions

Walking and Singing by Mary Rice Hopkins from "Miracle Mud" (Big Steps 4 U 2000)

Faith Will Do by Dean-o from "You Got It All" (FKO Music, Inc. 1997)

Walking and Leaping Traditional chorus

Jump into the Light by Jana Alayra from *Jump into the Light* (Montjoy Music 1997)

Lord I Give My Heart by Mark Thompson from "Yes Yes Yes!" (Markarts 2000)

 Craft for Younger Children: Show the Love
Needed: Large craft stick, craft foam heart.

Show children how to glue the heart onto the end of the craft stick. Write "God loves you" on the heart.

This is a special bookmark that you have made. Give it to someone you don't even know. When you give it to them, say, "I'm sharing God's love with you!"

Craft for Older Children: Pack of Joy
Needed: Storage bags, bottles of water, and individual packages
of crackers, other individual treats.

Say: Today we are going to make something special. It is called a Pack
of Joy. We will put together a bag of treats for someone who doesn't have
very much. Do you ever see homeless people? (Let children discuss.) Jesus
had many friends who were homeless; he really loved them.

Show children how to put one of each item into the bag. Encourage
them to take it with them and give it to a homeless person. (Tell them to
do this only while their parents are with them.) They may be
surprised by the reaction of the homeless person!

Snack: "Poor Boy" Sandwiches

 Needed: French rolls, condiments, cheese.
Say: A long time ago in our country, there were some
people who didn't have jobs. Other people created a special
sandwich just for them and gave them out for free. They
were called "poor boy" sandwiches.

Show children how to make their sandwich.

Say: Today we would never call something a "poor boy" sandwich, would
we? Why wouldn't we do that? (It might make some people feel bad.) We
need to be careful that we show only love and never make people feel bad.

Memory Verse: John 12:7, 8 ICB

*Jesus answered, "Let her alone. It was right for her to save this perfume for to-
day—the day for me to be prepared for burial. The poor will always be with you,
but you will not always have me."*

Alternate Version (New King James)
*But Jesus said, "Let her alone; she has kept this for the day of My burial. For the
poor you have with you always, but Me you do not have always."*

Memory Verse Activity: Act It Out!

Write the verse on a whiteboard where all the children can see it. Assign the following parts to the children: Jesus, the woman, the crowd, Judas.

Say: In our story today Jesus said these words. Let's act out what happened. (Let children read the verse together as they act out the verse.) Repeat several times until the children remember the verse.

Prayer Focus

Dear God, thank you for your Son, Jesus. Thank you for showing us how special he is. Help us always to remember him. Amen.

July 13, 2005

Leaders Take a Stand, Midweek
By Vicki Wiley

Scripture
Nehemiah 13:7–12

Lesson Aim
Children will see how a good leader can make a big difference.

Life Skill
Children will want to lead others in taking a stand against sin.

Bible Learning Activity for Younger Children: Say No!
Tell the children they are going to play a version of Simon says. You will be the leader, and they should do the good things you say but not the bad.

Say: Leader says jump up and down.

Leader says hit someone. (Don't do it!)

Leader says say hello to someone.

Leader says make a bad face at someone. (Don't do it!)

Continue playing.

Say: Sometimes leaders are good, and when we follow them, we do good things. Sometimes leaders do not lead well and tell us to do things that are wrong. We shouldn't do those things, even if our leaders tell us to do them!

Bible Learning Activity for Older Children: Leaders in the Bible
There were many leaders in the Bible. Sometimes these leaders were called judges, and sometimes they were called kings. Some of the most famous judges were Deborah, Gideon, Samson, and Samuel. Some of the most famous kings were Saul, David, and Solomon.

Who are the leaders in our country? What do they do for us? How are they like or unlike the judges or kings in Bible times? (They were liked or not liked by the people. They were appointed or chosen to be in their positions. Some are good, and some are bad.)

We always need to pray for our leaders and follow the laws that we have.

Enrichment for Younger Children: Follow the Leader

Lead children in a simple game of follow-the-leader. After several children have had a turn, say: What makes a good leader in this game? What should you do if you are the leader? When you are the leader, you need to know what you want to do. To be a good leader, you need to listen to other people and hear what they say.

Enrichment for Older Children: Tug of War!

Form two teams. Give each team one end of the rope. Draw a masking tape line on the floor. Tell one team they represent the Jews who did wrong. The other team represents Nehemiah.

Read Nehemiah 13:7–21. Tell children to pull on the rope according to the verse. Read the verses and try this ahead of time so you can yell "pull."

v. 7, I learned about evil. (Sin side pulls.)

v. 8, I threw them out. (Nehemiah's side pulls.)

v. 10, Levites portion had not been given. (Sin side pulls.)

v. 11, I rebuked the officials. (Nehemiah's side pulls.)

v. 15, Men in Judah were working on the Sabbath. (Sin side pulls.)

v. 17, I rebuked the nobles. (Nehemiah's side pulls.)

v. 18, Wrath against Israel. (Sin side pulls.)

v. 19, I stationed my men. (Nehemiah's side pulls.)

v. 20, Merchants and sellers stay in the temple. (Sin side pulls.)

v. 21, I lay hands on you and commanded the Levites to purify. (Nehemiah's side pulls.)

This tug-of-war continues today. God is looking for brave leaders like Nehemiah who will direct people back to God's laws. Boys and girls can lead their friends to Jesus by holding on to God's promises and following Jesus no matter what others do.

Memory Verse: Nehemiah 1:11 ICB
And listen to the prayers of your servants who love to honor you.

Alternate Version (New King James)
Please let Your ear be attentive to the prayer of Your servant, and to the prayer of Your servants who desire to fear Your name.

July 17, 2005

Leaders Take a Stand
By Pat Verbal

Scripture
Nehemiah 13:7–12

Lesson Aim
Children will see how a good leader can make a big difference.

Life Skill
Children will want to lead others in taking a stand against sin.

Bible Lesson: Leaders Take a Stand

Preparation: A pair of sunglasses, a rope long enough for a game of tug-of-war, and masking tape.

Say: Have you ever wondered what makes a good leader? Someone once said there is one thing you need to be a leader—followers! That may be true, but it only tells half the story. You can be a bad leader and still have followers. A good leader needs much more.

Look at Nehemiah for example. He didn't become a leader because he had followers. He became a leader because he was upset over injustice. That means Nehemiah saw a problem and could not rest. When God's people returned to their homeland from captivity in Persia, the walls of Jerusalem were left in ruins. Nehemiah felt this dishonored God. So he went to the governor and requested permission to lead a group in restoring the city's walls.

You might think that Nehemiah's efforts were rewarded, but you would be wrong. Doing the right thing often gets leaders in trouble. The rich people in Judah didn't want the Jews to become proud and strong. They liked cheating the poor. The Jews were comfortable breaking God's laws and didn't want to change.

Put on the sunglasses.

Say: Nehemiah could have saved himself a lot of trouble if he had just worn dark glasses and said, "I'm not going to look at these walls." But he couldn't do that because great leaders never run from trouble (or sin). They bravely take a stand. After Nehemiah rebuilt Jerusalem's walls, he served two terms as governor of Judah. But when he died, the people again disobeyed God.

Can children be leaders? Can they see problems in their community that need to be changed? How can children take a stand against sin?

Allow time for discussion.

 Song Suggestions

The Family of God by Kurt Johnson, a.k.a. MrJ from "Kid Possible" (Kurt Johnson 1995)

No One Else I Know by Mary Rice Hopkins from "15 Singable Songs" (Big Steps 4 U 1988)

This Is Love by Dean-o from "God City" (BibleBeat Music, 2001)

What a Mighty God We Serve Songsheets published by CEF Press P.O. Box 348, Warrenton, Mo. 63383

 Craft for Younger Children: Leader Necklace
Needed: Squares of construction paper or craft foam approximately 2 inches x 2 inches, felt-tip markers, cord for necklace.

Show children how to write one letter on each square to spell *leader*, and then string the letters onto the cord. Wear your "leader" necklace to remind yourself that you are a leader!

Craft for Older Children: Leader Light Switch Cover
Needed: Plastic light switch covers and permanent markers.

Say: We can all be great leaders for God. Sometimes we forget that we are leaders, even while we are children. Today we are going to make something to remind us every day that we are leaders.

Show children how to write, "God made me a leader," across the top of the light switch cover. Let children finish decorating as they wish.

Say: Every day when you turn on your light, read this and remember that you are a leader!

Snack: Leadership Cookies

 Needed: Square cookies, red licorice, icing.

Show children how to make a leadership cookie by adding a licorice *L* on top of the cookie. Attach with icing.

Say: *L* stands for *leader!* Today we are going to become leaders for God.

Memory Verse: Nehemiah 1:11 ICB

Listen to the prayers of your servants who love to honor you.

Alternate Version (New King James)
Please let Your ear be attentive to the prayer of Your servant, and to the prayer of Your servants who desire to fear Your name.

Memory Verse Activity: Missing Words

Write the verse on the whiteboard. Let children say the verse together. As they learn it, erase one word. Say it again. Continue erasing more and more words and repeating the verse until they know it from memory.

Prayer Focus

Dear God, thank you for the leaders that you have given us. Help us to become leaders that do what you say. Amen.

July 20, 2005

Measuring Up, Midweek
By Vicki Wiley

Scripture
2 Thessalonians 1:3–5

Lesson Aim
Children will understand that there can be measurable evidence to show that one is growing as a Christian.

Life Skill
Children will use some of these measures to assess how they are growing in Christ.

Bible Learning Activity for Younger Children: Growing!
In the Bible we find that Jesus was growing and that God was pleased with his growth. The Bible says that "Jesus continued to learn more and more and to grow physically. People liked him, and he pleased God" (Luke 2:52 ICB).

How are you growing? (I'm getting taller. I'm getting stronger.) How can you grow so that you please God? (Get to know him better.)

Bible Learning Activity for Older Children: Wiser and Taller
Let's look up and read Luke 2:52. It says, "Jesus continued to learn more and more and to grow physically. People liked him, and he pleased God" (Luke 2:52 ICB).

How are you growing when you learn more and more?
What does it mean to grow "physically"?
How does growing in these areas please God?

Enrichment for Younger Children: Measure Up!

Needed: Many different kinds of measuring instruments such as measuring cups and spoons, rulers, scales, and tape measures. Gather, also, different types of items that can be measured such as liquid, sand, flour, a box, or a ball.

Say: There are lots of ways to measure things. Let's try to measure these things. Let the children experiment with measuring these objects.

Talk with the children as they do this about what measuring things helps us to do.

Enrichment for Older Children: Measure Up!

Needed: Many different kinds of measuring instruments such as measuring cups and spoons, rulers, scales, and tape measures. Gather, also, different types of items that can be measured such as liquid, sand, flour, a box, or a ball.

Ask: Why do we measure things? Is it important to measure things? Let children experiment with measuring different items.

It is also important that we measure our growth as a Christian. If we want to learn to love God and do what God says, we need to keep growing. What are some things we can do to grow as a Christian? (Read the Bible, go to church, pray.) How can we measure how much we are growing as a Christian? (how we think, how we act)

Memory Verse: 2 Thessalonians 1:3

We must always thank God for you. And we should do this because it is right. It is right because your faith is growing more and more. And the love that every one of you has for each other is also growing.

Alternate Version (New King James)

We are bound to thank God always for you, brethren, as it is fitting, because your faith grows exceedingly, and the love of every one of you all abounds toward each other.

July 24, 2005

Measuring Up
By Ivy Beckwith

Scripture
2 Thessalonians 1:3–5

Lesson Aim
Children will understand that there can be measurable evidence to show that one is growing as a Christian.

Life Skill
Children will use some of these measures to assess how they are growing in Christ.

Bible Lesson: Measuring Up!
Needed: A tape measure, a notepad, and a pencil or pen.

Today I want to see how tall some of you are. (Pick several children. Ask them to stand up and then measure them with the tape measure. Say their height out loud and write it on the notepad.) After you have measured the children, ask them to be seated.

Ask: If I were to measure you again a year from today, what do you think we would find? (Allow time for a response.) That's right! You would probably all be taller than you are today. One of the ways we can tell that someone is growing physically is by measuring their height. Seeing how tall children are at a certain age helps us to know how well they are growing physically.

But sometimes we can grow in ways that we can't always measure with a tape measure. God wants us to grow in our faith in him. Our Bible story today helps us to see how we can measure our growing faith in God.

The apostle Paul helped to start a church a long time ago in the Greek city of Thessalonica. After he left the city, he continued to be concerned that the people in the church love God and follow Jesus, so he wrote them letters to help them understand more about God and Jesus. In one of the letters, he helped them understand ways to tell that they were growing in their faith in God.

He told them he could tell that they loved one another more and more every day. This was one way he knew they were growing in their faith. He said that he saw how they continued to trust God and follow Jesus even when bad things happened to them. When they did this, he could tell they were growing in their faith in God.

Even though this story happened a long time ago, we can still measure how well we're growing in our love of God and Jesus by looking at these two characteristics of a growing faith. We can look at how well we're doing in loving other people, even those people we don't like very much. And we can look at how we're doing in trusting God with our lives even when bad things happen to us. If you are getting better and better at doing these things, then you know you are growing in your faith in God just as you know you're growing physically when each year you are taller than you were the year before.

 Song Suggestions

Little Is Much by Mary Rice Hopkins from "15 Singable Songs" (Big Steps 4 U 1988)

He's Got Plans by Dean-o from "Soul Surfin'" (FKO Music, Inc. 1999)

I'm Not Too Little Songsheets published by CEF Press, P.O. Box 348, Warrenton, Mo. 63383

 Craft for Younger Children: Growth Chart
Needed: Strips of paper for each child at long as children are tall. You may attach several smaller strips together to form one long strip.

Say: Today we are going to make a growth chart. Give each child a strip of paper and mark his or her height on the strip.

Hang this strip up on your wall so that you can check how much you have grown. You are always growing physically, but did you know you are also growing as a Christian? How can you do that? (Get to know God better, pray, read the Bible, show kindness.)

Craft for Older Children: Growing
Needed: One small clay pot, paints, one craft stick and small bedding plant for each child.

Let children decorate the pot as they wish. Plant the bedding plant and then stick the craft stick in the pot beside the plant. Mark the height of the plant on the stick.

Say: Sometimes it is hard to notice when something is growing. We are going to measure the growth of this plant so that we can see how fast it really grows.

Next Sunday we will measure the growth again and make another mark. God causes all things to grow. God wants us to grow physically and get bigger but God also wants us to grow in our faith.

(Be sure plants receive the care they need during the week.)

Snack: Growing Food

 Needed: Assortment of veggies, wheat crackers, and water.
Say: What are some of the things we need in order to grow? (Good food, sleep, air, etc.)
This is some healthy food that will help us grow!

Memory Verse: 2 Thessalonians 1:3

We must always thank God for you. And we should do this because it is right. It is right because your faith is growing more and more. And the love that every one of you has for each other is also growing.

Alternate Version (New King James)
We are bound to thank God always for you, brethren, as it is fitting, because your faith grows exceedingly, and the love of every one of you all abounds toward each other.

Memory Verse Activity: Growing Up

Say the verse together in this manner.

We must thank God for you. (Put hands together as in prayer.)

And we should do this because it is right. (Thumbs up.)

It is right because your faith is growing more and more. (Start this part crouched on the floor and grow as you say this sentence.)

And the love (Touch your heart.)

That every one of you has for each other is also growing. (Form a heart with your fingers and let it grow.)

Prayer Focus

Dear God, help us to remember how important it is for us to grow as Christians. Thank you for helping us grow! Amen.

July 27, 2005

Carrying the Truth, Midweek
By Eric Titus

Scripture
Exodus 20:16

Lesson Aim
Children will learn the importance of telling the truth.

Life Skill
Children will learn the importance of being a good witness.

Bible Learning Activity for Younger Children: Biggest Lie
Ask: What is the biggest lie you ever told? Does anyone want to tell us? Did you get away with it?

Let children tell what happened when they lied. If no one wants to talk, begin by telling a story yourself and laughing at your mistake.

The Bible tells us in the Ten Commandments that we should not lie. When we lie, things get very mixed up.

Bible Learning Activity for Older Children: Hot Potato Lies
Needed: Potato or ball to toss.

Say: We are going to play a game about lying. When you get the potato, think really quickly of something that kids your age lie about. Say it and then pass it on to the next person.

Say: Why do you think kids lie? What would happen if they told the truth instead?

Enrichment for Younger Children: A Lie and a Truth

Say: Today we are going to play a game about lying. I want each person to think of something to tell us that is a lie and something to tell us that is true. After you tell the two things, we will guess which is a lie and which is true.

Help children think of true and false things such as: I have a dog. My favorite color is blue. I have my own room.

Is it better to tell the truth or to tell a lie? Is it hard to know which is which?

Enrichment for Older Children: Web of Deceit

Needed: Roll of toilet tissue or crepe paper.

Sir Walter Scott said, "Oh, what a tangled web we weave, when first we practice to deceive." Why would he compare a lie, or deceit, to a web? Lets' try an experiment to see if we can understand. I will start a story that is a lie.

Say: One day the teacher told me that I was the best student in the class. Hold onto the roll of paper but throw it to someone else and let them continue the story saying anything they want to make the lie bigger. Keep this going until a web is created by the paper.

We should not lie to anyone. When we do, the lie always grows and grows as we try to keep the story straight.

Memory Verse: Exodus 20:16 ICB
You must not tell lies about your neighbor in court.

Alternate Version (New King James)
You shall not bear false witness against your neighbor.

Carrying the Truth
By Eric Titus

Scripture
Exodus 20:16

Lesson Aim
Children will learn the importance of telling the truth.

Life Skill
Children will learn the importance of being a good witness.

Bible Lesson: Carrying the Truth

Preparation: One hard-boiled egg, one regular egg, a bowl, a felt-tip marker, and a towel.

One of the commandments on God's top ten list can be a little bit hard to understand. Does anyone know what it means to bear false witness? Those are some good answers. Sometimes you might see a TV show where someone is a witness to something that happened. Maybe you have seen the part where they promise "to tell the truth, the whole truth, and nothing but the truth so help me God." Judges, lawyers, and others trust people to tell the truth about things they may have seen or not seen other people do.

What do you think might happen to someone who was on trial for a crime, and a witness didn't tell the truth? That's right. Some really bad things might happen. The wrong person might go to jail. Someone who should be in jail might be out doing other bad things. It is important for a witness to be honest. It is important for a witness to *carry* the truth.

But a witness could also carry a lie instead of the truth. Another word for carry is *bear*. That word is often used when we hear this commandment of God. We can *bear* or *carry* a false witness; we can *bear* or *carry* the truth or a lie.

Look at these two eggs. They look the same, don't they? But we're going to write false on one (use the marker to write false on the raw egg) and true on the other (write true on the hard-boiled egg). It's hard to tell these apart at first, but if we were to look closer or even break these eggs open, we would find a big difference.

I'm going to crack the egg open that says false. Do you think it would be easy or hard to carry this egg around now? What if you didn't have the bowl? It would be really hard. What a mess it would make! When we say something that is not true about somebody else, it is really messy. We don't only mess up the person that we tell lies about, but we get the mess all over ourselves too!

Now we are going to crack the other egg. See, it looks pretty much the same on the inside as it did on the outside. Would this egg be easier or harder to carry around than the other one? I think easier too. And it's a lot more solid. It's not messy either. That's the way it is with being a witness. It is much better to be a true witness than to tell something false about someone else. So you should always bear true witness about other people; it is best for them, best for you, and it pleases God.

 Song Suggestions

You Are a Wonderful God Songsheets published by CEF Press, P.O. Box 348, Warrenton, Mo. 63383

You Reign by Kurt Johnson from "Kid Possible" (Kurt Johnson 1995)

Create in Me by Mary Rice Hopkins from "15 Singable Songs" (Big Steps 4 U 1988)

Outta Sight by Dean-o from "Soul Surfin'" (FKO Music, Inc. 1999)

This Little Light of Mine Traditional Chorus

Craft for Younger and Older children: Tell the Truth Banner
Needed: Felt or craft foam cut into banner or pennant shapes, scraps of craft foam or felt, already prepared letters, glue, felt-tip markers.

Have children write or use letters to spell *Tell the Truth* on their banner or pennant. Let them continue to decorate as desired.

Say: Telling the truth is important. God wants us to tell the truth, and our friends and parents want us to tell the truth. This banner will remind us to tell the truth.

Snack: Gavel Snack

Needed: Rod-type pretzels and large marshmallows.

Show children how to make a gavel by pushing the pretzel rod into the marshmallow.

Say: A judge uses a gavel like this when talking to people in the courtroom. How many of you have see this on TV? When you are in court, you are supposed to tell the truth only. When you do, everything works out for the best.

Memory Verse: Exodus 20:16 ICB
You must not tell lies about your neighbor in court.

Alternate Version (New King James)
You shall not bear false witness against your neighbor.

Memory Verse Activity: Don't Tell Lies

Chant this verse while doing these motions

You must not (Shake your hand and your finger "no.")

Tell lies (Place your hand near your mouth and go outward.)

About your neighbor ("Knock" as you would on a door.)

In court. (Hit your fist into the other hand as a judge would a gavel.)

Prayer Focus

Dear Lord, we ask that you will help us always to carry the truth with us about other people and to be a true witness for others. Amen.

August 3, 2005

God Wants Everyone to Know About Him, Midweek
By Vicki Wiley

Scripture
Romans 10:4

Lesson Aim
Children will want everyone to believe in Jesus and to find a life with God.

Life Skill
Children will want to find ways to tell others about Jesus.

Bible Learning Activity for Younger and Older Children: The Salvation Message
Needed: Colored objects. This can be made the following ways:

Sandy Candy (Place small amounts into tubes.)

Bracelet or necklace (Use colored beads on cord.)

Salvation Tube (Use small aquarium gravel with clear tubing found in home improvement store.)

Chain (Use colored chenille wire.)

Whichever plan you select, you will need these colors: yellow or gold, white, black, green, and red.

Choose the method you will use from choices above. Using your chosen method, tell the following message: Today we are going to learn the best part of the Bible, the salvation message. When your tube is filled, it will help you remember what we talk about.

Pass around the yellow or gold items.

Say: What does this gold remind you of? (money, jewelry) Those things are valuable and special. But today the gold is going to represent heaven. The Bible tells us that in heaven the streets are made of gold. God tells us many other things about his home. No one is ever sick there. No one ever dies.

There is no night there. Heaven is a special place. There is one thing that can never be in heaven. Does anyone know what that is? (sin)

Pass around the black items.

Say: Do you know what sin is? The black candy stands for sin. Sin is anything we think, do, or say that is wrong and does not please God. God cannot live with anything sinful, but it is impossible for us not to sin. Because God wants us to live in heaven and because we sin, God had to think of another plan for us.

Pass out the red items.

Say: God loved us so much and wanted us to be in heaven with him, so God sent his Son, Jesus Christ, to the world. Jesus lived on earth just like we do, but Jesus never sinned. The Bible tells us that Jesus died on the cross because he was being punished, even though he did nothing wrong. Instead of dying for his sin, he dies for our sin—all the sin we already did and all the sin we will do in our lives. The red candy stands for the blood of Jesus.

Pass out the white items.

Say: God wants to forgive your sins and make it so that they never happened at all. No matter how good you are, you still will sin. There is nothing you can do to take away your own sin, nothing except one special thing. You can receive Jesus. How do you do that? You tell Jesus that you know you are a sinner and that you are sorry for all the wrong things you have done. You tell Jesus that you believe in him and that you want him to be your Savior. That's it. That's all you have to do.

Then when God looks at you, he doesn't see the sin; he only sees the clean part of you that has no sin at all. The white candy will stand for a pure heart.

Pass out the green items.

Say: The color green reminds me of things that are growing, like trees, plants, and grass. When you are a Christian and have received Christ, you begin to grow too. You learn more and more about Jesus, and that means that you are growing in Christ!

Would anyone like to receive Jesus right now? We are going to pray, and when we pray, let's all bow our heads. I will tell you what to pray, and if you want to receive Christ, you can pray along with me, OK?

Dear Jesus, I know that I am a sinner. But I would like to receive you right now so that you can be the Lord of my life. I love you, and I want to follow you. Please forgive me for my sins and come into my life. Thank you God. Amen.

Let's review what the colors mean so you can tell others about Christ! (Review each color, and let the children tell you what the colors mean.)

Enrichment for Younger Children: Tell Someone!

Play a simple game of telephone with the children. Begin the round by saying to the first child: Jesus died for you, and he loves you. Have each child repeat that to the next child until it has gone all the way around. Have the last child tell what he heard.

Say: Telling other people about Jesus is important. Do you know what to say? "Jesus died for you, and he loves you" is one way to tell people about Jesus.

Enrichment for Older Children: RSVP

Needed: Card stock paper to make invitations.

Say: Today we are going to make an invitation. What should it be for? (Let children brainstorm.) Let's make one to invite people to our church.

Let the children make an invitation to invite someone to come to Sunday School or to another activity at your church. Explain to the children that this is one way they can help other people learn about Jesus

Memory Verse: Romans 10:4 ICB

Christ ended the law, so that everyone who believes in him may be right with God.

Alternate Version (New King James)

For Christ is the end of the law for righteousness to everyone who believes.

August 7, 2005

God Wants Everyone to Know About Him
By Tina Hauser

Scripture
Romans 10:4

Lesson Aim
Children will want everyone to believe in Jesus and to find a life with God.

Life Skill
Children will want to find ways to tell others about Jesus.

Bible Lesson: God Wants Everyone to Know About Him

Needed: You will need several teaching pictures/representations of the apostle Paul and, if you have them, pictures of great Christians from history like St. Patrick.

Much of the New Testament, the second part of the Bible, was written by a man named Paul. (Show pictures.) Because Paul lived so long ago, we don't really know what he looked like, but these pictures are what artists think he might have looked like. Paul wanted everyone in the world to know about Jesus and live the way God created us to live. So he traveled, wrote letters, preached, and started churches so that everyone in the world could know who Jesus was. Not everyone liked what Paul was saying, so sometimes he was chased out of town, and sometimes he was even put in jail. But that didn't stop Paul from telling other people about Jesus because he thought that was the most important thing he could ever do. It was the focus of his life.

Why do you think Paul thought it was so important to tell other people about Jesus? (Allow time for several responses.) Yes, he knew that living a life of following Jesus was the only thing that would make the world better and give people the chance to live forever with God.

The writings and activities of Paul in the New Testament have inspired other people to tell others about Jesus too. After Paul died, lots of people in the churches Paul started went out to start other churches and wrote books about the Bible and following Jesus. They, like Paul, thought that telling people about Jesus was the most important thing they could do. (At this point mention some important figures from church history or historical figures or missionaries from your denomination or church tradition, explaining the work they did in helping others all over the world to know and follow Jesus.)

It's not just people like Paul and other Christians from history who need to tell others about Jesus. People just like you and me need to do it as well. The Bible tells us that people who love and follow Jesus need to show love to other people, and one way we do that is to help other people understand who Jesus is and what it means to follow him.

Do you know some ways our church helps other people to know who Jesus is? (Allow time for responses. After the children have responded, add some specific things your church does such as supporting missionaries, supporting local social service organizations, outreach activities your church may sponsor, or other types of evangelistic programming done by your church.) These are ways we can tell people in our neighborhoods and around the world about Jesus.

We can tell other people about Jesus, too. Can you think of some ways we can tell our friends about Jesus? (Allow time for responses.) Those are all good ideas. We can invited friends to Sunday School or Vacation Bible School. We can show kindness and love to other people. There are lots of ways we can tell others about Jesus and show other people that Jesus loves them.

 Song Suggestions

Do You Know About Jesus? Songsheets published by CEF Press, P.O. Box 348, Warrenton, Mo. 63383

He Is Really God! by Dean-o from "You Got It All" (For Kids Only, Inc. 1997)

Can You Hear My Heart? by Jana Alayra from "Dig Down Deep" (Montjoy Music 1997)

Craft for Younger Children: New Creation
Needed: Old-fashioned clothespins (the kind without the spring), tissue paper of different colors.

Give each child a clothespin and some rectangles of tissue paper (about 4 inches x 6 inches)

Show children how to put the tissue paper inside the clothespin to form a butterfly.

Say: When we accept Christ into our lives, we become a new person just like this butterfly is new. This butterfly used to be a caterpillar, and it became a butterfly.

 Craft for Older Children: Tell Them About Jesus!
Needed: Clip art or sticker of the world, posterboard, glue.

Cut a piece of poster board for each child (depending on the size of the world sticker you are using). Let children glue the "world" onto the posterboard. Write across the top "Tell Them About Jesus."

Say: The Bible tells us that we should tell everyone about Jesus. How can we do this? Whom would we tell? Children can tell people about Jesus too!

Snack: Popcorn Ball Worlds!

 Needed: One popcorn ball for each child, blue and chocolate frosting.

Let children make a "world" by icing a popcorn ball. Make one for children to see.

Say: Jesus said that we should tell everyone about himself. That means the whole world!

Memory Verse: Romans 10:4 ICB
Christ ended the law, so that everyone who believes in him may be right with God.

Alternate Version (New King James)
For Christ is the end of the law for righteousness to everyone who believes.

Memory Verse Activity: The Law Is Ended!
Choose a child to be the judge. Stand him in front of the rest of the children and give him the "verdict" (memory verse) to read.
  Repeat until all children know the verse

Prayer Focus
Dear God, please help us to remember how important it is to tell other people about you. We love you, and we want everyone to know about you. Amen.

August 10, 2005

From Pots to Pans, You're in God's Hands, Midweek
By Michael Bonner

Scripture
Jeremiah 18:6

Lesson Aim
Children will learn that God gives us a second chance when we do something wrong.

Life Skill
God puts events in our lives that continue to mold us so that we can become just the right shape to be used by him.

Bible Learning Activity for Younger Children: God Is the Potter
Say: Do you know what a potter does? He makes pots out of clay. The Bible says that God is like a potter and that he makes us.

Let's make a clay person. What would he look like? God made each of us to look different from everyone else. Your clay people will also look different from others.

Bible Learning Activity for Older Children: Charades!
Needed: Play clay.

Play a game of charades using play clay. One member of the team has to make an item from play clay while the other team members try to guess the item. Go back and forth between teams just as you would in charades.

Say: The Bible tells us that God is like a potter. He makes us and molds us like you made and molded the clay. Were you careful while you molded? God is too!

Enrichment for Younger Children: Pots

Needed: Some pots of different types and clay.

Say: A potter is someone who makes pots like these. Do you think you could make something like this? Let children try to copy the pots that you brought in.

Say: God didn't need to copy anything the way we did. He made us all by himself just the way he wants us to be!

Enrichment for Older Children: What Does a Potter Do?

A potter in Bible times was one who made and decorated pottery. Pottery is an ancient and developed craft. In its early history, the nation of Israel had professional potters who sat on the edge of a small pit, turning the pottery wheel with their feet. In treading the clay or kneading it by foot, it was important to get the right consistency for a good end product. Many potters probably trod the clay themselves.

The potter's total control over the clay to do whatever he wants with it is likened to God's control over people.

Memory Verse: Jeremiah 18:6 ICB
"You are like the clay in the potter's hands."

Alternate Version (New King James)
"Look, as the clay is in the potter's hand, so are you in My hand."

August 14, 2005

From Pots to Pans, You're in God's Hands
By Michael Bonner

Scripture
Jeremiah 18:6

Lesson Aim
Children will learn that God gives us a second chance when we do something wrong.

Life Skill
God puts events in our lives that continue to mold us so that we can become just the right shape to be used by him.

Bible Lesson: From Pots to Pans, You're in God's Hands
Needed: Gather enough colored modeling clay to design a clay pot. You will also need one can of play clay and a bag of approximately 10-15 marbles.

Show a can of play clay to the children. Ask, "How many of you have ever played with this before?" (Wait for a show of hands.) Have several children name something they have created using play clay (a snake, a car). Respond by telling them how fun and interesting their creations must have been. Now take out the colored modeling clay that you will be using for the teaching time. Tell the children that your clay is similar to play clay, and that you are going to create something for them today.

Begin molding the clay into a pot as you share the following information with the kids. (You will want your pot to have some quarter-sized holes in the bottom when you are finished with it.) Say: In our Bible we read in Jeremiah 18 about a potter. A potter is a person who molds things out of clay—things like jars, bowls, pans, and pots. This particular potter was making a pot. Our story tells us that the pot didn't turn out right the first time, so the potter re-worked the clay and made another pot that was just what he needed.

Once you have finished your pot with the holes, say: I've designed this pot to hold these marbles. Will someone please help me by pouring these marbles in my pot?

Choose one child to pour the marbles into the pot. They will obviously fall through the holes in the bottom. As you gather the marbles, say: I've apparently not designed my pot just right to hold these marbles. I'm going to try it one more time.

Quickly rework the clay into another pot without holes this time. You may want to talk with the kids about other things they have designed with play clay to keep their interest while you are molding quickly.

When complete, ask another child to place the marbles in the pot again. This time they stay inside. Say: Wow! I messed up the first time, but I was able to have another chance and make the right kind of pot the second time. Boys and girls, that is how God handles you and me. He loves us so much that he gives us a second chance when we mess up, even a third and fourth chance! Just as the potter in our story from Jeremiah 18 is able to rework his clay into just the right pot, God is able to rework us into just what he wants us to be so he can use us.

The first pot wasn't any good for holding marbles. So I was able to rework the clay and make it into a great pot for holding marbles. If we make a mistake, maybe make a bad choice like not sharing a toy, God can help rework us and give us a second chance. Has anyone ever done something wrong and afterwards wished it hadn't happened?

Have children raise their hands and take a few examples.

Say: I know I have. But I'm thankful that God forgives me and gives me a second chance to do the right thing. One thing to remember is that we have to be willing to be reworked. Just as our clay is moldable, our lives have to be moldable so that God can teach us. We need to pray, read the Bible, and come to church to learn God's Word. He wants us to be his helpers, but we have to be willing to let him be our potter and shape us into whatever we should be!

Song Suggestions

I Am the Apple by Cindy Rethmeier from "I Want 2 Be like Jesus" (Mercy/Vineyard Publishing 1995)

Watch It Grow by Mary Rice Hopkins from "Good Buddies" (Big Steps 4 U 1994)

Children All Around the World Songsheets published by CEF Press, P.O. Box 348, Warrenton, Mo. 63383

G-Mail! by Dean-o from "Soul Surfin'" (FKO Music, Inc. 1999).

 Craft for Younger Children: You Are in My Hands
Needed: Construction paper, felt-tip markers.

Show children how to trace around their hands and cut out the shape of the handprint. Write on the handprint, "You are in my hands."

Say: God made us and holds us in his hands. This will help us remember that!

 Craft for Older Children: Handprint Ornament
Needed: 2 cups of flour, 2 cups of salt, and 1 cup of water. Mix together to form dough. If mixture is too sticky, add a little more flour.

Let children flatten their clay. Press their hand into clay and cut around handprint. Let dry.

Say: The Bible says, "You are like the clay in the potter's hands." That means that God formed us just the way he wants us!

Snack: Handprint Sandwich

Snack

Needed: Cream cheese or peanut butter, bread.

Cut two handprints for each child out of bread, spread with topping.

Say: This is a handprint sandwich! You formed and made this sandwich just as God formed and made you!

Memory Verse: Jeremiah 18:6 ICB
You are like the clay in the potter's hands.

Alternate Version (New King James)
Look, as the clay is in the potter's hand, so are you in My hand.

Memory Verse Activity: Molding Us!
Teach children this verse in this way. Pretend that you are molding something with your hands. While making that motion say the verse: "You are like the clay in the potter's hands." Repeat the verse making the motion until children know the verse.

Prayer Focus
Dear God, thank you for creating and shaping us. Please help us to be who you made us to be. Amen.

August 17, 2005

The Race of Your Life! Midweek
By Vicki Wiley

Scripture
2 Timothy 4:1–8

Lesson Aim
Children will understand that our ultimate goal as Christians is to live a faithful life.

Life Skill
Children will compare the life of faith to a race.

Bible Learning Activity for Younger Children: Sports in the Bible
Say: Did you know that the Bible talks about sports? Well, it does! Paul wrote about races in the Bible.

What happens in a race? (People run. There is a winner.) What do you think Paul said about races? (Let children discuss.) Paul wanted us to know that life is like a race.

In a race we train hard to do our best. In life we need to study the Bible, go to church, and pray so that we will do our best. In a race there is a prize, and in our life the prize is eternal life. In a race there is a ribbon or a trophy for a prize, and in our life the prize is a crown in heaven!

Bible Learning Activity for Older Children: Bible Times Sports
Needed: Whiteboard and felt-tip markers.

Say: Do you like sports? Did you know that people in Bible times liked sports too? Well they did! When Paul wrote books for the New Testament, he wrote about sports because he knew that people liked sports.

Paul also knew that sports involve a great deal of concentration, effort, and practice in order to win the prize. So he used sports to tell people that it also takes a great deal of concentration, effort, and practice in order to live a life of faith. Paul compares the Christian's spiritual life to the training of a runner and a boxer.

How are races and life the same? How are they different?

On the whiteboard, write *Life* and *Race* across the top. Let children list how they are different and the same. (They are the same because they each have a beginning and an ending. Both have a goal. There is a prize at the end of both. They are different because life is longer than a race. One difference is that in a race everyone starts and ends at the same time.)

Paul tells us that we need to practice for the game of life and be ready for everything that happens. How can we be ready? (by reading the Bible, going to church, praying)

Enrichment for Younger Children: Race for Life!

Needed: *Life* written on a piece of paper, masking tape to make a starting line.

Say: We are going to have a relay race. Divide kids into two teams and explain how to have a relay race. Race.

When the race is over, ask: What was racing like? (It was fun. I wanted to win.) What did you do to run faster? How did it feel to finish the race? (It felt great!)

Life is like a race. When we finish running a race, we want to feel like we were prepared and did a good job. When we finish our life, we want to have great faith in God and feel like we did a good job too!

Enrichment for Older Children: Fit to race!

Needed: Running shoes, trophy, whistle, numbers (like participants wear in a race), a Bible, a picture of a church (a sketch drawn on paper), offering money, Sunday school lesson, *faith* written on a piece of paper, and other items that may be used in an athletic contest or at church.

Say: All of these items can be used for a race. What are they for? (Let children discuss each one.)

In the Bible Paul writes that life is like a race. Which of these items are for a "running" race? Which are for the "race of life"? Which item do you think is the most important?

Memory Verse: 2 Timothy 4:7, 8 ICB

I have fought the good fight. I have finished the race. I have kept the faith. Now, a crown is waiting for me. I will get that crown for being right with God.

Alternate Version (New King James)
I have fought the good fight, I have finished the race, I have kept the faith. Finally, there is laid up for me the crown of righteousness, which the Lord, the righteous Judge, will give to me on that Day.

August 21, 2005

The Race of Your Life!
By Vicki Wiley

Scripture
2 Timothy 4:1–8

Lesson Aim
Children will understand that our ultimate goal as Christians is to live a faithful life.

Life Skill
Children will compare the life of faith to a race.

Bible Lesson: Fight the Good Fight
Needed: First-place ribbons or trophy, running shoes, Bible.

Say: Did you see any of the Olympic games last year? Have you ever seen a race at your school? Discuss races that the kids have seen.

When the runners get ready to run, what do they have to do? (Put on their shoes. Practice so they will be fast. Eat right.)

Yes, you're right! When a runner trains for a race, they need to prepare. They need the right equipment. They need the right nourishment, and they need a goal. What kind of equipment do they need? (Let children answer.) What kind of nourishment do they need? (Let children answer.) What is their goal? (Let children answer.) Some of them have a goal just to finish the race. Some have a goal of winning the race. Those who just wanted to finish the race wouldn't have to prepare as much, would they? If they wanted to win the race, they would have to do more.

In Bible times Paul wrote that life is like a race. When we run a race, we have a goal; and when we live our lives, we have a goal. The goal in our lives is to finish our lives with faith. When we finish our lives with faith in God, we will live with God forever. What do you need to do to prepare for the race of life? (Let children answer.) Who can help us with the race of life? (our parents, our teachers at church) What is our equipment for the race of life? (Bible, church, prayer) What is our goal for the race of life? (To be faithful so that we finish the race well.)

Whatever we do, we should train for the race of life and the goal of living with Christ!

 Song Suggestions

I Will Fight This Fight by Jana Alayra from "Jump into the Light" (Montjoy Music 1997)

Rad-Dude Attitude by Dean-o from "You Got It All" (FKO Music, Inc. 1997).

Running for the Prize by Mary Rice Hopkins from "15 Singable Songs" (Big Steps 4 U, 1988)

He's Got Plans by Dean-o from "Soul Surfin'" (FKO Music, Inc. 1999)

 Craft for Younger Children: Crown of Life!

Needed: Lightweight cardboard to make crowns or pre-made crowns, "jewels" to decorate crowns.

Say: Today we are going to make crowns. Who wears a crown? (kings, queens, beauty pagent winners) In Bible times, when there was a race, the winners were given a crown. They wore that crown to show that they had worn the race and that they had done well in their race.

We are not in a race, but we want to do well in our lives. We want to love God, love other people, do well in our work and school, and be kind to our friends and families. We will wear our crowns to show that we do well in life!

Craft for Older children: Blue Ribbon Time
Needed: Wide blue ribbon (1 1/2 inches wide), 3-inch paper circles, markers.

Today we are going to make blue ribbons. Have you ever won a blue ribbon? What does it mean when you win a blue ribbon? (That you were the best!)

Let's each make three blue ribbons. What do you do well? (I draw well. I am kind to everyone. I know how to make a sandwich. I am good at reading.)

Make your blue ribbon by gluing the circle onto the ribbon. On the circle, write what you do well.

Snack: Running Shoes

 Needed: Rectangular crackers, string cheese, cheese dip.

Show children how to make a "running shoe" using the cracker as the shoe and the cheese as the laces. Attach with cheese dip.

Say: A runner needs good equipment in order to finish a race. We need good equipment too. What kind of equipment do we need for the race of life? How can we finish it well?

Memory Verse: 2 Timothy 4:7, 8 ICB

I have fought the good fight. I have finished the race. I have kept the faith. Now, a crown is waiting for me. I will get that crown for being right with God.

Alternate Version (New King James)
I have fought the good fight, I have finished the race, I have kept the faith. Finally, there is laid up for me the crown of righteousness, which the Lord, the righteous Judge, will give to me on that Day.

Memory Verse Activity: Fight the Good Fight!

Needed: Paper with the following words lettered on them (one set for each team).

I have fought
the good fight.
I have finished the race.
I have kept the faith.
Now, a crown
is waiting for me.
I will get that crown
For being right with God.

Let each team have a set of the word papers. Attach small pieces of tape to each paper. Let the kids line up and race (relay race fashion) to the other side of the room taping up their papers in order.

When they have finished, they should sit down and say the verse together.

Prayer Focus

Dear God, we thank you for our lives and the race of life that we can live. Help us to do well! Amen.

August 24, 2005

Being Bold for God, Midweek
By Vicki Wiley

Scripture
Daniel 1

Lesson Aim
Children will learn the joy of doing what they know is right.

Life Skill
Children will know they can be bold for God.

Bible Learning Activity for Younger Children: Sometimes I Get Scared
Ask: Have you ever been scared? Have you ever had to be bold when you were really afraid? Being *bold* means courageously doing what is right even if you are afraid.

There is a story in the Bible about a young man that was very bold. He was probably scared; he was far away from home, and he had to do something he thought was right.

Have you ever been far from home and a little scared? Have you ever had to do something that was scary? Then you are just like Daniel!

Bible Learning Activity for Older Children: Scared or Bold?
Ask: Have you ever been afraid? When have you been the most afraid? Tell a story of when you were personally afraid.

Ask the kids when they have been the most afraid. Let them share stories with you.

Say: There are times in all of our lives when we are afraid. But when you are afraid, you can just think, *I'm just like Daniel.* Daniel was a young man in the Bible who had many scary adventures, but every time he did what was right.

Enrichment for Younger Children: Choices!

Needed: Pictures from magazines of different types of food; be sure to choose both healthy and junk foods.

Say: Daniel had to make a choice. He could have had all the food in the whole world! (Put out all the food pictures.) Do you know what he chose? What would you choose? What do you think would make you healthy? (Go through each picture and let kids choose if it is healthy.)

Daniel chose to eat only vegetables. Show pictures of veggies. He knew what was right, and he did what he knew God wanted him to do. Which foods do you think God wants you to eat?

Enrichment for Older Children: Good Reputation

Daniel had a great reputation. He always did what was right even when it must have been hard for him to do so.

Give each child a sheet a paper and a pencil, and ask them to write down at least ten ways they can build a strong reputation for doing good. While you are a child, you can begin to build a good reputation. Every time you do the right thing, your reputation grows. When people see that you have a good reputation and at the same time they see that you are a Christian, they will know that they can look up to you.

Memory Verse: Daniel 1:17 ICB

God gave these four men wisdom and the ability to learn. They learned many kinds of things people had written and studied. Daniel could also understand visions and dreams.

Alternate Version (New King James)
As for these four young men, God gave them knowledge and skill in all literature and wisdom; and Daniel had understanding in all visions and dreams.

August 28, 2005

Being Bold for God
By Vicki Wiley

Scripture
Daniel 1

Lesson Aim
Children will learn the joy of doing what they know is right.

Life Skill
Children will know they can be bold for God.

Bible Lesson: Being Bold for God!

Needed: A pitcher that is half full of water, a sheet of stiff paper, a clear drinking glass, and a table with a smooth surface.

Ask: What is the biggest problem you have ever had to face? What did you do about it? (Let children discuss.)

When you have a big problem, whom do you turn to for help? We all face many problems in our lives, and we all have to go to someone for help. Many times we can feel like our problem is too big if we don't have any help.

(Place the sheet of paper over the rim of the glass and then quickly turn the glass over and place it on the table upside down. Hold the glass tight against the table and pull the paper out. You now have an upside down glass of water!)

Say: Now here's a problem! How can I solve it? (Get suggestions.)

Put a pitcher under the side of the table. Push the glass firmly to the side of the table so that the water falls into the pitcher. Problem solved!

This was a silly trick, but it shows that no problem is too big to handle. The Bible talks about a young man named Daniel who had a problem. The king wanted him to eat food that he knew was not good for him. So he asked God to help him solve the problem.

Daniel had made up his mind that he was going to obey God no matter what. He wasn't going to eat the king's food. He was only going to eat what God had commanded.

But the king's helper said to Daniel, "The king has ordered what you are to eat. If you don't look as strong and healthy as the others, the king might kill me!" Daniel had a plan. "Let my friends and me eat what God has commanded us to eat. Give us vegetables to eat and water to drink. After ten days, compare us with the others who have eaten the king's food, and see for yourself who looks healthier." And so that is what they did.

Sure enough, after ten days, Daniel and his friends were healthier and stronger than the ones who had eaten the royal food. From then on Daniel and his friends were allowed to follow God and eat what God had commanded.

This was a hard problem to solve, but Daniel solved it by being bold for God!

 Song Suggestions

One Step at a Time Songsheets published by CEF Press, P.O. Box 348, Warrenton, Mo. 63383

Praise His Holy Name by Norm Hewitt from "Ablaze with Praise!" (Revelation Generation Music 2000)

He Is Really God! by Dean-o from "You Got It All" (FKO Music, Inc. 1997)

Did You Ever Talk to God Above Songsheets published by CEF Press, P.O. Box 348, Warrenton, Mo. 63383

Craft for Younger Children: Veggie Prints
Needed: Vegetables such as green peppers, potatoes, broccoli, tempera paints, construction paper.

Say: Daniel and his friends loved to eat vegetables. To help us remember the story, let's make a picture out of vegetables. Show children how to dip the veggies into paint and then print on the paper.

Craft for Older Children: Veggies Galore
Needed: Several types of veggies to paint with (see craft for younger children), paper, tempera paint.

Show children how to use veggies to paint with. Let them use a carrot stick as a paintbrush to title the picture "Being Bold for God."

As they are painting, ask: How do you think Daniel felt when he knew he had a problem? What would you have done? Have you ever felt that you were bold for God?

Snack: Kingly Veggies

 Needed: Simple-to-eat raw veggies: carrots, celery, broccoli.

Daniel and his friends asked to eat only veggies to see if they could be just as healthy as those eating rich food. Do you like veggies? Do you eat them often?

Let children eat veggies of their choice.

Memory Verse Daniel 1:17

God gave these four young men wisdom and the ability to learn. They learned many kinds of things people had written and studied. Daniel could also understand all kinds of visions and dreams

Alternate Translation (New King James)
As for these four young men, God gave them knowledge and skill in all literature and wisdom; and Daniel had understanding in all visions and dreams.

Memory Verse Activity

Needed: Whiteboard with verse written on it.

Read the verse with the kids. Talk about what it means. Ask these questions: How many young men were there? What did God give them? What did they learn? What could Daniel understand? What are dreams and visions? Now say the verse together again.

Prayer Focus

Dear God, thank you for the example of Daniel. Help us to be like him. Amen.

August 31, 2005

Protect God's Teachings, Midweek
By Tina Hauser

Scripture
Proverbs 7

Lesson Aim
Children will consider God's rules when making decisions.

Life Skill
Children will understand that God's rules apply all the time.

Bible Learning Activity for Younger Children: Remember to . . .
Needed: Mailing labels, object to pass around.

On mailing labels (or pieces of masking tape), write rules that God wants us to obey. (Love your neighbor. Honor your parents. Tell the truth. Put God first. Be kind to everyone. Love your enemies. Keep your marriage promises. Do not steal. Be happy with what you have.) You will need a mailing label for each child. If the group is large, you can repeat the rules. As you give each child a mailing label, read what it says. Children will stick their mailing labels to their forehead before beginning to play the game.

Everyone will sit in a circle. The children will pass an object around the circle while the music plays. When the music stops, the entire group will say together, "Remember to ..." and then read what is written on that child's forehead mailing label.

We put the mailing labels on our foreheads, close to our brains, as something kind of silly. God doesn't want us to write on our brains, but he does want us to remember the things we have been taught about him. He wants us to faithfully obey his rules.

Bible Learning Activity for Older Children: Protect Yourself!

Needed: A pair of shop safety glasses.

When we are riding in a car, what do we do to keep ourselves safe? (Put on a seat belt.) To protect a marker from drying out, what do we do to it? (Put the cap on it.) What does a construction worker wear to protect his head? (a construction helmet)

Put the safety glasses on. When would someone wear these special glasses? Before using a power tool where bits of wood or metal might be thrown through the air, the worker puts on safety glasses. Can workers wearing these special glasses still see what they are doing? Sure they can. If you have more than one pair of safety glasses, pass them around and let the children try them on.

The Bible tells us that we have to protect ourselves from things that go on around us that do not please God as seriously. We must remember the rules that God gave us to live by. When we have a decision to make, each one of us should think about which choice would make God happy and which choice would sadden his heart. We must protect ourselves from hating others because of the color of their skin. We must protect ourselves from listening to music that would make us want to do things against God's rules. Can you name other things we need to protect our hearts and minds against?

We don't protect our hearts with seat belts, construction helmets, or safety glasses. But we can protect ourselves by knowing God's Word and living by it.

Enrichment for Younger Children: Made You Blink!

Needed: Sponge ball.

Toss the sponge ball at each child, aiming for the face. If the soft sponge actually hits them, it won't hurt. After the ball has been thrown at everyone, ask the children to tell you what they did as the ball was coming at them. They put their hands up; they knocked it away; they caught it. Encourage them to explore the one thing they may have overlooked: they blinked!

When something is coming at your face, God made your brain so it will tell your eyelids that there is danger. When that happens, you blink. Blinking protects your eyes from danger. Your eyes can be damaged easily by even the smallest piece of something getting in them. Have you ever gotten something in your eye? How did it feel? Did your eyes get watery? That's because your eye was trying to get rid of whatever wasn't supposed to be there.

By knowing God's Word, knowing the rules He has given us for a happy life, and then obeying those rules, we protect ourselves from the many things that can take us away from God. When you are tempted to do something that would not please God, blink your eyes to remind yourself to let his words protect you.

Enrichment for Older Children: Reminders

Needed: Lots of Post-it notes.

When the children enter the room, there should be Post-it notes, with reminder messages written on them, stuck to everything. Some of the reminders you may want to write on the Post-its are: Pick up milk at grocery. Fix lunch for kids. Take clothes to dry cleaner. Meet Lydia for lunch. Water plants. Change the lightbulb.

Go through the Post-its, reading each one and becoming overwhelmed by all you have to remember. Say: If it weren't for these wonderful little reminder notes, I would forget to do something, I'm sure.

The Bible says we should write God's commands on our minds, just as we would write them in our notebook. We need to put them in our minds so we will be reminded of what God desires for us. Give each child a Post-it note so they can write down one thing God wants them to remember. Add these to the ones already posted around the room.

Did you know that Post-it notes haven't been around very long? They are only about twenty-five years old. Art Fry, a scientist for the 3M Company, kept losing his place in the hymnal when he was singing in his church choir. His bookmark would fall out every time he turned the page. Because he was a scientist, Art tried to think of some way he could mark the pages and keep them marked as the hymnal was being used. A friend of his had made a new kind of glue that you could use over and over. Art Fry took his friend's glue and put it on a piece of paper he was using as a bookmark, and the first Post-it note was made. The bookmark would stay where it was put, but then it could be moved to another page, and it would stay there just as well.

Memory Verse: Proverbs 7:2, 3 ICB

Obey my commands, and you will live. Protect my teachings as you would your own eyes. Remind yourself of them. Write them down in your mind as if on a tablet.

Alternate Version (New King James)

Keep my commands and live, and my law as the apple of your eye. Bind them on your fingers; write them on the tablet of your heart.

September 4, 2005

Protect God's Teachings
By Vicki Wiley

Scripture
Proverbs 7

Lesson Aim
Children will consider God's rules when making decisions.

Life Skill
Children will understand that God's rules apply all the time.

Bible Lesson: Protect God's Teachings
Needed: One-inch paper hearts cut from red construction paper, one heart for every two to three kids; drinking glasses filled with water.

Ask: What does it mean to hide God's Word in your heart? (Let kids respond.)

Say: When you hide God's Word in your heart, it means that you know what God wants you to do, and you remember it. When you remember what God wants you to do, it is easier to make good decisions in your life.

Pass out hearts and glasses of water. Have the kids hold up the heart next to the water. Ask: Can you see your heart? Yes! You can.

Now put the heart down on a table and set the glass of water on top of it. Have kids look though the sides of the glass. Can you see it now? No! You can't!

God always knows our thoughts. If we want to know God's thoughts, we have to learn about them in the Bible. When we memorize God's thoughts, they are "hidden in our hearts" just as the heart is hidden from you now.

Now let kids look down the glass at the heart. Now can you see the heart? Yes! You can. God sees our hearts just as we can see these hearts. God loves for us to remember his rules and do what he says because his Word is hidden in our hearts.

Song Suggestions

Up for the Word by Dean-o from "Soul Surfin'" (FKO Music 1999)

The B-I-B-L-E Traditional Chorus

Treasure of My Heart by Jana Alayra from "Jump into the Light" (Montjoy Music 1995)

God's Love by Mary Rice Hopkins from "Good Buddies" (Big Steps 4 U 1994)

 Craft for Younger Children: Scrolls
Needed: For each child two dowel rods (8 inches long) and paper 7 inches x 14 inches, glue.

Say: In Bible times they did not have books. Instead they used scrolls. The Bible was first written on a scroll too. Scrolls were made from a long piece of papyrus paper and wrapped around a stick on each end.

Let them copy the memory verse onto the paper, leaving a wide margin for gluing the paper onto the rods. Show children how to glue the ends of the paper onto the dowel rods.

 Craft for Older children: Hidden in My Heart
Needed: One sheet of construction paper for each child, many construction paper hearts, markers, glue.

Say: We know that God wants his Word hidden in our hearts. What are some of the things we can hide in our hearts? Let kids write them on their "hearts" and then glue onto the paper (Love everyone. Read the Bible. Take care of one another. Pray.)

Snack: Scroll Rollup

Needed: Fruit rollup for each child, stick pretzels.

Let each child make a scroll to eat. Talk about what a scroll is and how it was used in Bible times.

The first Bibles were written on scrolls. They were written by hand too!

Memory Verse: Proverbs 7:2, 3 ICB

Obey my commands, and you will live. Protect my teachings as you would your own eyes. Remind yourself of them. Write them down in your mind as if on a tablet.

Alternate Version (New King James)
Keep my commands and live, and my law as the apple of your eye. Bind them on your fingers; write them on the tablet of your heart.

Memory Verse Activity
Write the verse on board. Say the verse together and then let the kids make up a tune to sing the verse. Sing it until they know it.

Prayer Focus

Dear God, please help us always to stay moral and not to follow the world around us. Help us always to follow you. Amen.

September 7, 2005

(Special Activity, 9/11)
Remembering 9/11, Midweek
By Tina Hauser

Scripture
James 4:13–17

Lesson Aim
The children will be challenged to live for Christ today.

Life Skill
The children will realize that life can be taken away quickly, so today is important.

Bible Learning Activity for Younger Children: All Day Long
Needed: Kitchen timer and items to complete chosen tasks.

Provide several tasks for your children to complete. These could include:

Put a band-aid on someone.

Wipe off a chair with a damp cloth.

Fix a glass of chocolate milk for a classmate.

Rub the teacher's shoulders.

Sharpen a pencil.

Make a card for someone who is sick.

Compliment someone in your class.

Post the tasks in the classroom, and read through them before beginning. The students are to do any of the tasks they want to do as time allows. When they complete one task, they can move on to the next one they choose. Set a kitchen timer to go off in 8–10 minutes, but don't tell the children how much time they have. When the timer goes off, everyone should stop immediately and sit down where they are.

Ask: How old do you think you'll live to be? Do any of you know for sure? Some of us will live to be very old, and others of us will not. We really have no idea, do we? Ask children what they were doing when the timer went off. The Bible teaches us that it isn't so important how long we live but how we live while we are here on earth. God wants us to spend each day serving him. When we think about God all day long, it shows in the things we say and what we do.

Bible Learning Activity for Older Children: If God Wants . . .

Needed: A balloon for each child.

Give each child a balloon. (Before you begin, you will want the children to blow up their balloons a little and let the air out. This will stretch the balloon and get it ready for the activity.) Instruct the children to respond after each of your statements with the phrase, "If God wants," and then blow two big puffs of air into their balloon.

I will move to a different place without complaining (If God wants ... puff, puff)

I will be a friend to a new person in my class complaining (If God wants ... puff, puff)

I will listen to my friend's problem complaining (If God wants ... puff, puff)

I will learn to tell others about Jesus' sacrifice complaining (If God wants ... puff, puff)

I will be patient with my little brother complaining (If God wants ... puff, puff)

Now let the children add their own phrases of things they can do in the name of the Lord. Continue with the group responding and adding big puffs of air. At some point a balloon will pop. Did we know whose balloon would pop first? Even though you thought it was getting close, did it still surprise you when it actually popped? God wants us to live our lives for him with passion and with joy, even though we have no idea how long we'll be on this earth or how long we'll be able to serve others. God wants today. With God's help you can take care of tomorrow when it comes.

Enrichment for Younger Children: Space Shuttle Columbia

In February 2003, the space shuttle *Columbia* had completed its mission in outer space and was getting ready to land. As it flew over Texas on reentry, something terrible happened, and the *Columbia* exploded. The accident killed all seven astronauts on board. It was a terrible day for the country, for the astronauts' families and friends, and for the space program. Colonel Rick Husband was the commander on this flight.

The country will remember his name because of the contribution he made to the space program. But the people who knew him well and were closest to him will remember him for other reasons. Rick Husband was known for his tremendous love for his family and his Lord. Before he left on his space mission, he made videotapes of devotions to share with his two daughters and his wife while he was gone. Even though he wasn't going to be there, he wanted to teach them about his wonderful God. This man loved to sing, and he sang praises to God in his church choir. I think Rick Husband understood the meaning of the Scripture where God tells us that we don't know what will happen tomorrow so we need to serve him today. Colonel Husband worked hard to learn how to be an astronaut, but he worked even harder to make sure that he served God every day.

Ask each child to share what they want to be when they grow up and one thing they need to do to make that dream come true. Then ask them to share one thing they can do today to become a person of God for the rest of their lives. (Pray daily. Read my Bible. Talk to people who have been Christians for a long time. Faithfully worship with my church family.)

Enrichment for Older Children: Choo Choo!

Needed: Teapot of boiling water.

If you cannot take the children to a kitchen, then bring a teapot into the children's area straight from the burner where it has been boiling. Alert the children to the fact that only the teacher will touch the teapot. As you release the steam, instruct the children to observe what is happening. Lift the cover on the spout, and a small trail of steam should come out. Pull the lid off and let a larger amount of steam escape. Then return the lid to the teapot. Wait just a few seconds, and then ask the children if they can find the steam. Where did it go? It didn't stick around very long!

Did you know that steam is very powerful? Almost three hundred years ago two men figured out how to use steam to run engines. Steam is so powerful it can even make a train move! The engineers would boil huge amounts of water on the train and make steam, which would push parts of the engine to make the train move. The steam would build up and would have to be released. When it was released, it made a sound; and if you think real hard, you may be able to figure out what that sound was. When the valve released the steam exhaust, it made a "choo" sound as it left. The more steam they used, the more "choo" sounds the valve made. Choo, choo, choo, choo.

Steam can teach us a couple of lessons about ourselves. God used steam in a message for us in the Bible. Read James 4:14 together. Terrible accidents happen like the terrorist attack on September 11. People get sick unexpectedly, and car accidents sometimes take the lives of people quickly. Our lives can vanish quickly like the steam. The other thing the steam teaches us is that while the steam is around, it is strong. It does its work well. No matter how long we live on this earth before we go to live with God in heaven, we should use our lives as much as we can and be strong in our beliefs. If you get discouraged, just think "choo, choo, choo," and maybe that will help you go on with a strong spirit.

Memory Verse: James 4:14 ICB
But you do not know what will happen tomorrow! Your life is like a mist. You can see it for a short time, but then it goes away.

Alternate version (New King James)
Whereas you do not know what will happen tomorrow. For what is your life? It is even a vapor that appears for a little time and then vanishes away.

September 11, 2005

(Special Activity, 9/11)

Remembering 9/11
By Vicki Wiley

Scripture
James 4:13–17

Lesson Aim
The children will be challenged to live for Christ today.

Life Skill
The children will realize that life can be taken away quickly, so today is important.

Bible Lesson: Some Days Are So Sad
Needed: Pictures from 9/11, the *Challenger* or *Columbia* disaster, President Kennedy, Pearl Harbor, or any other natural disasters the children would recognize.

Let children have time to talk today. Give the lesson extra time if needed.

Say: Has anyone ever had a really sad day? (Let children discuss.)

There are some days when everyone is sad. (Show the pictures one at a time.) What is this? What happened here? Show all the pictures you brought, and let children have time to discuss.

Say: These are all sad days that happened in our country. When these events happened, everything stopped as the people in this country listened to the news, read the newspapers, and talked to one another about what happened.

One of the saddest days in our history was September 11, 2001, when the planes flew into the World Trade Center and the Pentagon. Many people died. We watched the TV and wondered what else was going to happen. We were scared and sad.

I was thinking … (Tell children what you were thinking about September 11 or another sad event.) Can you tell me what you were thinking? (Let children discuss.)

What do you think that God was thinking? In the Bible we learn that when bad things happen God cares very much. When bad things happen, God is sad.

What are some of the good things that have happened since 9/11? (We are more careful now. We try to understand people better. We realize how short life is. Let children discuss.)

We will always remember what happened on 9/11, just as we will always remember what happened at Pearl Harbor. We will always remember that it was a sad day. But we will also remember that only God knows what will happen to us. Isn't it great that God loves us and cares about us? We know our lives will be the best they can be when we love God!

 Song Suggestions

He Paid a Debt Traditional Chorus

Nothing but the Blood Songsheets published by CEF Press, P.O. Box 348, Warrenton, Mo. 63383

Love with the Love by Mary Rice Hopkins from "Miracle Mud" (Big Steps 4 U 1998)

Before We Say Goodbye by Jana Alayra from "Believin' On" (Montjoy Music 2002)

 Craft for Younger and Older Children: Remembering
Needed: Construction paper, crayons or markers.

After talking about 9/11, let children draw pictures of their memories of the day. Note: Some younger children will not remember the day, though they may know about it from seeing pictures or videos on television.

Discuss the pictures and address any fears that they may have.

Snack: Remember Cookie

Needed: Rectangle cracker or cookie for each child, small candies (20 for each child), icing.

Show children how to ice crackers or cookies and put the candies into the icing: 9 in the first line and then 11 below that.

Say: September 11, or 9/11, will always be remembered as a sad day. What can you do to remember what happened on that day? Why should we remember that day? (We can try to make life better so that it won't happen again.)

Memory Verse: James 4:14 ICB

But you do not know what will happen tomorrow! Your life is like a mist. You can see it for a short time, but then it goes away.

Alternate version (New King James)
Whereas you do not know what will happen tomorrow. For what is your life? It is even a vapor that appears for a little time and then vanishes away.

Memory Verse Activity: Life Is Short

Needed: Verse written on whiteboard.

Read the verse together. Ask: What do you think will happen tomorrow? (We will go to school. We will do our homework. We will see our friends.) We think we know what will happen tomorrow, but no one really knows except God.

What do you think this verse means? How is our life like a mist? How can we live a better life?

Prayer Focus

Dear God, thank you for our lives. Help us always to remember that our lives are short, and we should spend them doing things that are important. Amen.

September 14, 2005

Hearing Is Believing, Midweek
By Arlen Nagata

Scripture
Acts 13:47–49

Lesson Aim
Children will understand that Jesus wants all people to know him.

Life Skill
Children will think about what it means to help all people all over the world know Jesus.

Bible Learning Activity for Younger Children: All Around the World
Needed: Globe.

Ask: Have any of you ever been to another country? (Let children discuss.) Do you know anyone who lives in another country?

People who go to other countries to tell people there about Jesus are called missionaries. They go just to tell other people about Jesus. What do you think a missionary does? Let children discuss. Missionaries don't just hold church services; they also help the people with farming, schools, and all kinds of things. What do you think you could do if you were a missionary?

Bible Learning Activity for Older Children: Paul Was a Missionary
Did you know that Paul was a missionary? He went on three missionary journeys by ship. Paul's trip to Rome, recorded in Acts 27, is one of the most complete accounts of a sea voyage from ancient times. The account indicates that the ship they traveled on was carrying a cargo of grain (v. 38) from

Alexandria to Rome. In addition to the cargo, it carried a total of 276 passengers and crew, so it was a big ship.

The heavy seas threatened to break up the ship. The hull was strengthened by passing ropes around the beam and tightening them with wooden levers. Ships may have carried net-like webs for use in such emergencies, although ordinary ropes could be used if needed.

When the ship finally did run aground, the passengers escaped by using broken pieces of the ship as life preservers (v. 44). The dangers of winter navigation are clearly indicated in this account. But God's providence in rescuing Paul and the other people on the ship also comes through clearly in the graphic narrative.

Read this story in Acts 27 to see how Paul survived a shipwreck!

Enrichment for Younger Children: Missionary Tag
This tag game is great for a gym or outdoors. Have players line up along one edge of a basketball court or playing field. Choose one "missionary" per ten children to be in the field. When you yell "go" (or blow a whistle), the children run to the opposite side of the field/gym while the missionary tries to tag people. Anyone who is tagged joins the missionary. Close by explaining that missionaries try to teach others about Jesus. Once one person learns about Jesus, they can tell others!

Enrichment for Older Children: God's Assignments

Needed: Flashlight, Bible.

Ask: How many of you have assignments like chores to do at home? When you do your chores, do you get an allowance or a rewarded? Did you know God gives us assignments to do too? Often God's assignments can mean an adventure for us. One adventure God has given each of us is to be a light for people who don't believe in Jesus. Let's read in our Bibles: Acts 13:47–49.

I'm going to turn on this flashlight and turn out our lights in the classroom as we talk about what being a light for God means. (Tip: turn on flashlight before you turn off lights.)

Say: What are some things my light can do? (Allow answers.) Those are great answers, but you know what else my light can do? My light can also be used to help find something that's lost in the dark.

God tells us that without Jesus we are all lost; we don't know how to get to heaven when we die. But those of us who know about Jesus can be a light and find people who are lost and tell them what we know about Jesus. Does that sound like a hide-and-seek game? That's why I say this is an adventure. Looking for people to help find their way to God is a real hide-and-seek adventure. For our friends here in our community, we can help them find Jesus by inviting them to church with us.

But the Bible also says our light should also go to the ends of the earth. That means to other countries on the other side of the ocean, on the other side of the world! (Show children the globe.)

How are we supposed to get our light all the way across the ocean to the countries on the other side of the world? Do you have any ideas how we could tell people who live on the other side of the world about Jesus?

Memory Verse: Acts 13:48 ICB
When the non-Jewish people heard Paul say this, they were happy. They gave honor to the message of the Lord. And many of the people believed the message. They were the ones chosen to have life forever.

Alternate Version (New King James)
Now when the Gentiles heard this, they were glad and glorified the word of the Lord. And as many as had been appointed to eternal life believed.

September 18, 2005

Hearing Is Believing
By Ivy Beckwith

Scripture
Acts 13:47–49

Lesson Aim
Children will understand that Jesus wants all people to know him.

Life Skill
Children will think about what it means to help all people all over the world know Jesus.

Bible Lesson: Hearing Is Believing
Needed: Have a world map or a small world globe to show the children.

Ask: How do people learn about Jesus? (Ask for two or three responses.) How do other people in our neighborhood learn about Jesus? (Ask for two or three responses.) How do you think people in China or Australia learn about Jesus? (Take two or three responses.) Most people learn about Jesus when someone tells them about Jesus. Our Bible story today is about two men who helped people who didn't know about Jesus learn about him.

Our story today is from the book of Acts in the New Testament section of the Bible. This whole book is the story of how people all over the world started to learn about Jesus. Two men named Paul and Barnabas went to a city where people needed to hear about Jesus, but the people they went to tell didn't want to hear about Jesus. Instead of being discouraged, they went to another group of people to tell them about Jesus. And guess what happened; the Bible tells us that these people were glad that Paul and Barnabas came and told them about Jesus. They decided to believe in God and follow Jesus. And not only did they choose to believe what Paul and Barnabas told them about Jesus, but they were so excited that they went out into their neighborhoods and other nearby towns and told other people about Jesus. And lots of other people decided to follow Jesus.

Not everyone in town was happy that all these people were listening to Paul and Barnabas and deciding to follow Jesus. The people Paul and Barnabas went to first got really angry at them for telling all these people about Jesus, and they chased them out of their town. But the Bible tells us that Paul and Barnabas weren't upset about this because they were excited about all the people who did believe in Jesus. So they went to another town, and God was with them in a special way.

This story happened a long time ago, but just like the time when Paul and Barnabas lived, lots of people still need to learn about Jesus. (Show the map or the globe.) Who can tell me what this is? That's right; it's a picture of our world. Can you name some of the countries or places you see on this globe? (Allow time for several responses.) There are people in all these countries who need to learn about Jesus, and there are lots of people in our country and even right here in our town who need to learn about Jesus just like the people in our story did. So what can we do to help these people learn about Jesus? (Allow time for several responses.) Yes, we can do all those things. We can invite them to church. We can help them when they need help. We can move to a faraway country and be missionaries. God will help us know the best thing for us to do. But when we please God by helping other people to know about Jesus, just like Paul and Barnabas, God will be with us in a special way too.

♪ **Song Suggestions**

Who Is Your Neighbor? by Mary Rice Hopkins from "Come on Home" (Big Steps 4 U 2002)

Love the Lord Your God, Love Your Neighbor from "Kids on the Rock" (Gospel Light Publishers 1995)

I Do Believe by Jana Alayra from "Dig Down Deep" (Montjoy Music 1997)

Grow Me Up like You by Mary Rice Hopkins from "Come on Home" (Big Steps 4 U 2002)

More Precious than Silver Songsheets published by CEF Press, P.O. Box 348, Warrenton, Mo. 63383

Craft for Younger Children: Who Is My Neighbor?
Needed: Construction paper in different skin tones, blue construction paper cut into a large circle (globe shape), paste or glue.

Cut the skin-toned paper into simple child shapes. Let each child have several. Show children how to paste the child shapes onto the "globe" of blue paper.

Say: Who is your neighbor? (Lead children to know that our neighbors are more than those who live next door.) Our craft today will remind us that we have neighbors all over the world!

 Craft for Older Children: Rainsticks
Needed: Paper tube from wrapping paper, aluminum foil, rice.

Give each child a piece of aluminum foil and show how to roll it into a "snake" shape. Twist into "S" shape and insert into tube. Tape end of tube. Pour rice into tube and tape other end.

When it is turned over, the rice should hit the foil and sound like rain. Decorate the tube as you wish.

Say: Many children in foreign countries play with rainsticks that grow out of the ground. This will remind you to pray for all the children that play with rainsticks!

Snack: Quesadillas

Needed: Flour tortillas, grated cheese, electric skillet.

Show children how to put cheese onto the tortilla and cook until melted.

Say: Many people in South America like to eat quesadillas for lunch. Let's eat these and pray for the people in South America!

Memory Verse: Acts 13:48 ICB
When the non-Jewish people heard Paul say this, they were happy. They gave honor to the message of the Lord. And many of the people believed the message. They were the ones chosen to have life forever.

Alternate Version (New King James)
Now when the Gentiles heard this, they were glad and glorified the word of the Lord. And as many as had been appointed to eternal life believed.

Memory Verse Activity
Needed: Posterboard.
   Write the verse on the posterboard covering the whole board. Cut into puzzle shapes. Let the kids work the puzzle and then say the verse together.

Prayer Focus
Dear God, thank you for all the people you created. Help me to treat all of them like neighbors. Amen.

September 21, 2005

A Few Close Friends, Midweek
By Susan Harper

Scripture
Mark 2:1–12

Lesson Aim
Children will learn the importance of telling their friends about Jesus.

Life Skill
Children will learn how to tell their friends about Jesus.

Bible Learning Activity for Younger Children: Lame Man Crawl
Divide the class in two or more teams of five players. On "go" the first player on each team crawls to the other side of the room. When he touches the wall on the other side, he stands and runs back to his team where he tags the next player in line. This player crawls to the other side of the room and runs back to his team. The team to complete the relay first wins.

Bible Learning Activity for Older Children: Friends Tell Friends
Ask: Who can you tell about Jesus? (family and friends) What are some ways you can do this? What are some of the obstacles we have when we want to tell others about Jesus? How can we overcome them?

During our prayer time today, I want you to think of someone you know that you would like to tell about Jesus. Think about how you can do this, such as sharing your faith necklace with a friend. Say a prayer for Jesus to help you. This week when you wake up in the morning and before you go to sleep at night, say a special prayer for this person. Next week you will have an opportunity to share how you talked to someone about Jesus. Invite friends to come to Sunday school to learn more about your special Friend Jesus!

Enrichment for Younger Children: Tell Your Friends!

Supplies: A punch ball (or balloon).

Write the Bible verse on the board. Explain what it means and have players repeat it several times to help them remember it. Have players sit in a circle. Have one player start the game by punching the ball into the air. The player who is closest to the ball when it comes down says the Bible verse and punches the ball or balloon into the air again. Continue playing the game until all of the players have had a chance to punch the ball and say the Bible verse several times.

Enrichment for Older Children: Lame Man Blanket Carry

Needed: One blanket for each team.

Divide the class in two or more teams of five players. Have two of the strongest players on the team hold opposite ends of the blanket folded in half. Have the third player on the team lie down on the blanket.

On "go," the teams walk quickly to the other side of the room with the lame player lying on the blanket. When they get to the other end of the room, the lame player gets off of the blanket and all three run back to their starting line. The two strong players grab the ends of the blanket again, and the fourth player lies down on the blanket. Repeat the relay until all players have either been a carrier or the lame man. The team to complete the relay first wins.

Memory Verse: Mark 2:12 ICB

The people were amazed and praised God. They said, "We have never seen anything like this!"

Alternate Version (New King James)
All were amazed and glorified God, saying, "We never saw anything like this!"

September 25, 2005

A Few Close Friends
By Susan Harper

Scripture
Mark 2:1–12

Lesson Aim
Children will learn the importance of telling their friends about Jesus.

Life Skill
Children will learn how to tell their friends about Jesus.

Bible Lesson: A Few Close Friends
Needed: A cell phone in your purse or hooked on your belt loop.

Good morning boys and girls! How is everyone doing today? I get so excited when I think that I get to see all of you! *(Ring, Ring)* Oh, wait a minute! I have a phone call. Hello? Oh! Hi, Kathy! How are you? *(Whisper to the class, "This is my best friend, Kathy.")* What's up? You are kidding! Forty percent off all dresses! That's wonderful! What? You are going to treat me to lunch and tell me all about your date last night! Wow! I can't wait! Hey, I am in the middle of teaching my Sunday school class. Let me call you later, and we will make final plans to meet. *(pause)* Love you, too! Bye! *(Turn off the phone and put it back in your purse or on your belt loop.)* I am sorry for the interruption.

That was my best friend Kathy, and she was telling me about the big sale at the mall. I just love getting together with Kathy! We have so much fun together shopping, talking, eating! She is my very best friend, and there is nothing I would not do for her or she for me. I have known Kathy for a long time. One day soon after I first met her she was crying. She had had a fight with her mom, and it made her very sad. Her mom did not like some of the kids Kathy was hanging out with at school. Kathy wanted to be popular, so she decided she wanted to do what they did. She wanted to wear makeup and clothes like they did. She started to talk to others like they did. She even started to talk back to her mom and tell her she was not going to help with chores or do her homework!

Kathy knew she was not doing right, but she wanted to be popular so much that she did all theses things that were wrong. When her mom tried to talk with her about her behavior, Kathy got mad at her, and they had a fight. Now she was sad and did not know what to do. I really like Kathy, and I did not like to see her hurting.

I listened to what she had to say and knew that she wanted to do right. I told Kathy that I had a best friend who could help her. I told her about Jesus and how he forgives people for the things they do wrong. I told her that Jesus knew how important it was to her to be liked. The best way to do this was to be herself, not trying to copy others, especially when you know that they are not doing what they should. I then invited Kathy to go to Sunday school with me and meet some of my other friends who knew Jesus and wanted to be more like Him, loving others and being true to what was the right thing to do. She started going with me and soon asked Jesus to come into her heart and be her best friend! In our Bible story today we will learn how some men told their friend about Jesus and took him to see him even though he could not walk and there was a huge crowd at the house where Jesus was.

 Song Suggestions

Do You Know About Jesus? Songsheets published by CEF Press, P.O. Box 348, Warrenton, Mo. 63383

He Is Really God! by Dean-o from "You Got It All" (For Kids Only, Inc. 1997)

Can You Hear My Heart? by Jana Alayra from "Dig Down Deep" (Montjoy Music 1997)

Craft for Younger Children: God Is Love Cross
Needed: White cardstock with cross drawn on it, crayons or markers.

Give each child a cross. Let them color as they choose. Write "God is Love" across the top of the paper.

A cross reminds us of Jesus. This picture will remind us of God's love for us!

 Craft for Older Children: Colors of Faith Cross
Needed: Cardstock in the following colors—yellow, red, white, green, black, blue, purple, and brown; glue; markers; and scissors. You can use craft foam sheets instead of cardstock. Cut 2 inch squares out of the card stock.

Let the children form a cross with the colored squares.

Say: Each color stands for something. Let's try to memorize what they stand for:

Yellow	God's light
Black	Our sin
Red	Jesus' blood
White	Cleansing our sin
Green	New life in Christ
Blue	Baptism
Purple	Eternal life

Now you can use this cross to tell others about Jesus!

Alternate Craft: Faith Necklace

Needed: A piece of ribbon 18 inches long, a cross, and two beads of each color: black, red, white, green, and yellow for each student.

Give each child a ribbon, a cross, and two beads of each color. Have them string them with the cross in the middle, a yellow bead on each side, then the green beads, white, red, and black on the outside. Explain the meaning of each bead (see the first craft for older children) and how to share their faith with others.

Snack: A Few Close Friends

Needed: People shaped crackers or cookies.

As you are eating, say: These cookies look like people. What is the most important thing you can do for a person who has never heard of Jesus? Why is it important that you do anything at all? Who might tell your friend about Jesus if you don't?

Memory Verse: Mark 2:12 ICB

The people were amazed and praised God. They said, "We have never seen anything like this!"

Alternate Version (New King James)
All were amazed and glorified God, saying, "We never saw anything like this!"

Memory Verse Activity: Tell Your Friends

Needed: A punch ball (or balloon) for each team.

Write the Bible verse on the board. Explain what it means and have players repeat it several times to help them remember it. Divide the class in four teams. Have them sit in chairs or on the floor in a straight line. All players must remain seated during the game. Give the first player on each team a punch ball. On "go" the first player turns to the second player on the team and says the Bible verse to him. He then punches the ball to that player who catches it, turns and says the Bible verse to the next player in line. Repeat this until all players have said the verse and caught the punch ball. When the punch ball gets to the last player in line, he says the Bible verse again and punches the ball as hard as he can trying to get it to the first player in his line. Since all players must remain in their seat, the other players on his team may help him punch the ball to the first player if it does not make it all the way to the front of the line. The team to complete the relay first wins.

Prayer Focus

Dear God, thank you for everything you do for us. Help us to tell our friends all about you. We love you! Amen.

September 28, 2005

Obedience Brings Blessing, Midweek
By Vicki Wiley

Scripture
2 Kings 8:1–6

Lesson Aim
Children will discover that God rewards obedience.

Life Skill
Children will learn that God specifically directs their lives.

Bible Learning Activity for Younger Children: Go to the Blue!
Needed: Red, blue, green, and yellow paper (one sheet of each).

Tell the kids to stand in the center of the room. Place one paper in each of the corners of the room.

Say: When I say the name of a color, run to the corner of the room that has that color. Play the game for a few minutes.

It's easy to follow instructions, isn't it? When we follow instructions, we please God.

Bible Learning Activity for Older Children: Time Lines
Needed: A long sheet of white shelf paper to create a timeline for the Shunammite family's journey.

Write the following locations on the paper: Shunem, Philistine, Palace, Her Land.

Make circles to show actions in the story. Print one action on each circle: Elisha's Instructions, Move to Philistine, 7 Years, Move to Shunem, Retelling the Miracle, Woman's Request, King's Order, Home.

Cut out people shapes and decorate them to look like these people. Move them along the timeline: Elisha, Woman, Son, Gehazi, King, Official.

Enrichment for Younger Children: Journeys

Have you been on a journey? A journey is sort of like a trip. What do you take when you go on a trip? Where do you stop for food?

When the Shunammite woman and her son went on their journey, they had to take everything with them. What do you think they took? They probably took their food, their clothes, and most of what they owned.

Enrichment for Older Children: Come Home

Can you imagine how happy the Shunammite woman and her son were when they returned home? She probably called her old friends and neighbors together to celebrate. We know that in her earlier years she was a well-to-do woman because she entertained Elisha as well. See 2 Kings 4:8.

Plan a party to celebrate God's blessings for a time you obeyed God's leading. Invite your friends to praise God with you.

Memory Verse: 2 Kings 8:2 ICB
So the woman got up and did as the man of God said.

Alternate Version (New King James)
So the woman arose and did according to the saying of the man of God.

October 2, 2005

Obedience Brings Blessing
By Pat Verbal

Scripture
2 Kings 8:1–8

Lesson Aim
Children will discover that God rewards obedience.

Life Skill
Children will learn that God specifically directs their lives.

Bible Lesson: Obedience Brings Blessing!
Needed: Bible, real estate guide from your local newspaper, whiteboard markers, a roll of paper for a timeline, markers, scissors, and tape.

Ask: How long have you lived in your house or apartment? How many times have you moved? How far? What is the hardest thing about moving? What is the best thing about living in a new place?

Every year millions of American families move. Newspapers are filled with homes for sale in every price range, in big town and small rural cities. People decide to move for many different reasons. Let's list some. (Make a list on a whiteboard.)

Moving can be scary because a new place is filled with unknowns. In our story today a little boy and his family moved twice. They left their home the first time because a prophet warned about a famine in the land. Seven years later they returned to reclaim their property.

There is a story about moving in 2 Kings 8:1–8 ICB: "Elisha talked to the woman whose son he had brought back to life. He said, 'Get up and go with your family. Stay any place you can. This is because the Lord has called for a time of hunger. It will last seven years.' So the woman got up and did as the man of God had said. She left with her family. And they stayed in the land of the Philistines for seven years. After seven years she came back." She returned and went to beg the king for her house and land. Just at that moment, the king was talking with a man who knew Elisha. "Please tell me all the great things Elisha has done," he said, and the man told him all about Elisha. Just then the woman came up, and he said, "My master and king, this is the woman. And this is the son Elisha brought back to life." The king said, "Give the woman everything that is hers. Give her all the money made from her land from the day she left until now."

Let's play the "what if?" game. Look at the Bible story again with these questions in mind.

What if the woman had responded in fear? "I'm not leaving my home. I have no idea where to go. God will take care of me no matter where I live."

What if the boy had talked back to his mom? "Mom, you're kidding, right? It took me seven years to make new friends, and I like it here. You can just go without me."

God blesses you no matter where you live, but God wants to direct those decisions in your live. Always be ready to listen to what God wants you to do.

The psalmist David prayed for God to lead him and to make his way straight (Ps. 5:8 NIV). Do you think the Shunammite woman and her son prayed that prayer before returning to their homeland? If they did, we can clearly see that God's blessings were waiting for them. They lost nothing by following God's leading through Elisha. They could not see how bad the famine would be, so their action required blind faith.

 Song Suggestions

Walking and Singing by Mary Rice Hopkins from "Miracle Mud" (Big Steps 4 U 2000)

Faith Will Do by Dean-o from "You Got It All" (FKO Music, Inc. 1997)

Jump into the Light by Jana Alayra from "Jump into the Light" (Montjoy Music 1997)

I Will Fight This Fight by Jana Alayra from 'Jump into the Light" (Montjoy Music 1997)

Craft for Younger Children: Clay Tablet
Needed: Modeling clay, pointed stick.

Shape clay into rectangle and make the surface smooth. Let children write with the stick.

Say: In Bible times the children learned to write on clay like this. If they wanted to keep it, they would let the clay dry.

 Craft for Older Children: Writing in Bible Times
Needed: Wax or paraffin, a pointed stick, lid of shoe box, aluminum foil, wax paper.

Line the shoe box lid with wax paper, then with aluminum foil. Melt the candles or paraffin using a double boiler. Pour a thin layer of melted wax onto the shoe box lid. Let cool.

Let the children draw with the stick onto the wax as they did in Bible times.

Snack: Food in the Country

 Needed: Fortune cookies, tortillas, other ethnic foods.

Let children sample a variety of foods.

Say: No matter where we live, there are special foods. Where do people eat fortune cookies? Yes, in China. What about tortillas? Yes, Mexico. Wherever we go and whatever foods the people eat there, God is also there.

Memory Verse: 2 Kings 8:2 ICB

So the woman got up and did as the man of God said.

Alternate Version (New King James)
So the woman arose and did according to the saying of the man of God.

Memory Verse Activity: Get Up!

Have the kids lie on the floor (or sit in chairs). Say the verse as you do the action:

So the woman got up (get up) and did as the man of God said.

While they are standing, have the kids do the motions of something God might ask us to do.

Say: what did you do? What are some things that God might ask a kid your age to do? We never know what God will ask us to do; it might be to become a pastor, and it might be to sweep the floor. Whatever God asks you to do, God will bless your efforts!

Prayer Focus

Dear God, thank you for all you do for us. Thank you for caring where we live and what we do. Help us to serve you. Amen.

October 5, 2005

The Trap of Sin—Wanting Just a Little More Despite God's Incredible Blessing, Midweek

By Tina Hauser

Scripture
Joshua 7

Lesson Aim
The children will recognize ways Satan tries to trap us.

Life Skill
The children will name times when they have wanted more, just like the people in the Scriptures.

Bible Learning Activity for Younger Children
Play a game similar to London Bridge, where two children stand facing each other, holding hands, and then raising their hands in the air to form a bridge. The other children walk under the bridge and then around in a circle. As the children walk under the bridge, they sing this little chorus. Change the traditional words to:

I'm wanting just a little more,
Little more,
Little more,
I'm wanting just a little more,
But God says, "No!"

If using this chorus with the story in Joshua 7, use the words, "They wanted just a little more."

When the children say, "No!" at the end of the chorus, they drop their arms and capture the child who happens to be passing under the bridge at the time. The captured child will share a time when they have wanted more and have been told no.

Our parents tell us no sometimes when we ask for more because they want to keep us from getting sick or they are trying to protect us. They may tell you that you can't watch the next show on TV because it's not good for you to see. You may not want to stop watching TV, but you do because your parents say no more. You know the rule is that you can't leave your street, but you want to go to a friend's house two blocks away. That rule was made by your parents to protect you, so you don't go.

God loves us even more than our parents and knows what is best for us. He knows when having more will not be good for us, and he tells us no. Some of us got caught in our game when the bridge came down. In real life Satan gets hold of us, catches us in his trap, when we ignore what God tells us. Don't get caught wanting more than God has given you.

Bible Learning Activity for Older Children: Trap!

Needed: A marble and 5 small Styrofoam cups.

Before the game begins, encourage the students to think of times when they wanted more of something and their parents told them they couldn't have it.

Turn the cups upside down on a table. Choose one child to trap the marble underneath one of the cups. Move the cups around while the children watch and try to keep track of where the marble is. Once the cups have stopped moving, take turns letting one child at a time select a cup to look under for the marble. Continue choosing one child at a time until the marble is found. The child who locates the marble will share one of the times when they wanted more than they had. Trap the marble once again under a cup and keep playing until several of the children have had an opportunity to share their personal experiences.

The Bible tells us about some people who took more than God told them they could take, and then they didn't want to let go of it. They thought they could hide their wrong from God, but God knew they were trapped by their desire to want more. Be glad at what God has given you! Don't get caught in the trap of wanting more than you have been given!

Optional: Bubble gum balls can also be used instead of the marble and given to each child after their turn.

Enrichment for Younger Children: Mouse and the Trap

Needed: Mousetrap and a piece of cheese.

If you have mice in your house, you know it, even if you don't see them. You may find the corner chewed on a cardboard box, or some sawdust in a kitchen drawer, or just a little bit of a cookie left on the counter after you forgot to put the whole one away. You have to get rid of the mouse because mice sometimes carry diseases that will make people sick. To catch the mouse you put a little piece of cheese, his favorite food, in the trap cage. Show the mousetrap. The mouse just has to have some, even if he's already eaten until he's full. Just a few more bites. He creeps up on the cheese, and when he takes a nibble, the cage door slams shut, and he's caught.

People sometimes think that disobeying God just a little won't do any harm. Wanting just a teensy-weensy more when God has already made clear that more is not wise surely couldn't hurt anything. Or could it? The mouse found out that a little bit more cheese got him into a whole lot of trouble.

Enrichment for Older Children: Flytrap

Needed: A photo of a Venus flytrap plant.

Ask: Have you ever tried to catch a fly? Why is it so difficult? Flies are so fast that by the time you lift your hands, they have flown away and you don't even know where they are. Did you know that there is a plant that can catch a fly? It must really be fast! It's called a Venus flytrap. This special plant has two halves that slam shut when an insect, like a fly, brushes against one of the tiny hairs on one of the halves. It closes so quickly that the fly cannot get away. Once it's caught inside, the Venus flytrap eats the insect. In a few hours it opens up again, and the hard outside of the insect is left to be washed away by the rain or blown away by the wind.

Have you ever wanted to keep something that you knew you weren't supposed to keep? Give the children opportunity to share what that was. Sometimes we want to hold onto our bad attitudes. Or we don't want to stop saying bad words. Or we want to keep being mean to one of the kids in our class. God wants us to let go of those things, but we hold onto them. We get caught in Satan's trap just like the fly got caught in the Venus flytrap plant. Satan makes it easy to get caught in his trap, but the Bible says we are commanded to destroy Satan's traps. The Venus flytrap was so quick that the fly had no idea what was happening. We get caught by Satan's trap so quickly that we don't even know how it happened.

Memory Verse: Joshua 7:13 ICB
"The Lord, the God of Israel, says some of you are keeping things he commanded you to destroy."

Alternate Version (New King James)
Thus says the LORD God of Israel: "There is an accursed thing in your midst."

October 9, 2005

The Trap of Sin—Wanting Just a Little More Despite God's Incredible Blessing
By Vicki Wiley

Scripture
Joshua 7

Lesson Aim
The children will recognize ways Satan tries to trap us.

Life Skill
The children will name times when they have wanted more, just like the people in the Scriptures.

Bible Lesson: Sin Trap!
Needed: Bible, scarf, several rolls of mint roll candy (circle shaped with a hole in the middle), string cut into two-foot lengths, and paper towels.

Before the lesson bite a mint candy in half. Wet the ends and put it back together again. This will help it break easily during the lesson. Cover another whole piece of candy with a scarf.

Have a partner hold the string by each end and ask: What are some things we do that we know God may not want us to do? (Let kids list items: evil video games, bad music, etc.)

Many things take us away from God and put us in a "sin trap." A sin trap is something we get into, and it is very hard to get out of! We get in the habit of doing something wrong, and it is hard to stop!

Thread the mended candy onto the string. Partner should continue holding the string.

When we are tied to bad things, how can we stop? How can we start to follow God again? While kids are discussing, slide that scarf off the table with the candy under it. Keep candy hidden.

Put the scarf over the mended candy on the string. Break it so that it falls off, and hide it in the fabric. Say: When we get rid of the bad things in our lives, we get out of the sin trap.

Show string with no candy and show the whole piece of candy. Kids will think it is the same one that was on the string.

Now we can be free just like this piece of candy. Jesus is our "life saver." He saves us from sin and doing things wrong. Jesus takes us from the sin trap!

 Song Suggestions

Jesus Loves the Little Children Traditional Chorus

Turn It Over by Dean-o from "God City" (BibleBeat Music 2001)

Faith Is Just Believing Songsheets published by CEF Press, P.O. Box 348, Warrenton, Mo. 63383

It's Gonna Rock! by Dean-o from "God City" (BibleBeat Music 2001)

 Craft for Younger Children: Treasure Jar

Needed: One small jar for each child, rice, small symbols of God such as rainbow, heart, cross.

Show children how to fill each jar with rice and the "treasures." Shake the jar to reveal the treasure inside.

Say: What is a sin? (A sin is a wrong thing that we do.) God does not want us to sin, and God gives us things to help us remember that. The things that help us remember can be called treasures. Why is a rainbow a treasure? (It reminds us that God will never destroy the earth.) Why is a heart a treasure? (It reminds us that we should love as God loves us.)

Treasures are better than sin! Let's look for treasure!

Craft for Older Children: Sin Trap
Needed: Small box for each child such as a baby wipes box, markers, slips of paper.

Have the kids decorate the boxes as they choose, writing "Sin Trap" on the top of the box. Pass out the slips of paper, and have kids write things they do that may become a trap for sin.

Say: A sin trap is easy to fall into. This will remind us of the sins we want to get rid of!

Snack: Jesus Is a Lifesaver

 Needed: Bagels and spreads.

Let kids spread topping on their bagel.

Say: This bagel is shaped like a lifesaver on a boat. What is a lifesaver for? How can Jesus be like a lifesaver to us?

Memory Verse: Joshua 7:13 ICB

"The Lord, the God of Israel, says some of you are keeping things he commanded you to destroy."

Alternate Version (New King James)
"Thus says the LORD God of Israel: 'There is an accursed thing in your midst.'"

Memory Verse Activity
Needed: Circles cut from construction paper in the shape of lifesavers.

Write the words of the verse around the circle. Let kids arrange the words in the proper order and say the verse together.

Prayer Focus

Dear God, thank you for everything that you give us. Help us to be satisfied with what you have given us. Amen.

October 12, 2005

Get Real! Midweek
By Tina Hauser

Scripture
Revelation 3:1–6

Lesson Aim
The children will recognize words and actions that represent a Christian.

Life Skill
The children will understand that God does not want us to pretend to be Christians.

Bible Learning Activity for Younger Children: Actions of a Christian
Needed: Slips of paper, container.

On slips of paper write different occupations that are easy to act out. Include circus performer, construction worker, race car driver, farmer, teacher, and nurse. Make sure there are enough slips for each child to have one. Put the slips in a container. Each child will draw a slip of paper and then act out that occupation without using words. They can use sounds, though, like a drill or hammer sound for the construction worker. The other children will try to guess what occupation is being portrayed. When the occupation is guessed, say to the child, "You did a wonderful job pretending to be a construction worker, but you're really not a construction worker, are you?"

Allow the children time to act out being a Christian. What would you see a Christian doing? The Bible tells us that God does not want us to pretend to be Christians. His love should fill our hearts, and then what we do will be because we are real followers of Christ.

Bible Learning Activity for Older Children: What Is a Hypocrite?

Needed: A large piece of butcher paper, small pieces of paper, tape.

Let's learn a new word today. The word is *hypocrite*. A hypocrite is someone who pretends to be something he is not. The Bible warns about people who say they are Christians but don't act like it.

Lay a large piece of paper on the floor and let the children work cooperatively to draw around one child and cut out the drawing. Hang the silhouette on the wall. This will be our pretend Christian, someone who says he's a Christian but doesn't act like it. On small pieces of paper, the children will write things that a pretend Christian might do or say. Some suggestions are:

He is always grumpy and never shows God's joy.

He gets angry quickly.

He always wants to go first so he's sure to get what he wants.

He waits for other people to serve him.

He puts down his classmates.

He makes fun of someone who is sick.

When we say we are Christians, God wants us to use words that are pleasing to him and to act in a way that would make him proud.

Enrichment for Younger Children

Needed: Your driver's license.

How many of you are old enough to drive? I can drive, but there is something I have to have before the police will let me. What is that? (a driver's license) On a driver's license there is a lot of information about the person. It describes what that person looks like. If the driver's license gets lost, whoever finds it knows exactly who lost it and where to return it. Look at my driver's license and tell something you know about me by reading what is written there.

When we become Christians, people should be able to tell by the way we act. The things we do and say identify who we are. They are like our driver's license, only in a more special way. If we are cheating, then no one will actually believe we are Christians. If we are lying, no one will think we are Christians. But, if we love people, even when they aren't easy to love, then the people around us will know that we are different; we are Christians.

The children will make a pretend driver's license by drawing a picture of themselves (head only) and including information about themselves. Instead of putting eye color, height, and weight, ask them to write one way people notice they are Christians.

Enrichment for Older Children

A man named Frank Abagnale was born back in 1948. When he was a teenager, he ran away from home because his mother and father got a divorce. Although he had no training in any special field, he pretended to be good at all kinds of jobs. He even pretended to be an airplane pilot. The people at the ticket counters believed him and gave him free airplane tickets so that he was able to fly all the way around the world. The police were always after Frank for deceiving people. How do you think the people at the ticket counter felt when they found out that Frank really wasn't a pilot after all? Do you think Frank would've been happier if he had learned how to do one job and not lied about who he was and what he could do? Why?

Have you ever had someone tell you that they got to do something special and then you found out that they really didn't get to do that at all? They were just making it up so people would think they were better than everyone else. It doesn't matter to God what kind of job you have or what places you get to see, who you've met, or what you've been asked to do. God is interested in us being real Christians, not just pretending to be Christians.

Memory Verse: Revelation 3:3 ICB

Change your hearts and lives! You must wake up, or I will come to you and surprise you like a thief.

Alternate version (New King James)
Hold fast and repent. Therefore if you will not watch, I will come upon you as a thief, and you will not know what hour I will come upon you.

October 16, 2005

Get Real!
By Vicki Wiley

Scripture
Revelation 3:1–6

Lesson Aim
The children will recognize words and actions that represent a Christian.

Life Skill
The children will understand that God does not want us to pretend to be Christians.

Bible Lesson: Get Real!
Needed: Some pictures of real and pretend such as a tree, house, person, real rabbit for real items and an Easter Bunny, Santa Claus, tooth fairy, cartoon character for pretend items; salt and sugar; dark chocolate bar and unsweetened chocolate.

Ask: Which of these things are real and which are pretend? (Let kids discuss.) What is the difference between real and pretend? (Let kids discuss.)

Now let me ask you a really hard question. What is a Christian? (Let kids discuss.) Yes, you're right. A Christian is someone who believes in Jesus, loves other people, and has faith in God. Is there such thing as a pretend Christian? What would that person do? How could someone pretend to be a Christian and not really be one? What would they do?

Let's try an experiment. Show kids the sugar and the salt and the two kinds of chocolate. They should be in identical containers.

Which one is the real candy bar? (Let kids guess.) Which is the real sugar? (Let kids guess.)

The only way to find out is to taste them! These two look like sugar. Which one is sugar? (Let kids taste.) That's right! This one is sugar, and this one is salt. (Do the same with the chocolates.)

Salt is not the same as sugar. Salt has a good purpose, but it is not sugar, is it? We can cook with this kind of chocolate, but we don't eat it like we do a candy bar, do we? It isn't sweet enough.

Pretend Christians can be nice people. They can look just like Christians, and they can act like them too. But if they don't really love Jesus, they aren't real Christians. We want to be real Christians. We want to really love God, others, and really be able to know Jesus.

 Song Suggestions

Believin' On by Jana Alayra from "Believin' On" (Montjoy Music 2002)

Little Is Much by Mary Rice Hopkins from "15 Singable Songs" (Big Steps 4 U 1988)

Faith Will Do by Dean-o from "You Got It All" (FKO Music, Inc. 1997)

God's Power Songsheets published by CEF Press, P.O. Box 348, Warrenton, Mo. 63383

 Craft for Younger Children: God Is Real!
Needed: Salt, sugar, and paper.

Let kids write "God is real" with glue on their paper. Sprinkle salt and sugar on top of the glue and shake off the rest. Let salt and sugar stick to the letters to say "God is real."

God is not make-believe; God is real! How do we know God is real? (Let children name some of the beautiful things in creation that show that God is real.)

Craft for Older Children: Salt Sunset
Needed: Small jars for each child; powered tempera paint—orange, red, yellow, and blue; salt (large bag). Mix powered paint with the salt to form colors of the sunset.

Let kids layer the different colors of salt in a jar to make a sunset. Top it off with blue for the sky.

Say: One of the best ways to remember God is when you see a sunset. God decorates the sky to remind us of his presence and love!

Snack: Rainbow Cracker

 Needed: Colored small round candy, graham crackers, icing.

Show children how to ice the graham cracker and then make a rainbow with the candies.

Say: Whenever you see a rainbow, you can remember that God is real!

Memory Verse: Revelation 3:3 ICB

Change your hearts and lives! You must wake up, or I will come to you and surprise you like a thief.

Alternate version (New King James)
Hold fast and repent. Therefore if you will not watch, I will come upon you as a thief, and you will not know what hour I will come upon you.

Memory Verse Activity
This is a great verse to act out. Make up motions for the key words and then say the verse together using the actions. Repeat until kids know the verse.

Prayer Focus

Dear God, thank you for being so real in our lives. We praise you and we love you. You are an awesome God. Amen.

October 19, 2005

Joined Together, Midweek
By Tina Hauser

Scripture
Proverbs 5

Lesson Aim
The children will realize that marriages need loving attention.

Life Skill
The children will understand that God intends marriage to be a permanent commitment.

Bible Learning Activity for Younger and Older Children
Needed: Different colors of play clay.

The children will choose two different colors of play clay and take a piece of each. They will need a sampling of each about the size of a ping-pong ball. Combine the two pieces of play clay until the color becomes consistent throughout. Allow each child to tell what two colors they began with and what color they now have.

When two people get married, they are different from each other, just like our colors of play clay were different from each other. If I asked you to separate your play clay so it would be divided into the two colors you started with, could you do that? No, you can't because they have made a brand-new color. When two people get married, they make something brand-new, a brand-new marriage, like no other marriage has ever been before. God intends for them never to be pulled apart. He wants them to stay together, even though they may have to go through some difficult times.

Enrichment Activity for Younger Children

Needed: Items that are very fragile such as china teacup, egg, crystal vase/glass.

Does anyone know what the word *fragile* means? Something that is fragile can break or can be injured easily. Let the children know that the items you have brought today are very fragile. They must be handled with great care. Pass the items around slowly and carefully. Don't start a second item until the first has completed its time of viewing. We don't want to be careless with any of these. If any of the items have great sentimental value to you, briefly tell why. When something is fragile and it is very special, you handle it with extra care.

When people get married, God expects them to treat their marriage with tender loving care. Some people treat their marriages roughly when they say cruel things and do things to hurt each other's feelings. A marriage will stay beautiful, kind of like the china teacup, if we treat it with respect and take care of it. God wants every couple to take good care of their marriage.

Enrichment Activity for Older Children

What is the highest place you have ever been? Give the children opportunities to share briefly about where they have been that was very high. What could you see from there? You can see things from up high that you can't see when you're on the ground. Sometimes people go upstairs in their house to look out the window when they are trying to find their dog. You can see much more when you are up high.

In Bible times the people used towers to climb up in so they could see better. They put towers in their fields so they could see if animals were bothering the crops. Built into the walls of the cities were towers so the people could watch for attacking enemies.

God doesn't have to climb up in a tower to see us. He sees everything we do and hears everything we say. It doesn't matter if we are kids, or teenagers, or married adults. God gives special instructions to kids and teenagers to honor their mothers and fathers. He also gives special instructions to married couples to love each other and never to do anything that would make either person want to leave the marriage. God sees our troubles, even when we think no one knows.

Memory Verse: Proverbs 5:18 ICB

Be happy with the wife you married when you were young. She gives you joys as your fountain gives you water.

Alternate Version (New Kings Version)
Let your fountain be blessed, and rejoice with the wife of your youth.

October 23, 2005

Joined Together
By Vicki Wiley

Scripture
Proverbs 5

Lesson Aim
The children will realize that marriages need loving attention.

Life Skill
The children will understand that God intends marriage to be a permanent commitment.

Bible Lesson: Joined Together

Needed: A nail puzzle with two bent nails connected which you try to separate or a similar magic type puzzle that has rings or other parts joined together and cannot be separated without knowing the secret to separating them.

Say: Have you ever seen one of these puzzles? This is really great. These two nails have been joined together, and the object is to get them apart. Watch, I'll show you how it's done. (Try to separate them without success.) Let's see now, maybe if I pull this way. Oh, that didn't work. Maybe if I twist this way. (Keep on trying without success and perhaps even let one of the children try it.)

Well, I give up. Do you know what I think? I think that once these two nails are joined together like this, they are just supposed to stay that way!

You know, that is what Jesus said about marriage. One day some men asked Jesus if it was all right for a man to divorce his wife. Jesus told them that God created man and woman to be joined together as man and wife. When they are, Jesus said, they are no longer two; they become one. Then he told them that what God has joined together, man should not try to separate.

In our world today families are being twisted, turned, and pulled in all directions, just like this puzzle. Many families are coming apart, but the simple truth is, when God puts a family together, it is meant to stay that way!

Even though God meant for families to stay together, it doesn't always happen that way. There are some here today from families that have been "pulled apart." If you are one of those, there is good news for you because God still loves you just the same!

 Song Suggestions

A Dad Like You by Mary Rice Hopkins from "Good Buddies" (Big Steps 4 U 1994)

The Family of God by Kurt Johnson, a.k.a. MrJ from "Kid Possible" (Kurt Johnson 1995)

No One Else I Know by Mary Rice Hopkins from "15 Singable Songs" (Big Steps 4 U 1988)

This Is Love by Dean-o from "God City" (BibleBeat Music, 2001)

 Craft for Younger Children: Puzzle Families
Needed: Construction paper.

Have kids draw a picture of their family on the paper. When they are finished, make a puzzle out of their picture by cutting into puzzle shapes.

 Craft for Older Children: Our Family
Needed: Fabric scraps, construction paper, markers, yarn scraps.

Let children take time to draw a family portrait. Let them cut fabric for clothes, use yarn for hair, etc. to make this project a "keeper" portrait.

Snack: Wedding Cake

Needed: Two round cakes with different diameters that can be put together to form a wedding cake. Decorate to look like a wedding cake.

Say: What does this look like? Yes, a wedding cake. A wedding is a special time in our lives, and we get a special cake to show how special it is. A wedding cake is another way to tell everyone, "Our wedding is important."

Memory Verse: Proverbs 5:18 ICB

Be happy with the wife you married when you were young. She gives you joys as your fountain gives you water.

Alternate Version (New Kings Version)
Let your fountain be blessed, and rejoice with the wife of your youth.

Memory Verse Activity: Wedding Bells

This is a silly activity that can be effective. The point today is not memorization as much as that the kids will remember the point.

Have two children volunteer to be the bride and groom. The rest of the kids will be the audience. Set the room up like a wedding chapel.

Read the verse to the "bride and groom" and have them repeat after you, just as in a wedding. Talk about vows and how important it is to keep vows that you make. Repeat as necessary with a new "bride and groom."

Prayer Focus

Dear God, thank you for marriage. We pray that we will be prepared for marriage and that you are preparing just the right spouse for us. Thank you! Amen.

October 26, 2005

Someone's Knocking at the Door, Midweek
By Vicki Wiley

Scripture
Romans 1:16, 17

Lesson Aim
Children will understand the power of God in salvation.

Life Skill
Children will learn what the gospel is.

Bible Learning Activity for Younger and Older Children: Gospel Message Chain

Needed: Tape, strips of construction paper one-inch wide in the following colors: gold, black, red, white, and green. Instruct children that each time you give them a color strip they will add it to the chain with tape.

Say: Today we are going to learn the best part of the Bible, the gospel. *Gospel* means "good news." This chain will help you remember what we talk about.

Pass out the gold strip of paper. Ask: What does this gold remind you of? (money, jewelry) Those things are valuable and special. But today the gold is going to represent heaven. The Bible tells us that in heaven the streets are made of gold. God tells us many other things about his home. No one is ever sick there. No one ever dies. There is no night there. Heaven is a special place.

There is one thing that can never be in heaven. Does anyone know what that is? (sin)

Pass out the black strip of paper. Ask: Do you know what sin is? The black paper stands for sin. Sin is anything we think, do, or say that is wrong and that does not please God. God cannot live with anything sinful, but it is impossible for us not to sin. Because God wants us to live in heaven and because we sin, God had to think of another plan for us.

Pass out the red strip of paper. Say: God loves us so much and wants us to be in heaven with him. So God sent his Son, Jesus Christ, to the world. Jesus lived on earth just as we do, but Jesus never sinned. The Bible tells us that Jesus died on the cross because he was being punished, even though he did nothing wrong. Instead of dying for his sin, he dies for our din. All the sin we already did and all the sin we will do in our lives. The red paper stands for the blood of Jesus.

Pass out the white strip of paper. Say: God wants to forgive your sins and make it so that they never happened at all. No matter how good you are, you still will sin. There is nothing you can do to take away your sin except one special thing. You can receive Jesus. How do you do that? You tell Jesus that you know you are a sinner. You tell Jesus that you believe in him and that you want him to be your Savior. That's it. That's all you have to do. Then when God looks at you, he doesn't see the sin; he only sees the clean part of you that has no sin at all. The white paper will stand for a pure heart.

Pass out the green strip of paper. Say: The color green reminds me of things that are growing like trees, plants, and grass. When you are a Christian and have received Christ, you begin to grow too. You learn more and more about Jesus, and that means that you are growing in Christ!

Would anyone like to receive Jesus right now? We are going to pray. Let's all bow our heads. I will tell you what to pray, and if you would like to receive Jesus, you can pray along with me, OK?

Dear Jesus, I know that I am a sinner. But I would like to receive you right now so that you can be the Lord of my life. I love you, and I want to follow you. Please forgive me for my sins and come into my life. Thank you God. Amen.

Let's review what the colors in the chain mean.

Enrichment for Younger Children: The Gospel

Do you know what the gospel is? The gospel is the story of Jesus and how he saves us. Do you know how to tell your friends about Jesus? You can tell them that: Jesus loves them. Jesus died for them. Jesus takes their sin away if they ask him to. Jesus will live with them forever in heaven!

Enrichment for Older Children: The Gospel

What is the gospel? (Let kids talk.) The gospel is the joyous good news of salvation in Jesus Christ. The Greek word translated as *gospel* means "a reward for bringing good news" or simply "good news." In Isaiah 40:9, the prophet proclaimed the "good tidings" that God would rescue his people from captivity. In his famous sermon at the synagogue in Nazareth, Jesus quoted Isaiah 61:1 to characterize the spirit of his ministry: "The Spirit of the Lord is in Me. This is because God chose me to tell the Good News to the poor" (Luke 4:18 ICB).

The gospel is not a new plan of salvation; it is the fulfillment of God's plan of salvation that was begun in Israel, completed in Jesus Christ, and followed by all of us.

Why is it important to know the gospel? It is how we are saved!

Memory Verse: Romans 1:17 ICB

The Good News shows how God makes people right with himself. God's way of making people right with him begins and ends with faith.

Alternate Version (New King James)
For in it the righteousness of God is revealed from faith to faith; as it is written, "The just shall live by faith."

October 30, 2005

(Special Activity, Reformation Sunday)

Someone's Knocking at the Door

By Eric Titus

Scripture
Romans 1:16, 17

Lesson Aim
Children will understand the power of God in salvation.

Life Skill
Children will learn what the gospel is.

Bible Lesson: Someone's Knocking at the Door
Needed: This will take a little advanced preparation, but it's worth the effort. You will need a door in a frame from a dollhouse. In a pinch you can take a piece of cardboard and cut a door in it and fold it so that it stands on its own and opens. Behind the small door, out of sight of the children, place a small Bible. Place a marker in the Bible at Romans 1:16, 17.

Say: Who can tell me what important day is coming up (Halloween). What happens on Halloween? (We put on costumes. We get candy.) That's right. Children get lots of candy. Do you have to do something to get the candy? Did you have to knock on a door? (Knock on the dollhouse door.) Did you have to give the people inside the house a special message to get the candy? Isn't it great to get the candy and other stuff people give to you? It's even better to eat it all up, isn't it!

Would you believe that there is another special day, a very special day that the church celebrates this week? That's right, we remember it this Sunday, but it really happens the same night as Halloween, and it has to do with a door too! (Point to the door.)

At one time the church didn't want or help Christians read their Bibles! But one special man, Martin Luther, thought it was important that people read their Bibles and understand what the Bible teaches. He thought it was so important that even though his life was in danger for doing so, he took a hammer and nailed a paper to the door of the church he worked at in Wittenberg, Germany, way back in the year 1517. The paper had 95 sentences. Luther said it was important for people to understand the message of the Bible so that they wouldn't be fooled by some false teaching some people were saying about God, the Bible, and the church. One of the worst things that was being said was that people could pay their way to heaven!

When Luther nailed that paper to that door, it might have sounded a lot like a trick-or-treater knocking on a door at Halloween. The good thing Luther did when he took the hammer and pounded on the door was to give us the greatest treat of all, the truth of the Bible. (Open the door and pull out the Bible.)

Some pastors of his time were saying that we had to buy our way to heaven, but Martin Luther had discovered in the Bible that God had given us a wonderful gift—his love and acceptance for free, if we only believe in Jesus. Now that is something special to find when you knock on a door!

This Halloween, when you hear knocking on doors, remember Luther hammering on the door at Wittenberg, and remember the gift of the Bible, and the great gift of God's love for you.

 Song Suggestions

Oh, How Great a Love by Jana Alayra from "Believin' On" (Montjoy Music 2002)

Little Is Much by Mary Rice Hopkins from "15 Singable Songs" (Big Steps 4 U 1988)

You Got Game (It's in the Name) by Dean-o from "Game Face" (BibleBeat Music, 2003)

We Will Shout for Joy by Cindy Rethmeier from "I Want to Be like Jesus" (Mercy Vineyard 1995)

Craft for Younger Children: Pumpkin Time
Needed: Orange and green craft foam cut into pumpkin and leaf shapes. Cut pumpkin shapes out of orange craft foam and let children attach green leaves to their pumpkins.

Say: These pumpkins can remind us of fall and all the good things God gives us.

 Craft for Older Children: Crosses of Faith
Needed: Small sticks, twine.

Show children how to make a cross with the small sticks, tying them together with the twine.

Say: Christians use the cross as a symbol of Jesus. Why is that? (He died on the cross.) What else can we use to remember Jesus? (Let kids discuss.)

In our story today Martin Luther wanted people to know who Jesus was and always to remember him.

Snack: Pumpkin Treats

 Needed: Any sort of seasonal pumpkin treats—muffins, cookies, bread.

Say: At this time of year, we celebrate fall by eating things made of pumpkin. What else can you do with a pumpkin? (Carve it; make a pie.) When you think of a door, what do you think of? (going home, the entrance to our house)

Today we learned about a special door that changed Christianity. Whenever you see a door now, remember that a door can remind you of Jesus and how he wants you to come in to him!

Memory Verse: Romans 1:17 ICB

The Good News shows how God makes people right with himself. God's way of making people right with him begins and ends with faith.

Alternate Version (New King James)
For in it the righteousness of God is revealed from faith to faith; as it is written, "The just shall live by faith."

Memory Verse Activity

Needed: Long sheet of butcher paper. Write on each end *Faith*. Write the verse between the words at each end.

Say: God makes people right through their faith. What does that mean? It means that our faith is what makes us known by God.

Read the whole verse together and say it until kids become familiar with it.

Prayer Focus

Dear Lord, we thank you that you used Martin Luther to help people be able to read and understand the Bible. We thank you for your gift to us of love and acceptance through Jesus Christ.

November 2, 2005

Following God's Direction and Vision for Us, Midweek
By Vicki Wiley

Scripture
Exodus 14:10–22

Lesson Aim
Children will learn that God will protect them.

Life Skill
Children will realize that God always has a plan.

Bible Learning Activity for Younger Children: Fishing in the Red Sea
Needed: Fish or can of tuna, salt water. You can make this by simply adding salt to water.

Moses led the Hebrew people over a sea. The Bible says they walked across on dry land. Even though it was dry land, they still could smell fish and maybe taste the salt water.

Have you ever tasted salt water? (Let kids taste.) What do you think it was like when they walked through the sea? (Let children smell the fish.) I think it might have smelled like this!

Bible Learning Activity for Older Children: Red Sea Isn't Red?
The Red Sea is a narrow body of water that separates two large portions of land. On the east are Yemen and Saudi Arabia. On the west are Egypt, the Sudan, and Ethiopia. It is a large sea.

The Red Sea is actually bright turquoise, not Red! Sometimes algae grow in the water, and when they die, the sea becomes reddish-brown, thus giving it the name, the Red Sea. This body of water has the reputation of being one of the hottest and saltiest on earth.

Enrichment for Older Children: Red Sea Relay

Needed: Simple fish shapes cut from paper, spray bottles.

Let children run a relay race. Give each person on the team a fish shape. Let the kids race as they take their fish across to the other side. While they race, spray the kids with water from the spray bottles.

Say: The Hebrew people went across the Red Sea and got to the other side. Do you think they saw any fish? We don't know because the Bible doesn't tell us, but we do know that it was a real sea that has real fish living in it!

Enrichment for Younger Children: Crossing the Red Sea

Play this simple game of "Mother, may I" using, "May I cross?" instead of the traditional saying. One child will be Moses. Other children will be on other side of the room asking, "May I cross?" Moses will answer with one of the following: You may cross with giant steps, baby steps, backward steps, etc. The game ends when all the children have "crossed" the Red Sea.

Memory Verse: Exodus 14:13, 14 ICB

But Moses answered, "Don't be afraid! Stand still and see the Lord save you today... You will only need to remain calm. The Lord will fight for you."

Alternate Version (New King James)

And Moses said to the people, "Do not be afraid. Stand still, and see the salvation of the LORD, which He will accomplish for you today... "The LORD will fight for you, and you shall hold your peace."

November 6, 2005

Following God's Direction and Vision for Us
By Eric Titus

Scripture
Exodus 14:10–22

Lesson Aim
Children will learn that God will protect them.

Life Skill
Children will realize that God always has a plan.

Bible Lesson: Following God's Direction and Vision for Us
Preparation: Large plastic or Styrofoam cup, diaper, pitcher of water. Cut the diaper open and pull out all of the absorbent material inside. Place this in the cup. When you pour the water into the cup, you will be able to turn the cup upside down with nothing coming out. You will need to spend some time experimenting with the correct amount of absorbent material and water. Don't let the children look into the cup before or after the sermon.

Say: Do any of you ever have trouble following directions at school or at home? No, I didn't think so. But wouldn't it be hard to follow directions if they were confusing or didn't make sense? What about if they were dangerous? Moses had some directions from God; he was supposed to lead the people of Israel out of Egypt up to a land that God had told them about. These were hard directions to follow because the people of Israel were slaves to other people called Egyptians, and the Egyptians didn't want Israel to leave. They also had a huge, powerful army to make Israel stay. But God had given Moses a great vision about Israel being free and living in a wonderful land.

Because of God's miracles, Israel did leave Egypt, but the Egyptian army followed them so they could bring them back. Moses had followed God's directions and believed in the vision God had given him. He brought Israel to the edge of a huge sea. So there was a lot of water in front of them and a great big army behind them. Sometimes, even when we follow directions, it seems like things just don't work out too well.

God gave some new directions. God said, "Go forward!" Some of the Israelites must have been confused by those directions. Maybe some of them were thinking, *Does God think we're Noah? We don't have a boat!* Those must have seemed like impossible directions. And then Moses got new directions too. He was supposed to stretch his staff over the water and make the water part so Israel could cross! (Pick up the cup and pour the water into the cup while you talk.) Moving water that way must have seemed like a confusing instruction to Moses. But Moses knew that if Israel was going to get freedom and that wonderful land, he needed to obey God, even if it seemed a little odd. Because Moses followed God's instructions, something amazing happened. The water parted, and the land became dry (turn the cup upside down) so that Israel could cross and receive the vision God had given to Moses.

If God makes a promise to us, it is important for us to follow God's instructions, even if they are hard or confusing. God has a wonderful way of making things work out when we obey; and when we do, we see that the promises and visions God gives us come to pass.

 Song Suggestions

He Is Really God! by Dean-o from You Got It All (FKO Music, Inc. 1997)

Superman by Mary Rice Hopkins from "15 Singable Songs" (Big Steps 4 U 1988)

My Very Best Friend by Cindy Rethmeier from "I Want 2 Be Like Jesus" (Mercy/Vineyard Publishing 1995)

Holy, Holy, Holy Traditional Hymn

Craft for Younger Children: Parting of the Red Sea
Needed: Blue construction paper, tan construction paper, and people shapes. Putting the tan paper down first, cut waves from the blue paper and attach to the sides of the tan paper. Glue people shapes to the center so they are walking on "dry land."

Say: Today we learned about Moses and his vision. Moses followed God's instructions, and the people were saved as they walked on dry land.

 Craft for Older Children: Coiled Pots
Needed: Clay.

When the Hebrew people wandered through the desert, they had to make their own pots. They made them out of clay. Let's make some just like they did in Bible times.

Show children how to make coils with the clay and then form them into pots. Let pots dry.

Snack: Crossing the Sea Snack

 Needed: Bananas, ice cream, gummy people.

Show children how to make a "crossing the Red Sea snack" using the above ingredients. Eat and enjoy!

While children eat, say: Moses listened to God and led the Hebrew people to safety. How can we listen to God?

Memory Verse: Exodus 14:13, 14 ICB

But Moses answered, "Don't be afraid! Stand still and see the Lord save you today... You will only need to remain calm. The Lord will fight for you."

Alternate Version (New King James)
And Moses said to the people, "Do not be afraid. Stand still, and see the salvation of the LORD, which He will accomplish for you today… The LORD will fight for you, and you shall hold your peace."

Memory Verse Activity: Stand Still and Be Calm!

Moses told the people to stand still and be calm and wait for God to save them. Why do you think he said this? Do we ever need to stand still and wait? Can you tell about a time that you needed to wait when you wanted to do something else?

Let's learn this verse. Say the verse several times together. Then have the children stand up and say the verse again, this time acting it out. Emphasize the words: Don't be afraid, stand still, Lord will save you, fight for you.

Prayer Focus

Dear Lord, help us always to obey you even when it is hard. And show us that you are faithful to your promises when we do. Amen.

November 9, 2005

Warm Welcomes! Midweek
By Vicki Wiley

Scripture
2 Kings 4:8–17

Lesson Aim
Children will discover that their home and example can bring glory to God.

Life Skill
Children can prepare for and serve guests at home.

Bible Learning Activity for Younger Children: Taking Care of Others
Needed: Cookies or crackers.

When someone comes to your house, what do you do to make them feel that you want them to be there? (Play with them. Let them choose the games we play.)

Another way we make people feel comfortable is to give them a snack. Today we are going to serve one another.

Let children serve the snack to one another.

Ask: Do you feel welcome? When you go to someone's house and they give you a snack, do you feel special? God wants us to help others feel special in our homes.

Bible Learning Activity for Older Children: Hospitality
Hospitality was important in Bible times. In the New Testament the Greek word translated *hospitality* literally means "love of strangers" (Rom. 12:13).

In the Old Testament Abraham was the host to angels unaware; he invited strangers into his house, washed their feet, prepared fresh meat, had Sarah bake bread, and later accompanied them as they left (Gen. 18:1–15). Even today a traditional greeting to the guests among the Bedouin people of the Middle East is, "You are among your family."

Hospitality was specifically commanded by God, and it was to be characteristic of all believers. When we love God, we are hospitable.

Enrichment for Younger Children: Being Kind

What does it mean to be kind? How can we be kind? (Let children discuss.) When we are kind, we are serving God because we are giving hospitality. In our story we learn about a woman who was kind to God's servant, Elisha.

When someone comes to your house, how can you be kind? Did you know you are serving God when you do that?

Enrichment for Older Children: Hospitality

Needed: Whiteboard and felt-tip markers.

Say: In our story today the woman gave hospitality. What is hospitality? To discover what hospitality is, let's see how many words we can make out of the word *hospitality*. Write the word *hospitality* on the whiteboard and let kids create a list using the letters. H is for *humble*, O is for *open door*, etc.

Memory Verse: 2 Kings 4:10 ICB

"Let's make a small room on the roof. Let's put a bed in the room for Elisha. And we can put a table, a chair and a lampstand there. Then when he comes by he can stay there."

Alternate Version (New King James)

"Please, let us make a small upper room on the wall; and let us put a bed for him there, and a table and a chair and a lampstand; so it will be, whenever he comes to us, he can turn in there."

November 13, 2005

Warm Welcomes!
By Pat Verbal

Scripture
2 Kings 4:8–17

Lesson Aim
Children will discover that their home and example can bring glory to God.

Life Skill
Children can prepare for and serve guests at home.

Bible Lesson: Warm Welcomes
Needed: Bring to class 3-inch x 5-inch cards, pencils, a thesaurus, paper for an invitation.

Ask children to write their answer to this question on a note card. What does the word *hospitality* means. Most of the answers will be right because hospitality takes many forms. Help the children look up *hospitality* in a thesaurus (Synonyms include *generosity, cordiality, consideration, warm reception, warm welcome, graciousness*.)

Ask: Whose house do you like going to most besides your own? Why to you like to visit here? Whom do you enjoy inviting to your house? What do you do to get ready for his or her visit?

It does not matter whether people have a big house or a small one, fancy furniture or furniture that is well worn, T-bone steaks or hot dogs, X-Boxes or cardboard puzzles, swimming pools or sprinklers, we like to go to places where we feel loved and welcome.

The prophet Elisha felt that way. When he visited Shunem, he stopped for dinner at one family's house. Why? Because he always felt special in their home. Read 2 Kings 4:8–17. Think about the things the Shunammite woman did to serve Elisha. She served out of a generous heart, not expecting anything in return.

The Shunammite woman wanted to be a good host to Elisha. She felt pity on him because he had no home in the area. So, she washed some furniture and made Elisha a room on the roof. The roof was cooler on hot days.

She went to shop at the best stores to find rich foods to cook. Elisha especially enjoyed her delicious pot of stew. She lit a lamp in her window so Elisha would always be greeted with a warm welcome.

Elisha wanted to help her in some way for her kindness. So he asked her how he could help her. Her answer was that she didn't need anything. Elisha wanted to get her something, and he remembered that the woman needed a son to help her because her husband was old. So Elisha told her she would have a son.

Elisha was right! The next year at the same time, the woman had a baby boy, just as Elisha said she would. Her hospitality was richly rewarded.

 Song Suggestions

Lord I Give My Heart by Mark Thompson from "Yes Yes Yes!" (Markarts 2000)

Say Thank You by Mary Rice Hopkins from "Miracle Mud" (Big Steps 4 U 1995)

Outta Sight by Dean-o from "Soul Surfin'" (FKO Music, Inc. 1997)

God's Power Songsheets published by CEF Press, P.O. Box 348, Warrenton, Mo. 63383

 Craft for Younger Children: Bible Times Lamp
Needed: Clay and picture of clay lamp from Bible times.

In Bible times the people used lamps because they didn't have electricity. Let's make a lamp just like they used to have.

Show children what a clay lamp looked like and let them copy it.

Say: This looks just like a real Bible times lamp!

Craft for older children: Bible Time Oil Lamp
Needed: Baby food or other small jars, oil for lamps, wicks, picture of Bible times lamp, screwdriver to poke hole, hammer.

Show children how to poke a hole into the lid of the jar by hammering a screwdriver through the lid. Pour oil into the jar and put the wick through the hole into oil.

Say: This is just like a real oil lamp! In Bible times the people used lamps like this. This is just like the lamp that the woman gave Elisha.

Snack: Bible Times Snack

Needed: Pita bread, fruit, cheese.

In Bible times the people ate different food from what most of us eat today. Here are some of the foods they served their guests. Let children try the foods.

What do you give to your guests when they are hungry? What are your favorite foods? We show love when we give our guests the best!

Memory Verse: 2 Kings 4:10 ICB

"Let's make a small room on the roof. Let's put a bed in the room for Elisha. And we can put a table, a chair and a lampstand there. Then when he comes by he can stay there."

Alternate Version (New King James)

"Please, let us make a small upper room on the wall; and let us put a bed for him there, and a table and a chair and a lampstand; so it will be, whenever he comes to us, he can turn in there."

> ## Memory Verse Activity: Banner Bible Story
> Needed: Banner paper and felt-tip markers.
>
> Read the verse to the children. Say: Today we are going to make a banner Bible story.
>
> Let children draw this verse out on the paper. Assign one group of children to the first part, another to the second part, etc. When the banner is complete, say the verse together.

Prayer Focus

Dear God, please help us to be hospitable to others. Thank you for this great example of hospitality in the Bible. Amen.

November 16, 2005

God Made the Church, It's the Home Christians Grow Up In, Midweek

By Tina Hauser

Scripture
1 Corinthians 1:1–9

Lesson Aim
The children will identify reasons it is important to be faithful to the church.

Life Skill
The children will realize that God created the church.

Bible Learning Activity for Younger Children: The Church Is Our Church

Needed: Masking tape, long rope.

Using masking tape, outline a church building on the floor. It needs to be large enough for all the children to stand on the tape. Lay the rope on the masking tape so it traces the outline of the church and the ends come together. Choose a child to stand on the masking tape outline and pick up the rope in that place. As the child does this, using the family name, he or she will say, "The _____s will be faithful to God's church." (Example: The Johnsons)

If the child attends church without parents, use the first name instead of the family's last name. Continue doing this until all the children are standing on the outline and holding the rope. Make the observation that together we make up God's church.

Say: Right here we are connected by the rope, but we are joined together in the church by God's grace, forgiveness, and love. Push down on the rope in front of one child. When one person hurts and is feeling down, it affects the other people in the church who love them. See how the rope that others were holding went down a little also. Now lift high the rope that one child is holding. The rope that the children on both sides are holding will also be raised. When we are celebrating God's goodness, others around us feel that joy. God wants us to stay connected to the church and help one another follow him.

Bible Learning Activity for Older Children: God's People

Have you ever watched someone take care of a lawn? Or have you ever helped with the lawn care? What do you have to do to keep the lawn looking nice? The grass needs to be cut. The lawn needs to be fertilized. The bushes need to be trimmed. The flowers need to be planted, and the weeds need to be pulled! As you name these, the children will join you in frantically acting out each one. Just about the time you get it all done, it's time to start over again! When it's all just the way it should be, the owner of the house is happy.

The Bible tells us that "God is always at work on us." God uses the people in the church to remind us to read our Bibles. God uses the people in the church to remind us to show his joy. God uses the people in the church to remind us of all kinds of things that will help us live the lives that our heavenly Father wants for us. Can you name some other things God reminds us of through our church family? The children will put their hands together so that their fingers are tucked inside. (Like the old rhyme: "Here's the church, here's the steeple; open the door and see all the people.") Every time they suggest a way God uses the church to remind us, the children will open their hand-church, wiggle their fingers, and say together, "God uses the church."

Being faithful to the church is important because God wants to speak to us and be with us through our special family here.

Enrichment for Younger Children: Elephants and Church?

Needed: A picture of an elephant, drawing supplies

Ask each child to draw a picture of one elephant. Now describe an elephant for me. What can you tell me about elephants? You have done very well at telling me what an elephant looks like, but I want to tell you more about how an elephant acts and lives.

Elephants live together in groups or elephant communities. Let's put all our elephants together on the wall so we have an elephant community. Elephants live in their group for their entire life. They look for food together; they wash in the river together; and they travel together. Sometimes one elephant will wander away from the group but will find his way back because the others make sounds to help him. The entire group has a greeting ceremony when the wanderer returns. They will run to him, spin, click tusks, trumpet, and rub heads. If one elephant gets in trouble, the rest will risk their lives to protect him. When a baby is born, how do you feel? We are happy for the new mother and father. Elephants celebrate together when a baby elephant is born, too. When someone dies, what do we do? We are sad and cry. People have actually seen elephants shed tears when one member of their family dies. God made elephants so they need their group.

God also made an extra special group for people. It's called the church. The church is more important to God than any group of animals. The church prays together when people are celebrating and when something bad has happened. The people of the church cry together when they are sad and laugh together when they are happy. When someone needs something, the church is willing to help. And the most important thing about the church is that the people help one another grow closer to God.

Enrichment for Older Children: God's Great Idea

Needed: One low-wattage lightbulb, a lamp, black permanent marker, yellow highlighter.

One of God's incredible ideas was the church. One of God's messages to us from the Bible is to come together and worship him. Groups of people all over the world get together to worship, to learn, to pray, to enjoy being together, and to support one another when they are going through something difficult. The people at your church are your own special church family!

Have you ever seen in the cartoons or on a comic strip a lightbulb over someone's head to show that they have an idea? When the idea comes through their head, the lightbulb comes on. Using a permanent marker, write on the light bulb, "The Church ... God's Great Idea." Put the lightbulb into a lamp. Turn the lights off in the room and turn the lamp on. Isn't the light a wonderful thing in this dark room? God wants the church to be a wonderful experience for all of us as we live in a world where many people do not know him.

Sketch a lightbulb on the board or have one ready on a piece of posterboard. Draw lines, or light beams, out from the lightbulb with a yellow highlighter. On each line the children will write their family's last name. These are the families that worship together at this church. We love one another and need one another as we live for God. It is important for all of us to be faithful to God's church.

Memory Verse: 1 Corinthians 1:2 ICB

You were called to be God's holy people with all people everywhere who trust in the name of the Lord Jesus Christ—their Lord and ours.

Alternate Version (New King James)

To those who are sanctified in Christ Jesus, called to be saints, with all who in every place call on the name of Jesus Christ our Lord, both theirs and ours.

November 20, 2005

God Made the Church, It's the Home Christians Grow Up In
By Eric Titus

Scripture
1 Corinthians 1:1–9

Lesson Aim
The children will identify reasons it is important to be faithful to the church.

Life Skill
The children will realize that God created the church.

Bible Lesson: God Made the Church
Needed: A posterboard with pictures of a small child, a father, a mother, other children, a teacher, a classroom, books, food, and other elements from the story below that you wish to include. As you tell the story, take a red marker and put a line through the things the child says he doesn't need. On the other side of the posterboard, draw or paste pictures of a pastor, a pulpit, Sunday school, people at worship, and any other church events you wish to include.

Say: There once was a small child. This child was different from all other children. The child didn't have a father or a mother. He didn't have a sister or a brother. You might think this child was very sad, right? Well, he wasn't. The child didn't have any friends because he didn't want any friends, and he didn't want a family. The child said that he had seen some fathers and mothers that he really thought weren't what they should be, and he said that he always saw brothers and sisters fighting, and he just didn't want to be a part of that. The child never went to school. He said it was really boring, and he didn't get anything out of it. He never learned anything about what it meant to be a child or an adult. The child never ate, never read, never drank, and never talked to anyone. The child never grew. Years and years went by, but the child never gained a pound and never grew an inch. The child never listened to any advice that people tried to give. The child insisted that he didn't need any help; he was doing just fine on his own. What do you think happened to that child? How do you think this child looked to other children?

As Christians, we are all children of God. God has created a beautiful home for his children, and that home is called the church. (Turn the posterboard to the other side.) The church is where we grow up in our Christianity. We learn about God; we learn about Jesus; we learn about the Holy Spirit. We learn about how to live as Christians from sermons, Sunday school lessons, and other times of teaching. We can look at other Christians who are more mature and watch how they live. The church is filled with people we call our Christian brothers and sisters. The church gathers, like Paul says, to be together, grow together, and to share our gifts together. Saying that we are Christians but not belonging and being a part of the church is a lot like being that child we talked about. We would never grow in our Christianity, not one inch! It is important to be a part of the church because that is the people and house God has given us to grow up in spiritually.

 Song Suggestions

I'm Not Too Little Songsheets published by CEF Press, P.O. Box 348, Warrenton, Mo. 63383

Purest of God by Kurt Johnson, a.k.a. MrJ from "Pure Gold" (Mr. J Music 1995)

Miracle by Mary Rice Hopkins from "Juggling Mom" (Big Steps 4 U 1999)

He's Got Plans by Dean-o from "Soul Surfin'" (FKO Music, Inc., 1999)

You're in My Heart to Stay by Jana Alayra from "Dig Down Deep" (Montjoy Music 1997)

Craft for Younger Children: The Church

Needed: Tan craft foam or construction paper (cut into a church shape), people shapes cut from paper, cross for steeple.

Let children make the church by adding windows, a door, and a cross. Let them add the people.

Say: What is the church? Is this building the church? Or are the people the church? God wants all his people to go to church; it's the place where we grow as Christians.

Craft for Older Children: The Church

Needed: Large envelopes, people shapes.

Let children draw a church on the outside of the envelope. Let them color the people shapes.

Ask: Which of these is the church, the drawing on the envelope or the people? The church is really the people; the building is just where we meet together. When God's people come together, it is a church.

Snack: Potluck Supper

Needed: A variety of foods for snacks to resemble a potluck.

Say: Many times when people get together at church, they have a potluck meal. In some cultures it is called a "pot blessing." People like to have a meal together this way, and when everyone brings a different food, it is easy for everyone to participate.

Let's try this "pot blessing" now.

Memory Verse: 1 Corinthians 1:2 ICB

You were called to be God's holy people with all people everywhere who trust in the name of the Lord Jesus Christ—their Lord and ours.

Alternate Version (New King James)
To those who are sanctified in Christ Jesus, called to be saints, with all who in every place call on the name of Jesus Christ our Lord, both theirs and ours.

Memory Verse Activity: Echo the Verse
Lead kids in the verse as follows. You say the first part and instruct them to echo you:
You were called (you were called)
to be God's holy people (to be God's holy people)
with all people everywhere (with all people everywhere)
who trust in the name (who trust in the name)
of the Lord Jesus Christ— (of the Lord Jesus Christ—)
their Lord and ours. (their Lord and ours.)
Repeat until the kids know the verse.

Prayer Focus
Thank you, God, for creating the church, for giving us a home to grow up in as Christians. Amen.

November 23, 2005

The Whirlwind into Heaven, Midweek
By Tina Hauser

Scripture
2 Kings 2:1–18

Lesson Aim
The children will realize that preparation takes time and patience.

Life Skill
The children will understand that they need to have patience as they trust God to prepare them.

Bible Learning Activity for Younger Children: Colors, Colors!
Needed: One-minute egg timer, markers, drawing paper.

Tell the children that you want them to draw a picture of themselves and someone who teaches them. This may be a parent, a schoolteacher, a piano teacher, a Sunday school teacher, the pastor, or a scout leader. Give each child one marker. Make sure the colors of markers are spread out so that all the dark ones aren't with the children on one side of the table and the light colors on the other side of the table. Give them one minute to work on their picture using only the marker they have been given. When the egg timer indicates that one minute is up, say, "Switch," and everyone will pass their one marker to the person to their right. Set the timer again for one minute and the children will work on their pictures with the new marker. Determine before beginning how many times you will allow the markers to be switched.

How did this make you feel? Were you anxious to get a color a neighbor had and you knew would be yours in a minute or two? What were some of the things you were thinking? You had to have patience as you waited for the next marker to come to you. When the teacher said it wasn't time yet, you had to trust that they were telling you that for a reason. The teacher also has to have patience. It would be easy to say that we can change the rules and just throw all the markers in the middle so that we can use whatever we want. But if the teacher lost patience and said that, then the students wouldn't learn the lesson they were supposed to learn by doing this. God wants us to have patience that he is working in our lives and trust him to work everything out for good.

Bible Learning Activity for Older Children: Training for the Job

Needed: A six-foot stepladder, a beanbag.

Ask: Has anyone ever asked you what you'd like to be when you grow up? (Allow the children to tell you their answers.) If you really have your heart set on doing a special job, then you have to take certain steps to get there. When you're fifteen years old, you just can't say, "I think I'll build a skyscraper." Let's think about the steps someone would have to take to become a pastor. There are things that even children can do to start preparing.

Set up the ladder with a piece of masking tape about eight feet away as the stand-behind line. The children are going to take turns tossing a beanbag at a certain open area between two of the rungs. Make sure they know which opening they are aiming for. If they get their beanbag to go through that space, then they can tell you one thing that can be done to prepare to be a pastor. Write their contribution on a strip of paper and tape it to one of the ladder supports. As more strips are added, try to put them in order of how they should take place. (Study the Bible. Write a sermon. Learn how to talk to hurting people. Ask questions of older ministers. Go to college. Go to seminary. Volunteer in a church. Teach a class.) Point out that as a child you can't go to seminary, but you can begin to study your Bible and develop a prayer time. We have to be patient as God prepares us while we're growing up. He will show us the right time for each step.

Enrichment Activity for Younger Children: Patience! Patience!

Needed: A quart jar with a tight lid, chilled whipping cream, cheesecloth, salt, crackers.

Place the whipping cream in the jar and check to make sure the lid is secure. The children will take turns shaking the jar vigorously for a minute at a time. In 10–15 minutes you will notice the whipping cream changing form. It will get thick at first and then turn to a clump. When there is a definite clump, pour the contents of the jar through a piece of cheesecloth. Put the clump that is left in a small dish. Sprinkle with salt and mash it into the butter. Give each child a sample of the butter on a cracker. We had to be patient as we waited for the cream to turn to butter, but this delicious butter was worth the wait. Can you name other times when you have to be patient?

Butter is made when cream is beaten so hard that the fats in it separate from the liquid. When they separate, the liquid is called buttermilk, and the solid part is called butter. Most of our milk is from cows, but milk can also be made from goat, camel, buffalo, sheep, and horse milk. The butter made from each of these is different in color because the animals eat different things. In Bible times the cream was put in an animal skin and suspended between two poles. It would then be pushed back and forth on the poles, shaking the cream up, and eventually turning it to butter.

Enrichment Activity for Older Children: Strong Bricks

In Bible times bricks were made to use as a building material. There were several steps in making the bricks, so people had to be patient in waiting for the bricks to be finished. The first thing a brickmaker had to do was find a place to get clay. There weren't stores where you could purchase clay, so you had to find a place to dig it out of the ground. Then chopped straw would be added to the clay along with some water. The straw kept the brick from cracking when it was done. The mixture was then shaped by hand, or it was put it a form to make it the shape they wanted. The wet brick was laid out in the sun to dry, and then they waited and waited and waited! The sun was doing its work. The brick had to be completely dry before it could be used.

As you grow up, God will add people and experiences to your life that will move you one step closer to the person he has in mind for you to be. Sometimes we just have to wait. God is working in you!

Memory Verse: 2 Kings 2:4 ICB

But Elisha said, "As the Lord lives, and as you live, I won't leave you."

Alternate Version (New King James)

But he said, "As the LORD lives, and as your soul lives, I will not leave you!"

November 27, 2005

The Whirlwind into Heaven
By Vicki Wiley

Scripture
2 Kings 2:1–18

Lesson Aim
The children will realize that preparation takes time and patience.

Life Skill
The children will understand that they need to have patience as they trust God to prepare them.

Bible Lesson: The Whirlwind into Heaven
Needed: A pan of water (cake pan size), a wooden ruler, a washcloth, a plastic lid.

Can you divide this water? (Let kids try to divide the water with the ruler, washcloth, and lid.) Did any of these things divide this water? No, of course they didn't!

The Bible tells us about water being divided. Does anyone know that story? Yes, you're right! Moses parted the water. And yes, Joshua parted the Jericho River. And yes, in creation God divided the water from the dry land.

There were two more times when water was parted. This time it was parted using a coat and the Jordan River. Let me tell you about it.

One day Elisha and Elijah were standing by the Jordan River. There were fifty men who were prophets watching to see what would happen to the prophet Elijah. Right before their eyes Elijah took off his coat, rolled it up, and hit the water. The water divided to the right and to the left, and Elijah and Elisha crossed over on dry ground.

After they had crossed over, Elijah said to Elisha, "What can I do for you before I am taken from you?"

Elisha said, "Leave me a double share of your spirit." He loved Elijah and wanted to be like him.

Elijah said, "You have asked a hard thing. But if you see me when I am taken from you, it will be yours. If you don't, it won't happen."

As they were walking and talking, a chariot and horses of fire appeared and separated Elijah from Elisha. Then Elijah went up to heaven in a whirlwind.

Elisha did see it! He saw Elijah go up to heaven! But now Elisha was sad because Elijah was gone. When the Hebrew people were sad when someone died, they tore their clothes. That is exactly what he did. He picked up Elijah's coat that had fallen from him. Then he returned and stood on the bank of the Jordan.

Elisha hit the water with Elijah's coat and said, "Where is the LORD, the God of Elijah?" When he hit the water, it divided to the right and to the left, and Elisha crossed over. When this happened, he knew that he now had Elijah's spirit, just as he had asked.

We don't want to have Elijah's spirit because we can now have God's own Holy Spirit. How do we do that? How can we have this Spirit of God? Just ask! Ask God to fill you with his Holy Spirit, and he will!

 Song Suggestions

Day by Day by Jana Alayra from "Jump into the Light" (Montjoy Music 1995)

Rad-Dude Attitude by Dean-o from "You Got It All" (FKO Music, Inc. 1997).

Sharing Comes Round Again by Mary Rice Hopkins from "15 Singable Songs" (Big Steps 4 U 1988)

Hallelujah Ballad Songsheets published by CEF Press, P.O. Box 348, Warrenton, Mo. 63383

Craft for Younger Children: Hebrew Headgear

Needed: Nine-inch circles of felt or craft foam, decorations cut from foam or precut shapes, glue.

The Hebrew people wore a special hat. These hats were always worn when they were going to worship.

Show children how to decorate their hats and let them wear them during the lesson.

Craft for Older Children: Bible Times Instrument

Needed: Disposable pie pans, beads, nails and hammer to poke holes, string.

Let children poke four holes in the pans along the sides. (You can also do this ahead of the class.)

Show children how to string a few beads onto a string and tie through a hole. Repeat for each hole. Clank away!

In Bible times the Hebrew people loved to celebrate! Shaking a praise shaker was one of the ways they celebrated!

Snack: A Cloak over Blue Water

Needed: Fruit rollups, blue gelatin.

Give each child a cup of blue gelatin and a section of fruit rollup that will resemble the coat Elijah used to part the sea.

Say: This will help us remember what we learned today!

Memory Verse: 2 Kings 2:4 ICB

But Elisha said, "As the Lord lives, and as you live, I won't leave you."

Alternate Version (New King James)
But he said, "As the LORD lives, and as your soul lives, I will not leave you!"

Memory Verse Activity

Have kids form partners. Write the verse on a whiteboard where all can see it. Have the kids face each other and say the verse to each other.

Say: Elijah and Elisha were special friends; they were both prophets who loved God. Special friends can say things like this to each other and make promises they will always keep.

How would you say the same thing now? How would a kid like you tell a friend you will never leave them?

Prayer Focus

Dear God, thank you for your prophets and the words they gave us. Please help us to be diligent like they were. Amen.

November 30, 2005

The Sermon on the Amount, Midweek
By Tina Hauser

Scripture
2 Corinthians 8:1–13

Lesson Aim
Children will be challenged to serve God by serving others.

Life Skill
Children will realize that God wants to be our top priority and serving others our second.

Bible Learning Activity for Younger Children: I Can't Believe You Did That!

Needed: Three buckets, masking tape, two beanbags.

Say: God wants us to serve him by loving other people. He also wants us to serve beyond what is expected. Isn't it nice to hear someone say, "I can't believe you did that for me!"

Place the three buckets against a wall. Each bucket will have one of these labels: for my family, at my school, for my friends. Place a piece of masking tape back from the buckets about eight feet. Each child will get two tries to toss the beanbags into the buckets. If a beanbag goes in one of the buckets, the child will tell a way he or she could amaze someone with their serving attitude at the place on the bucket label. Continue playing as long as the ideas keep flowing.

Bible Learning Activity for Older Children: Serving Others

Needed: Lined paper, pencils, number cubes.

Give each child a piece of lined paper and a pencil. Divide children into groups of three or four and give each group a number cube. The children will take turns rolling the cube, trying to get the numbers in order, one through six. If they get the number one on the cube, then they will write on the paper what they consider to be most important in their lives. Now they will try to roll for the number two. When they roll the two, they will write down what is second in importance in their lives. Continue doing this until each child lists the six most important things in his or her life.

Say: God knows what will make us happy. God knows what is best for us, and God tells us in the Bible that the most important thing in our lives is to be close to him. He also tells us that the second most important thing should be to serve other people.

Enrichment for Younger Children: Surprising Service

Needed: Toilet tissue rolls, wrapping paper.

Prepare a surprise gift for each child. Cut a toilet tissue roller in half. Put a few pieces of individually wrapped candies inside the roller. Wrap a piece of Christmas wrapping paper around it and secure with one small piece of tape. Twist the excess paper on each end, close to the roller. Use a piece of ribbon to hold each end, or use a small piece of chenille stick and simply twist.

Express to the children that you were thinking of them and wanted to do something special to show them your love. Give them the presents

Say: How did it make you feel when you received a gift you weren't expecting? Two things delight God's heart: (1) for his people to love and serve Him, and (2) for his people to love and serve one another. He smiles when we make him the most important part of our lives. Because God is important, we show our love to the people around us. Our love surprises people sometimes.

Would you like to give an unexpected love gift to someone today? Provide supplies for the children to make one of the candy filled-rollers (like they received from you) to give away. Encourage them to think of someone to give it to who would not be expecting it.

Enrichment for Older Children: Paying Your Tithe

Needed: Miniature marshmallows

Give each child ten small marshmallows and put a sign in the middle of the table with the word *God*. Before we can have our marshmallow snack, we need to give one-tenth of our marshmallows to God. Does anyone know how many marshmallows each one of us should give? Out of each group of ten, the Bible says we are to give one. There is a special word for this. Giving one-tenth of what we earn to God is called a tithe.

All the way back in the first book of the Bible, Genesis, we read about tithing. The tithe was given to the priests at the temple. It was used to take care of the temple and the priests, to feed people who were hungry, and to take care of orphans and widows. When God's people gave part of their money, crops, and belongings, it was one way they could show how dedicated they were to God and to let God know that they were thankful for everything they had. God is most interested in our reason for giving. He wants us to give generously because our hearts are glad to be his children.

The nine marshmallows you have left are ones you get to use however you want. Do you have any ideas?

Memory Verse: 2 Corinthians 8:5 ICB

And they gave in a way that we did not expect: They first gave themselves to the Lord and to us. This is what God wants.

Alternate Version (New King James)

And not only as we had hoped, but they first gave themselves to the Lord, and then to us by the will of God.

December 4, 2005

The Sermon on the Amount
By Vicki Wiley

Scripture
2 Corinthians 8:1–13

Lesson Aim
Children will be challenged to serve God by serving others.

Life Skill
Children will realize that God wants to be our top priority and serving others our second.

Bible Lesson: The Sermon on the Amount
Needed: Twenty dollars and a jar full of pennies and other coins. Be sure the coins add up to more than twenty dollars.

Show the twenty-dollar bill and the jar to the kids. Say: Which do you think is more money? (Let them guess, but most will say the $20.)

Say: Actually, the jar has more money in it! Lots of people gave me a little bit of change, and when I put it all together, I had a lot of money.

That's how it is in the church. The church needs lots of people to give the money they can give, and when it is put together, we have a lot of money—enough to have a ministry here in _____ Church.

In the Old Testament a system for giving is taught. It is called a "tithe." A tithe is 10 percent of the money you have. So if you have twenty dollars and you give a tithe on that, you will give two dollars. Lots of people use that system when they decide how much money to give to God.

Giving to God means more than giving money. What else can you give to God? (your time, your skills) God wants us to give him our time. How can you do that? (We can come to church. We can help our teachers. We can take time to pray. We can read the Bible.)

God does not tell us exactly how much to give to him, but God does want us to give our best!

 Song Suggestions

Believin' On by Jana Alayra from "Believin' On" (Montjoy Music 2002)

Little Is Much by Mary Rice Hopkins from "15 Singable Songs" (Big Steps 4 U 1988)

Faith Will Do by Dean-o from "You Got It All" (FKO Music, Inc. 1997)

God's Power Songsheets published by CEF Press, P.O. Box 348, Warrenton, Mo. 63383

 Craft for Younger Children: Giving Bank
Needed: Small jars (baby food jars works great) with slit cut in the lid for money, stickers to decorate jars.

Say: Let's make a bank to help us save our money. Each Sunday you can bring some of your money to church to give to God.

Show children how to decorate their jar. Talk about the importance of giving to God while they work.

 Craft for Older Children: Giving Our Best Poster
Needed: Construction paper, markers, pictures of kids from magazines, and plastic money.

Write *Give Our Best* across the top of the paper prior to class.

Say: Giving our best can be fun. Let's make a poster to remind us that God wants us to give our best to him.

Instruct children to think of ways that they can give their best to God. Let them draw a picture or paste plastic coins and pictures on their paper to show how they choose to give their best.

Snack: Money Muffins

Needed: Peanut butter (check for allergies) and English muffins.

Let children spread peanut butter on the English muffin and create a large "coin."

Say: Today we are going to talk about money. What kind of money does your "coin" look like? Some look like pennies; some look like money from another country. We all need money, no matter where we live, and we all give a part of our money to God.

Memory Verse: 2 Corinthians 8:5 ICB

And they gave in a way that we did not expect: They first gave themselves to the Lord and to us. This is what God wants.

Alternate Version (New King James)
And not only as we had hoped, but they first gave themselves to the Lord, and then to us by the will of God.

Memory Verse Activity: Buckets of Pennies!
Needed: Two buckets of pennies and two empty buckets. You'll need twenty pennies for each child. Make two lines of masking tape on the floor four feet apart.

Form two pairs. Have each pair select a thrower and a catcher. Have partners stand across from each other on the taped lines. The catcher on each team holds the empty bucket. The thrower on each team digs into the penny bucket and tosses as many pennies into the empty bucket as possible in thirty seconds.

Play high-excitement music as the children play. Have the observers cheer while the clock is ticking. Play several rounds of this game.

When the last pairs have played, give each child twenty pennies. Say the verse together and talk about what a tithe is.

Prayer Focus
Dear God, thank you for all that you give us. Please help us to give back to you. Amen.

December 7, 2005

Master and Commander, Midweek
By Vicki Wiley

Scripture
Luke 5:4–12

Lesson Aim
Children will understand a reason for obeying Jesus.

Life Skill
Children will learn to obey Jesus in all areas of their life.

Bible Learning Activity for Younger Children: Fishing for Fish or People
Needed: Pictures of fish and fishermen.

Say: Have you ever gone fishing? (Let children discuss.) Have you ever caught a fish?

In Bible times there were many fishermen. Some of Jesus' disciples were fishermen. What do fishermen do? If your job is to be a fisherman, what would you do? How would you feel if someone told you that you were going to now catch people instead of fish?

Bible Learning Activity for Older Children: What Did the Fishermen Do?
Gather several Bible dictionaries, encyclopedias, or books about life in Bible times together. Have the children do research on the life of fishermen during the time of Jesus. This will help them understand the context of this story.

Enrichment for Younger Children: Catching People!

Say: If you were going to catch people, what would you do? What "bait" could you use? (Be nice. Give them something.)

Catching people is sort of like making friends. When we make friends, they listen to what we say; they like to be with us. Jesus wants us to catch people so that they will want to be with us so that they can learn about Jesus!

Enrichment for Older Children: Best Friends

Needed: Fish shapes cut from paper. Cut each fish into two parts and give both parts to a child. Let each child give one half to another child.

Say: Fishing for people is easier when we are friendly. When we are friendly, people want to be with us. Today we are going to fish for people. Give someone else half of your fish and say, "I love Jesus, and Jesus loves you!"

Memory Verse: Luke 5:10 ICB

Jesus said to Simon, "Don't be afraid. From now on you will be fishermen for men."

Alternate Version (New King James)
And Jesus said to Simon, "Do not be afraid. From now on you will catch men."

December 11, 2005

Master and Commander
By Ivy Beckwith

Scripture
Luke 5:4–12

Lesson Aim
Children will understand a reason for obeying Jesus.

Life Skill
Children will learn to obey Jesus in all areas of their life.

Bible Lesson: Master and Commander
Needed: A small fishing net, a picture of a nativity scene.

Hold up the net. Ask: Does anyone know what this is? (Allow time for several responses.) People use this to help them catch fish. In Bible times many fishermen used large fishing nets to help them catch all the fish they needed. Our story today is about a fisherman Jesus helped because the man chose to obey him.

The fisherman's name was Simon. Jesus was walking by a lake teaching people about God. He saw several fishermen washing and mending their fishing nets. This meant they had finished fishing for the day. Jesus got into the boat that belonged to Simon. He asked Simon to take the boat out a little ways into the water. Simon did as Jesus asked, and Jesus was able to teach the large crowd of people from Simon's boat.

When Jesus finished teaching the people, he told Simon to take the boat further out on the lake. And he told him to put the nets down for fishing. Now this was not the time of the day the fishermen usually fished. They usually fished at night. So Simon thought this request was a little unusual. Maybe he thought Jesus didn't know too much about fishing. But, he said to Jesus, "Master, we've fished hard all night and we didn't catch anything." But

Simon didn't stop there. Even though he wasn't sure about Jesus' request, he knew there was something about Jesus that compelled him to obey, to do what Jesus said. He finished by saying, "But because you say so, I will let down the nets."

Now I'm not going to tell you how the story ends. I'm not going to tell you whether Simon caught any fish. You can find the story in your Bible and read the ending. I'm not going to tell you because it really doesn't matter whether Simon caught any fish. What was really important was that Simon obeyed Jesus. Even though he may have thought Jesus' request was a colossal waste of time, something about Jesus gave Simon no choice but to obey Jesus. Simon called Jesus "Master," and a master is someone the servant must obey.

Hold up the picture of the nativity. Say: We're not too many days away from Christmas, which I'm sure you are all really excited about. What does this picture remind us that we celebrate at Christmastime? (Allow time for several responses.) At Christmas we talk about the birth of the baby Jesus. And we celebrate that God came to earth as a human being just like us. But we don't want to forget that Jesus grew up and called all sorts of different people, just like Simon, in this story to follow and obey him. And just like Simon, these people knew they needed to do what Jesus said. And do you know what? Just like he did with Simon, Jesus asks us to obey him, to do what he says.

What are some ways Jesus asks us to obey him? (Allow time for several responses.) Yes, Jesus wants us to love others. Jesus wants us to be generous. Jesus wants us to love him and love God. And because Jesus is God, we must do what he says.

♪ **Song Suggestions**

It's Jesus Love by Dean-o from "Game Face" (Biblebeat Music 2003)

Wrap It All Up by Mary Rice Hopkins from "Mary Christmas" (Big Steps 4 U 1993)

Glory by Mary Rice Hopkins from "Mary Christmas" (Big Steps 4 U 1993)

O, Come Let Us Adore Him Traditional Carol

Silent Night Traditional Carol

Craft for Younger Children: The Master Fisherman
Needed: Fish shapes cut from colored paper, the same number of each color, each with a paper clip attached; a "fishing pole"—a stick with string attached and a magnet attached to the end of the string; blue construction paper; glue sticks.

Say: Today we are going to go fishing! Let's see what you can catch! Let children "catch" fish with the fishing pole.

After all the fish are caught, let children sort the colors of fish and glue them onto the "water" (blue construction paper) to make a picture.

Say: In Bible times Jesus had many followers who were fisherman. Fishermen catch fish, just like you did today!

 Craft for Older Children: Fishers of Men
Needed: Net bags like those that onions come in or use netting from a fabric store, small people-shaped crackers or cut small people shapes from craft foam or construction paper.

Show children how to put "people" into the net. Staple a paper on top of the net and write, "Fishers of Men," across the top.

Snack: Fishy Snack

 Needed: A variety of fish snacks—gummy type, cracker type, cookie type.

Say: These are all fishy snacks. In Bible times Jesus was often with fishermen, and they often ate fish!

Let children choose the snacks they want to eat!

Memory Verse: Luke 5:10 ICB

Jesus said to Simon, "Don't be afraid. From now on you will be fishermen for men."

Alternate Version (New King James)
And Jesus said to Simon, "Do not be afraid. From now on you will catch men."

Memory Verse Activity: Fishers of Men
Needed: Simple fish shapes cut from paper with a paper clip on each one. Write one word of the verse on each fish. Use a dowel rod "fishing pole" with a magnet attached to a string on the end.

Put the fish shapes on the floor with the words up so the kids can see them. Say the verse together one word at a time and "catch" the word/fish as you say the word. When all fish are caught, say the verse together again.

Prayer Focus
Dear God, thank you for all you do for us. Please help us, as we become fishers of men. Help us to serve you by serving others. Amen.

December 14, 2005

Worshiping the Trinity at Christmas, Midweek
By Vicki Wiley

Scripture
Exodus 20:1, 2

Lesson Aim
Children will gain a better understanding of the Trinity.

Life Skill
Children will understand that there are three parts to God.

Bible Learning Activity for Younger Children: Three in One!
Needed: An apple, a knife.

Cut the apple into halves. See the different parts of the apple? What are they? (peel, seeds, fruit) Are all the parts the same? (no) Do they all belong to the apple? (yes)

God is like that too; there are three parts of one God: the Father, the Son, and the Holy Spirit.

Bible Learning Activity for Older Children: Three in One
Needed: Raw egg and hard-boiled egg.

Say: An egg has three parts—the yoke, the white, and the shell. Three parts make one egg. The Trinity is similar: God the Father, God the Son, and God the Spirit. Together they form one God.

Break the egg and let the kids see the three parts; cut the hard-boiled egg into halves, and let the kids see the three parts.

Enrichment for Younger and Older Children: The Trinity

Needed: Food coloring (three different colors in powder form from a cake decorating shop) or alternate idea: three different color/flavors of powered drink mix, three glasses, jar of water, sticky tape.

Stick small pieces of double-sided, sticky tape to the inside bottoms of three glasses. Put a little food coloring on each piece of tape.

Show a jar of clear water and say: There is one God, represented by the water in this jar, who is made up of three different persons—Father, Son, and Holy Spirit.

As you talk, pour some water into your three glasses to produce the three different colors. Say: What did I put into this glass? You are right. In each glass there is a special color and some water.

The Trinity is not about colored water, but it is all about three parts of the same thing. God is Father, Son, and Holy Spirit. There are three parts to one great God.

Memory Verse: Exodus 20:1–3 ICB

Then God spoke all these words: "I am the Lord your God. I brought you out of the land of Egypt where you were slaves. You must not have any other gods except me."

Alternate Version (New King James)

And God spoke all these words, saying: "I am the LORD your God, who brought you out of the land of Egypt, out of the house of bondage. You shall have no other gods before Me."

December 18, 2005

Worshiping the Trinity at Christmas
By Eric Titus

Scripture
Exodus 20:1–3

Lesson Aim
Children will gain a better understanding of the Trinity.

Life Skill
Children will understand that there are three parts to God.

Bible Lesson: Worshiping the Trinity at Christmas

Preparation: A mailbox (a shoebox with a "door" cut in it and covered with paper will do); three cards in envelopes. The cards are handmade (or computer made) and should be elaborate and attractive. The first card should have a large bill (it can be play money) and say: "Christmas is a time when we all think about money. I am sending you money since that is what you should think about at Christmas. Merry Christmas, Mr. G. R. EED."

The second card will say: "Christmas is all about the things we get, so I'm sending you a great big present; it will bring the true meaning of Christmas to you. Merry Christmas, Sally Stuff." For the second card, you will need a large wrapped box and someone to make the delivery to you.

The third card says: "For God so loved the world that he sent his only Son. Merry Christmas, I love you. God the Father, Son, and Holy Spirit."

Ask: Do you all like Christmas as much as I do? It's great, isn't it? What do you like about Christmas? Yes, those are all great things, and I like some of those too. Do you know what else I like about Christmas? The mail—isn't it fun to get mail? I like getting Christmas cards. I brought a mailbox with me. Let's look inside to see what kinds of cards I got. (Reach in and pull out the "greed" card.) This card is from Mr. G. R. EED. It says: "Christmas is a time when we all think about money. I am sending you money since that is what should think about at Christmas. Merry Christmas, Mr. G. R. EED." Well, what do you think about that? Should my Christmas be all about money like G. R. says? Shall we look at another?

Oh look, this is from my old friend Sally Stuff. What a great-looking card. Sally says, "Christmas is all about the things we get, so I'm sending you a great big present; it will bring the true meaning of Christmas to you. Merry Christmas, Sally Stuff." (At this time a volunteer should call out "special delivery from Sally Stuff" and bring the present to you). Wow, I bet Sally Stuff sent me something really great. Doesn't this present look beautiful? Maybe my Christmas should be about presents, I mean this looks pretty special, doesn't it?

Should we open the third card? "For God so loved the world that he sent his only Son that the world might be saved. Merry Christmas, I love you: God the Father, Son, and Holy Spirit." That's a wonderful message, isn't it? It means that God sent his Son into the world to save us. Maybe that's what we should think about at Christmas!

There are a lot of things that could become more important to us at Christmas than God. Maybe money like Mr. G. R. EED says, or things like Sally Stuff says. But God says that he has to be the most important thing in our lives and that we aren't supposed to have any other god than God. At Christmas it can be easy to forget God because of all the presents, lights, and busy people. But let's remember that last card, with that wonderful message: God gave us the greatest gift of all by sending his Son into the world to save us. If we remember that, we will keep God in first place at Christmas.

Prayer

Dear God, we thank you that you are our only God. Help us always to keep you in first place at Christmas and everyday of our lives. Amen.

 Song Suggestions

The Best Gift by Mary Rice Hopkins from "Merry Christmas" (Big Steps 4 U 1990)

Silent Night Traditional Carol

Treasure of My Heart by Jana Alayra from "Jump into the Light" (Montjoy Music 1995)

It's Jesus Love by Dean-o from Game Face (Biblebeat Music 2003)

Craft for Older and Younger Children: Snow Globe
Needed: Baby food jar, small plastic Christmas toys (from cake decorating section of store), silver or white glitter (or small beads), corn syrup (or mineral oil), super glue.

Show children how to glue the plastic figurines to the inside of the jar lid. Wait for the glue to dry.

Fill the jar almost to the top (leave a little space) with corn syrup. Then add the glitter or beads. Put the lid on the jar and glue it around the edges (to make sure it's sealed). Let it dry.

Flip it over, and your snow scene is right-side up! Shake it to see the blizzard!

Snack: Three in One Pizza

Needed: English muffins, pizza sauce, and grated cheese

Show children how to make simple pizzas. Cook for two minutes or until the cheese melts.

Say: What is this? (a muffin!) No, its just sauce. (no!) Or is it just cheese (no!) When all three things are together it is pizza! It is the same with God. God has three parts, but he is still the only God we should ever worship.

Memory Verse: Exodus 20:1–3 ICB

Then God spoke all these words: "I am the Lord your God. I brought you out of the land of Egypt where you were slaves. You must not have any other gods except me."

Alternate Version (New King James)
And God spoke all these words, saying: "I am the LORD your God, who brought you out of the land of Egypt, out of the house of bondage. You shall have no other gods before Me."

Memory Verse Activity: No Other Gods!

Needed: Toys that can be stacked into a statue.

Say: What is this? It is a pretty silly pretend idol. Some people worship things just like this. Let's read this verse about it.

Read the verse and say together several times. Knock down the idol!

Prayer Focus

Dear God, we thank you for all the parts of you—the Father, the Son, and the Holy Spirit. Help us to worship you well this Christmas season. Amen.

December 21, 2005

Listen to the Angels, Midweek
By Vicki Wiley

Scripture
Luke 2:10, 11

Lesson Aim
Children will understand what angels are and what their place is.

Life Skill
Children will begin to assimilate into their thinking the true meaning of Christmas.

Bible Learning Activity for Younger Children: Angels Afraid!
Appoint one person to be the angel. Play a form of tag, but the "angel" will tag people saying to them, "Do not be afraid."

End the game when all have been tagged.

Say: In the Bible people sometimes saw angels. When they did, the angels always said, "Be not afraid."

Ask: Why do you think they said that? Would you be afraid if you saw an angel?

Bible Learning Activity for Older Children: Where the Angels Appeared
Needed: A concordance or topical Bible to find all the biblical references to angelic visitation. Have the children look these up in their Bibles.

Ask: What is an angel like? What is an angel's job? Why does God need angels?

Say: God made angels so they could announce things and protect us. Let's thank God for angels!

Enrichment for Younger Children: Angels Appearing

Needed: Pictures of angels or other forms of angel artwork (ornaments, statues).

Show the angels to the children and ask: What does an angel do? Why do we need angels?

Get all their ideas and let them discuss angels as long as they wish. Assure them that angels protect them.

Enrichment for Older Children: Be Not Afraid!

Needed: The list from the Bible Learning Activity of biblical references to angels or use this list:

Personal angel: Acts 12:11, 15

Role of guardian angels: Psalm 91:9–12; Exodus 23:20[1]

Angel subdued lions: Daniel 6:22

Gabriel, Daniel: Daniel 9:20, 21

Ministry following temptation: Matthew 4:11

Children's angels: Matthew 18:10

Angelic birth announcements: Luke 1:5–38

Frightened by angel: Luke 1:11, 12

Gabriel's two assignments: Luke 1:11–38

Firstborn's name given by angel: Luke 1:13

What is something angels often say to people when they see them? (Be not afraid!) Why do you think they say this? Do you think they are scary?

Memory Verse: Luke 2:10, 11

The angel said to them, "Don't be afraid, because I am bringing you some good news. It will be a joy to all the people. Today your Savior was born in David's town. He is Christ, the Lord."

---

1. Ken Anderson; illustrated by John Hayes, *Where to Find It in the Bible [computer file]*, electronic ed., *Logos Library System*, (Nashville: Thomas Nelson Inc., 1997), © 1996 by Ken Anderson.

Alternate Version (New King James)

Then the angel said to them, "Do not be afraid, for behold, I bring you good tidings of great joy which will be to all people. For there is born to you this day in the city of David a Savior, who is Christ the Lord."

December 25, 2005

Listen to the Angels
By Ivy Beckwith

Scripture
Luke 2:10, 11

Lesson Aim
Children will understand what angels are and what their place is.

Life Skill
Children will begin to assimilate into their thinking the true meaning of Christmas.

Bible Lesson: Listen to the Angels
Needed: Several representations of angels (pictures, Christmas decorations).

Show the children the various angels. Ask: What do angels do? (Allow time for several responses.) We find angels appearing in many Bible stories. Usually their job is to bring some kind of message from God to human beings.

At Christmastime we see angels almost everywhere we turn. Why do you think that is? (Allow time for several responses.) Yes, it's because angels play a big role in the story the Bible tells us about the birth of Jesus.

The Bible tells us that at the time Jesus was born shepherds were out in the fields around Bethlehem watching their sheep. It was probably pretty quiet out in the country where the shepherds and the sheep were. Maybe a few of them were even nodding off, beginning to fall asleep. All of a sudden an angel appeared to them. How do you think the shepherds felt when they saw the angel? (Allow time for several responses.) The Bible tells us the shepherds were terrified; they were really scared. But the angel told them not to be scared because he had brought them good news about the Savior being born in Bethlehem. And the angel told the shepherds where to find the Baby. Then all of a sudden many angels appeared before the shepherds. And they praised God for sending Jesus to earth.

Now who can tell me what a savior is? (Allow time for several responses.) It's a person who comes to rescue us from something dangerous that could hurt us very badly. And that's just what Jesus came to do. Without Jesus human beings are in danger of living the kind of life that could hurt us. But if we decide to follow Jesus, he will help us live a life of a friendship with God, and this is the way human beings were created to live.

The angels in the story knew how special this newborn Baby was. They wanted the shepherds to know how special that baby was too. And who knows the rest of the story? What did the shepherds do after the angels appeared to them? (Allow time for a response.) That's right; the shepherds went off to see Jesus, and then they told other people about what they had seen and heard. Not only did they tell other people about Jesus, but they worshipped God too. The Bible tells us they praised God for all they had seen and heard about Jesus.

Probably a real angel won't come to any of your houses this Christmas, but we can still celebrate the message the angels brought to the shepherds and the rest of the world. We can be just as excited as the shepherds were that Jesus came to earth to be the Savior. And like the shepherds, this Christmas we can tell other people about Jesus and praise and thank God for sending Jesus to us.

 Song Suggestions

It's Jesus Love by Dean-o from "Game Face" (Biblebeat Music 2003)

Wrap It All Up by Mary Rice Hopkins from "Mary Christmas" (Big Steps 4 U 1993)

Glory by Mary Rice Hopkins from "Mary Christmas" (Big Steps 4 U 1993)

O, Come Let Us Adore Him Traditional Carol

Silent Night Traditional Carol

Craft for Younger Children: Christmas Light
Needed: Small jar, old Christmas cards, small votive candle.

Let children cut pictures from the cards and glue on the jar. Place the candle in the jar.

Say: This is a special Christmas candle. When we light it today, we will remember that Christmas is all about Jesus, the light of the world!

Craft for Older Children: Glitter and Sugar Ornament
Needed: Christmas cookie cutters, 1/2 cup sugar with 1 teaspoon of glitter added. Stir in 1 teaspoon of water.

Let children press mixture into cookie cutter. Let mixture dry for 1/2 hour.

Makes four ornaments.

Snack: Christmas Trees!

Needed: Green icing, pointed ice cream cones, decorations.

Show children how to make a Christmas tree snack by icing and decorating the inverted cones.

Say: A Christmas tree is a tradition that was begun around the time of Martin Luther a long, long time ago. We still have Christmas trees today!

Memory Verse: Luke 2:10, 11
The angel said to them, "Don't be afraid, because I am bringing you some good news. It will be a joy to all the people. Today your Savior was born in David's town. He is Christ, the Lord."

Alternate Version (New King James)
Then the angel said to them, "Do not be afraid, for behold, I bring you good tidings of great joy which will be to all people. For there is born to you this day in the city of David a Savior, who is Christ the Lord."

Memory Verse Activity: Touched by an Angel
Needed: Whiteboard with verse written on it.

Say the verse together. Then appoint an "angel" who will go to each child and say the verse as she/he touches each child's hand. Continue saying the verse until each person has been touched.

Prayer Focus
Dear God, thank you for this very special day. It's Christmas! Thank you for your son, and please help us to honor him today. Amen.

Feature Articles

Children's Perceptions of God

By Karl Bastian

Jean Piaget was a pioneer in studying the developmental stages children pass through as they develop as moral persons. Piaget had a gift of crafting questions which would be answered differently by children of different ages, thereby revealing insights into how they think and how they arrived at the answers they gave.

While Piaget's studies were not religious at their core, or in purpose, there are important ramifications to Christian education. After all, teaching the way that "is good and right" goes back to the Old Testament (1 Sam. 12:23 ICB). Also, 2 Chronicles 6:27 ICB says that we are to "teach them the right way to live." At the core of Christian education, after preaching the gospel, is training people to live for God (Ex. 18:20; Deut. 4:9; 5:31; 6:7; 11:19; 1 Kin. 8:36).

But to what level, or what depth, are children able to understand religious concepts? At how young an age can we begin to instruct children about God and his attributes? William Hendricks, in his book *A Theology for Children* (Nashville: Broadman, 1980), compares religious education (theology) to mathematical education, when he notes that "the argument for modern math suggests that children learn elementary principles in their formative years which they can relate to and build upon when they come to 'higher math.' This will enable the child to use both elemental and sophisticated forms of mathematics all through life" (p. 12). The same seems to be true of Christian education or moral education. Early concepts of God are later built upon and added to. One analogy is that of young children learning the letters of the alphabet and their sounds long before they can appreciate their use in forming words, then sentences, and ultimately creative or profound thoughts.

Long before children can contemplate the deeper concepts of God or his attributes, we can begin to provide them with the spiritual "alphabet." The importance of laying a correct and helpful spiritual foundation for young children is critically important. As Hendricks later adds, "Relearning theology is as bad as relearning to play the piano. There is not one musical scale for children and another for adults. There is only one basic musical scale, and it must be mastered first in simple terms before it can be used in complicated patterns" (p. 13). The challenge, then, is to determine what that "basic scale" is as it relates to God and to religious education.

In order to determine what the religious concepts of children are on the very general subject of God, I prepared the following assignment for the children in my local church ministry. I created an optional essay contest, in which the children were invited to write on just a few pages their answer to the question: Who is God? What is He like? What does He do? These three questions were offered as a suggestion, but they were given freedom to address the concept or person of God in any manner they chose. About 25 percent took the offer and returned results. The submissions that were turned in do shed some insight into the concept of God as found in different ages of children. Here is a summary of the results, broken down by age:

First Grade

First graders were allowed the help of parents in writing but, hopefully, not in content.

General descriptions of God—"God is loving, and God is a very good and nice King."

Visual descriptions—"God wears a white robe. He also wears a blue sash and sandals."

Activities very parent-like—"He watches us to see if we are acting good or bad."

Many first graders chose to draw pictures, such as a colorful heart, or pictures of Jesus doing things.

Second Grade

Growing understanding of the attributes of God—Getting beyond "loving and nice" to "holy, forgiving," "sees everything and knows everything."

Sense of a future rather than just temporal traits—"He answers our prayers. ... He is preparing a place for us in heaven." Another wrote: "The award for dying is meeting God. We live because He wants us to know a little bit about Him before we meet Him."

Physical attributes sometimes still attributed to God—"Nobody knows what God looks like, but ... I think He can run real fast. I think He looks like He's really bright."

Able to repeat teachings learned, even if not fully understood—"God is ... Father, Son, and Holy Ghost. The beginning and the end. He owns heaven."

Growing understanding of God's power— Miracles are things you never thought could happen. God makes miracles because He knows we want them to happen and He doesn't want to disappoint us."

The problem of evil—"God lets bad things happen to us so that we know what it feels like ... If things go bad, we pray and He will make it better. Even if things are going well, we should remember to pray and say, 'Thank you for this wonderful time.'"

Third Grade

Growing understanding of the need for others to know God—"Jesus is my Savior. Is He yours?"

Impact of belief in God on daily life—"He wants you to be honest. And obey the Ten Commandments. But mostly He wants you to believe in Him. When you believe in Him, He will always forgive you, and you will not have to worry."

Repeat of general descriptions and look to the future—"If you pray, God will help you through tough times. If you do good deeds, someday God will reward you. Someday God will come back."

Fourth Grade

Essays begin to take on better form, as more writing is done in school. Introductory paragraphs and conclusions appear.

Repeat of things seen before but with more details—"He helps me through rough decisions like when I have to pick what's right or what is wrong. ... God teaches me through the Bible."

Evidence of personal relationship with God—"After the past few years I've been a Christian, God has made a big difference in my life."

Much more use of Scripture in answers—"He is my stronghold, my shield, and my horn of salvation. Found in Psalm 18."

Expression through poetry—"Here is a poem I wrote about God.

> God, God He's our man!
> If He can't do it, nobody can.
> So let's go on and see the Lord,
> And praise Him, praise Him,
> Shout His name forever!

Starting to ask abstract questions—"Here are some of the questions I have wondered about for a long time. ... How can something have no beginning and no end?"

Understanding of sovereignty—"God is the Creator of the earth. God is the one and only God. He decides what happens to you. ... If we didn't have God, we wouldn't be here."

Fifth Grade

The true size and scope of the subject becoming more clear—"This essay is very difficult to write because to explain God in such a short page is impossible. I'll try to explain as much as I can about our awesome and amazing God."

Very clear understanding of the gospel—"God's Word tells us that everyone needs to be forgiven from their sins. In Romans 3:23, it says, [quoted]. God is fair. In the Bible it says that at the end of the world He will decide who goes to heaven and who does not. If you trusted that Jesus died on the cross for your sins and asked Him into your heart, then your name will be written in the 'Book of Life' [goes on in great detail].

Understanding of need to learn even more—"Since God left us His Word, I can learn and study more about Him."

One boy took a unique approach to the essay: "On these questions, ... I think that these 160 different attributes of God will best answer all three of these questions: [list of 160 attributes of God!].

Another unique approach (much less technical than the preceding) was to describe God in tangible, poetic ways: "God is a warm fuzzy blanket on a cold day. God is cold water with ice in it on a hot day. ... God is ... hopefulness when you are hopeless. ... Fresh bread from the oven when you are hungry ... good news after you've heard the bad. ... God can bring happiness to the saddest person."

From this limited research we can draw some limited conclusions. Obviously, some children developmentally could be ahead or behind of the grade they are enrolled in, but some patterns can be seen.

At the lower elementary grades, God is seem as similar to a parent. Adjectives such as *loving* and *nice* are heard often in relation to God as well as His expectation of good behavior. The gospel message tends to be more of a works salvation as in every area of life children are constantly being instructed on how to behave. It is only natural, and expected, that God, too, would have some instructions on behavior.

As children reach middle elementary, they begin to realize that God is more than just a loving force that protects and provides and requires good behavior. They begin to see that God can have a personal impact on their life. They also begin to notice that not everyone obeys God or even necessarily believes in Him. They start to understand that they can choose how they are going to respond to God. They also begin to see the dark side of the subject of God. Hell becomes more real, as well as the need of others to learn about and accept God.

By upper elementary, children have a pretty good foundational understanding of God (if they have grown up in the church; if not, their understanding will reflect the popular culture's view of God). They are beginning to ask good questions about both the nature of God and the problems of the world. They can start to see the apparent problem of evil. They are willing to challenge what they have learned and would like to come to the same conclusions on their own.

The ramifications for Christian education are important. At every age children can be taught the gospel message and invited to receive Christ, but our focus can be tailored to each age. Younger children need to be assured of God's love and care and that they need to obey God. Middle elementary need to be challenged to invite friends to church and to tell them about God. Upper elementary children can be challenged, in addition, to study the Bible and about God on their own. They can be challenged to make life decisions about how they are going to live and the things they will pursue in life.

The other application to a study such as this is the importance of teachers to evaluate their teaching not on what they have said to the children but on what the children say back reflecting what they have learned. These essays contained some surprises: ("If you are good enough, God might let you into heaven.") We need to make an effort to measure the learning of the children in our ministry—not to test them, as to what they are learning, but to test ourselves as to what we are really teaching. After all, it is not what we say that matters in the end; it is what our students believe. Neither is it what they memorize that counts but what decisions they make. We are not about creating little theologians but disciples of Jesus Christ.

Foundations of Faith

By Pat Verbal

By the time many children get to the preteen class, they've spent ten years in Sunday school. They can retell most of the Bible stories and quote a list of memory verses. But do they truly understand the basic doctrines that shape their faith? Some do! Yet all preteens can benefit from a class designed to teach basic Christian truths and prepare them for baptism or church membership.

At my church students in fifth grade spend six weeks each spring in a Foundations of Faith class. The class name comes from two Scriptures. In Psalm 11:3 NIV David asks this question, "When the foundations are bring destroyed, what can the righteous do?" The apostle Paul answers David's question in 2 Timothy 2:19 NIV: "God's solid foundation stands firm, sealed with this inscription: 'The Lord knows those who are his,' and, 'Everyone who confesses the name of the Lord must turn away from wickedness.'"

Can savvy preteens, soaked in modern culture, grasp the absolutes passed down from their parents and grandparents? Can Bible concepts make a difference in their day-to-day lives? Yes! Students in our Foundation of Faith class write statements of faith that are published in the church newsletter. Here is what some of them had to say.

"God is the head of the church. He created the heavens and the earth. He died on the cross for me." Jamie Adams

"I come to church to worship God and learn more about Him. He helps me during tests at school that I'm not ready for. He is my Savior and my Father God." Ben Meyer

"God is important to me because He is Abba-Father and the head of the church. God helps me in every situation, big or small. He hears every prayer that I pray." Mallory Radford

"God was there for me when I had brain surgery when I was six years old. With His help I have made it through some tough times. He healed me so I could start school three weeks after surgery. If it wasn't for God, I would not be alive. I thank Him so much for saving my life and saving me from my sin." Ryan Dorrell

"I think this is a good class because I learned about the kingdom of God. I also learned about conversion, which is like transforming from an ugly caterpillar into a beautiful butterfly." Bethany Chatman

"I was four years old when I got saved. I was in my dad's van driving down the road, and I asked Jesus for forgiveness. I wanted to do the right thing so that I would not go to hell. I want to be baptized, and I look forward to the future living like Christ." Jared Webber

Build a Spiritual House

To help your students understand doctrine, build a "spiritual house" out of wooden or cardboard blocks

Row 1—Use three foundation blocks to symbolize what you believe about God the Father, Son, and Holy Spirit.

Row 2—On the next row of blocks, talk about what you believe about people (born in sin, have free choice, need forgiveness).

Row 3—Use blocks to represent what Jesus did for us (came as a baby, suffered and died, was resurrected).

Add as many rows as needed to connect preteens to your church's statements of faith. These might include what you believe about the Bible, Christ's second coming, heaven, healing, holy living, the Lord's Supper, or spiritual gifts. You can also insert Bible verses on each block. A cardboard roof with your church's mission statement completes the house.

Next, talk about things that can knock down our spiritual houses (or lives). Students will begin to see the dangers in accepting only part of their doctrine. This is also a good time to invite parents to discuss their struggles as preteens and their conversion experiences. Our senior pastor always stops by with words of encouragement on being part of the family of God.

Never underestimate the potential of your preteens. As you can see from the written testimonies of our fifth graders, they have a strong message for their generation. Their God is real! And with a little tutelage, young faith can stand firm!

Moment + Moment = Eternity

By Michael Bonner

Have you ever felt like time is passing you by at warp speed? My life has felt that way lately. I am not sure if it is my increasing amount of gray hair or the fact that my children are growing so quickly. It is probably a little bit of both. Whatever the reason, I have recently been overcome with a desire to grab the clock and slow it down! Moments are adding up, and I wonder if I am making the most of them.

This thought came to mind as I was reading in the Book of John, chapter 1. There we find John the Baptist preparing the way for "the one who comes after me, the thongs of whose sandals I am not worthy to untie" (John 1:27 NIV). Verse 32 NIV continues, "Then John gave this testimony: 'I saw the Spirit come down from heaven as a dove and remain on him.'" Imagine that moment—to be present at the very time God sent His Spirit to earth. I think I would want to grab that moment for sure and hold on to it forever!

The reality is that life is made up of many moments, each one important and powerful in its own way. I think we just frequently miss them. Eternity is made up of a collection of moments—some good, some not so good. The question is not really whether the moments are good or bad but whether we make the best of the moments we are given. We need to realize that every encounter we have in life—with family, friends, coworkers, and neighbors—may be our last. Our next breath is a gift from God. What we choose to do with that breath, that moment, defines who we are and what God is doing in our lives.

Think about athletes who compete at the Olympic Games. Talk about some moments! I cannot imagine the feeling an athlete would have standing on the podium during a medal ceremony, knowing he or she had earned something few people in life will ever experience. However, it really is not about just that one moment, is it? That moment was made possible because of a number of other moments that were carefully planned, executed, and played out with success.

My hope for us today is that we make the most of each moment. May we take every moment and make it count for eternity. The journey makes the destination all the sweeter. May we forever understand that "Moment + Moment = Eternity."

Some Thoughts on Children's Sermons

Considerations of Form: Construction and Delivery

By Rev. Eric J. Titus

In the church we are quick to say that children are important and have priority. I believe this is a true expression of heart and intent. Certainly many churches stretch resources in order to hire children's ministers because of this commitment to the children within the congregation. There is something, though, that I think we should think about. On Sunday morning we expect that our pastor or priest has taken a great deal of time to research, prepare, write, execute, and deliver a particular message for the congregation on each and every Sunday morning of the year. The message is for those people at that time, or at least this is the theory.

Yet in much of our homiletic practice, we state in no uncertain terms that the children in our congregations do not enjoy the same status as adults. Oftentimes the children's sermon is a last-minute item with little preparation, thought, or insight. Children's sermon books are great in so far as we use them to spark our imagination and excite us about truly preaching to children, but I fear that many of us (especially pastors!) spend too little time reflecting on the children's message. It is my hope that we will look with renewed attention at the importance of investing in our children's sermons.

Perhaps one reason we don't do a better job with children's sermons is that we don't really understand how to prepare and present them. I want to share a few of my thoughts on construction and delivery of children's sermons. Some of this may seem basic, but I have seen enough children's sermons to know that some practitioners might benefit from such a discussion.

Observations About Construction

Theology divides itself into two considerations with respect to construction: form and content. Form really asks how and in what way will we say things. Much of the church operates with the idea that form really doesn't matter much as long as the content is present. This is a big mistake, especially in regard to children's sermons (and with regard to all other questions of ministry too!). We use any tool, any means, any *form* in a variety of ministry settings with the practical aim of getting the message across. But we have spent too little time of late on what the message of the form is saying. How we say or present something says something too.

Consider the simply complex message: I love you. *I love you* constitutes the content of the message, but the form by which the message is sent conveys perhaps more of the raw message than simple content. I can say, "I love you," with a hug. I can say it to my brother, and the content will be contingent upon the form that it rests upon, and it will mean something different when I deliver the same message to my wife. I can say it with expressions, gestures, and emotion that will clearly change the meaning of the content although the content itself remains the same.

When we fail to spend time on constructing a children's sermon, if we ramble, if we do not have focus, then the content may say, "I care," but the form will clearly alter the message to "I could care less." A children's sermon then should have the following elements:

1. The sermon should capture attention at the beginning. This can be done through a number of techniques. You can begin with a question. You can focus on an object. You can start with an action without speaking. You can begin with a story.

2. Children's sermons generally should have one point. The sermon should lead to that one point, or that one point should be repeated in different ways throughout the course of the sermon.

3. The form of children's sermons should also respect the capacities of the audience. Usually a short, well-constructed children's sermon is preferable to a long, well-constructed sermon. Content will be lost when form disavows the children's developmental levels.

4. I strive to have an object integrated into the construction of the sermon. Things are inherently interesting to children and adults. More than this, an object conveys an important theological message, that is intrinsic to Christian theology; it can be seen and touched: "We declare to you what was from the beginning, what we have heard, what we have heard, what we have seen with our eyes, what we have looked at and touched with our hands, concerning the word of life" (1 John 1:1 NRSV).

We are teaching with form, that Christianity is concrete, and this is a testimony about the resurrection, and you just can't convey that theology enough. Objects also acknowledge in form that children are concrete learners. Using objects conveys that you have taken enough time, thought enough about me, the child, and demonstrates that it is important to you that the child understands this message. Only form can truly convey that message; content alone will never accomplish this.

Construction of Delivery

Form of delivery is also crucial when preaching to children. You should examine your content before you speak it.

1. Theological concepts are oftentimes abstract. They are difficult even for adult minds. But for children that operate on concrete levels, they are even more obtuse. If you say "Lamb of God" to adults (provided they have been in Christian circles long enough), they may immediately make the connection to Jesus Christ. Say it to a child, even with a good deal of context around it, and you will undoubtedly have created the image of an old man carrying a lamb in his arms. You have to scan your construction for language like that, get rid of it, or replace it. Sometimes this will be challenging, and in some cases you just have to live with it, but if you can simplify and concretize, do it.

2. I find that children's sermons are dialogical. Children love to dialogue. They learn in dialogue better than through monologue, so my delivery usually incorporates dialogical elements, allows them to respond and to respond safely (usually little right-and-wrong answers, more feeling and opinion). Listening to them demonstrates in form that I care about their heart, and hopefully it communicates that God does too.

3. You have to be sincere. Children really do have an uncanny sense of when someone is being disingenuous. You have to care and mean it. The best way I know of doing this is to get to know the children. Nothing makes children (or parents) light up with joy as knowing you know their name. They take this as a sign of importance and priority. Call them by name, and you have children and their parents hooked.

4. Speak with animation and modulation. Some children's sermons are delivered with all of the enthusiasm of a snail on its way to a salt factory. When you're animated, the message is exciting, and it's that simple.

5. Finally, always keep in mind that these are real people we're talking about here. They feel, react, think, sense, and wonder just like adults. So treat them like people. If you wouldn't talk down to your head elder, then don't talk down to them. If you wouldn't embarrass or shame an adult during worship service, then don't do this to a child. You can enter into the joy and fun children are having at the sermon, but never make them the butt of your jokes; that's just bad form. Make yourself the butt of jokes; that's acceptable, and it also conveys to the children that their pastor is human too!

Keeping Current with Kids

By Karl Bastian

Kids' interests and needs are constantly changing; staying current takes effort. It takes even more effort, if you are in leadership, to keep your teachers and volunteers current! Here are two ideas I have used.

Pass out a kid survey to every kid in your ministry. Ask some of the following questions, and add some of your own. (A sample you can photocopy and use is in the *Kidology Handbook*.) What is your favorite TV show? Who is your favorite actor? What is your favorite movie? cartoon? What do you like best about church? What don't you like about church? What do you like about your mom? dad? If you could change one thing about your mom, what would it be? (then dad) (NOTE: I will not show this to your parents!) If you were God for a day, what would you do? If you could ask God one or two questions, and He would answer you, what would you ask? What would help you read the Bible more? What would make it easier to invite a friend to church? If you were the kids' pastor for one Sunday, what would you do?

You get the idea.

Then either publish the results (minus kids' names) for the teachers, or do a game where they try to guess what kids wrote. Award prizes or points to the teachers or teams and give a prize to the winner(s). Works well at a teacher training luncheon.

Give the kid survey to your teachers and have them interview their students over the phone during the week. The answers will not be as open as an anonymous survey, but it gets the teachers in the process of keeping current with kids.

Whatever you do, take the time and make the effort to listen to the kids—not only to what they like but also to their questions, hurts, and advice for your program's success!

And then, be willing to change as a result of what you learn.

10 Ways to Build Thanksgiving Memories with Your Children

By Susan Rutledge

1. Start a Thanksgiving scrapbook. Take a family snapshot and have each member write a short message about what they did and enjoyed the most this Thanksgiving. Add to it each year.

2. Turn grocery shopping for your Thanksgiving meal into a family scavenger hunt. Instead of pitting family members against one another, keep everyone on the same team and race the clock!

3. Create place mats to use for the Thanksgiving meal. Sign, date, and laminate them for preservation; reuse every year.

4. Write and mail "I'm thankful for you because …" notes to family members and close friends.

5. Bake and decorate cookies to deliver on Thanksgiving afternoon to your fire station, to shut-ins at a nursing home, and/or to neighbors.

6. Produce a family Thanksgiving movie. Videotape each person stating what they are thankful for. Save the video and add to it year after year. Everyone will enjoy going back to watch footage from previous holidays.

7. Play board games or cards as a family on Thanksgiving afternoon. (Use your VCR and turn off the TV!)

8. Make real pumpkin pie. Remove the insides of pumpkin, roast seeds, and enjoy!

9. Dress up for Thanksgiving dinner and serve the meal on your best china.

10. Skip the Thanksgiving meal and volunteer as a family at a homeless shelter or soup kitchen.

What Does Your Heart Symbolize?

By Michael Bonner

The heart is an interesting thing, isn't it? It carries so much symbolism with it, often misunderstood symbolism. Hearts can be found on many things from a hospital billboard to a piece of candy that says, "Be Mine." You can find heart-shaped cookies, stuffed animals, dinner plates, door decorations, balloons; the list is endless. My daughter recently told me that people go to heaven by asking Jesus "into their hearts." I know that she understands that phrase, but I wonder how she ever got there in a world filled with so many variations on the "heart."

February is often filled with "hearts" because of Valentine's Day. With that in mind, what should our hearts be like? What do our hearts represent? Undoubtedly, the heart is a primary symbol for love. Scripture says, "Love the Lord your God with all your *heart*, soul and strength" (Deut. 6:5 ICB). Is that where you are today? It is a daily struggle—surrendering the will—to love in this way. Sometimes we fail at it, but that doesn't mean we quit trying. God doesn't give us that option. Scripture isn't based on suggestions but rather on commands.

Galatians 5:22 ICB tells us, "But the Spirit gives love, joy, peace, patience, kindness, goodness, faithfulness, gentleness, self-control." I doubt these thoughts were written in random order. Love precedes the others in the list and in life. If we don't have a heart that symbolizes love, it is going to be difficult to demonstrate the other things.

Here is the challenge. Let's evaluate our hearts, understanding that God knows full well what's on the inside. Are we loving God with everything we have? Are we loving our spouses in a biblical and God-honoring way? What about our kids? Would they say we have a heart that symbolizes love or one that is more like a heart balloon, which appears full from the outside but is empty on the inside?

Robert Wolgemuth, in his wonderful book *She Calls Me Daddy*, details some great tools every man needs to build up "complete daughters." The author himself admits that the principles in his book are applicable to other relationships beyond the daddy-daughter relationship. Wolgemuth suggests we recommit ourselves to "being" rather than just "doing." That's my prayer for each of us. Let's commit ourselves to *being* truly *in love* with God and then sharing that love with others around us. Who knows, they might create a Valentine's candy that says, "Be His" instead of "Be Mine!"

An Investment Guide to Special Needs Ministry: Tackling the Tough Questions!

By Pat Verbal

The Real Me
By Joe Bishop

Don't just see my legs not running;
Don't just see my hands not writing;
Don't just see my mouth not talking;
These broken pieces are not me.
See instead the light in my eyes;
See instead my loving soul;
See instead my thinking mind;
These inner pieces are the real me.

Joe Bishop has a congenital condition in which there is an absence of transverse fibers that connect the brain's two hemispheres. "My body doesn't seem to want to do what my mind tells it to do," says Joe. "My disability overrides many things in my life, but it can't rob me of my mind."[1]

My passion for investing in children like Joe began in 1990 when I became children's pastor at a church with an exciting special needs ministry. Supervising that amazing program of twenty-five children, ages two to fifteen, changed my life. When their regular teachers were absent, my husband and I substituted in the Royal Hearts class. We quickly discovered they loved doing everything a regular class does, but they needed a little more help—and more hugs, laughter, puppets, music, and fun! The class met on Wednesday evenings, allowing parents to enjoy a support group or Bible study at Rose Drive Friends Church in Yorba Linda, California.

Two years later a precious little girl with Down syndrome became a part of our family. Jessica won our hearts instantly, and the special needs ministry at church took on a new perspective. We soon realized, however, that Joe and Jessica, and children like them, don't always find a warm welcome at church.

---

1. Joe Bishop, "The Real Joe," *Exceptional Parent Magazine*, June 2001, 108.

Why Is Church Stock in Special Needs So Low?

- Ninety-five percent of people with disabilities are unchurched.
- Four out of five marriages that produce a child with disabilities end in divorce.
- Many companies (and churches) never think of hiring disabled workers to fill jobs.

According to Dr. James Dobson, in a broadcast titled "Mothers of Handicapped Children," the church as a whole is not meeting the needs of the disabled. "People who have handicaps come to churches and see the absence of anybody else like themselves," says Dr. Dobson. "They feel a wall of misunderstanding and disapproval. I really feel that the Christian church is going to have to examine its values at this point because there but for the grace of God go I or my child."

Pam and Alex attended the Christian school at Rev. Miller's church but rarely visited Sunday school. One Friday he invited the children to Christmas services and even offered to pick them up at their house. "I don't think we can come because of our brother Jerry," said Pam sadly. "Dad says if we can't go as a family, we'll all just stay home." As the children turned to get on their bus, the pastor breathed a prayer for guidance.

On Saturday Rev. Miller visited Pam and Alex's home where he met Jerry, one of the most beautiful children he'd ever seen. Jerry's big, dark eyes remained fixed on a colored piece of yarn as the eight-year-old rocked back and forth on the floor. "Jerry is autistic," explained his weary, young mother. "He lives in his own little world and can get aggressive with strangers." She told Rev. Miller that she grew up in a country church and longed for her family to worship together, but she felt trapped.

The church and school worked together that Christmas to give Jerry's family the gift of one-on-one care. They found an available classroom, recruited caregivers who rotated one Sunday each month, and held a training night with Jerry's parents. As the months passed, Jerry's mom and dad often knelt at the altar for special prayer support. Pam and Alex smiled more and talked openly about Jerry with their friends. Jerry challenged his caregivers, but they all agreed their investment was worth it.

If your church offers a special needs ministry, chances are it began with one family who touched the heart of your congregation. The question is, would families like Jerry's find a place of worship in your church?

What Should We Keep in Mind About Special Needs?

Let's talk profit and loss. What are the liabilities? Why pay attention to such a small part of our community? Doesn't ministry for those with special needs take more money, time, and resources? What's the bottom line?

If Jesus walked the earth today, what would his ministry be? Some people believe it would be with children and adults who have special needs because they are so close to God's heart. Churches that serve these families report great blessings and a growing maturity throughout their congregation. In Luke 14 Jesus said, "But when you give a big dinner, invite those who are poor. Also invite those who can't walk, the disabled and the blind. Then you will be blessed." Teachers of special needs children agree.

"When we open our arms to children with disabilities, we open our hearts to God," says Tami Segura of Celina, Texas. Tami left her singles class to serve in a new special needs department. She meets quarterly for training with the special needs team and attends events sponsored by Joni and Friends Ministries[2]. "These kids radiate Jesus and inspire me throughout my week," Tami confesses.

Special needs programs do not cost more than other ministries in the church. New buildings and playgrounds are required by law to meet the Americans With Disabilities Act. Older buildings may need some upgrades. Including those with disabilities in choir, missions, VBS, prayer groups, and parties will only appreciate the church's investments in these programs. The bottom line is this ministry can be an outreach to the community resulting in greater church growth and evangelism.

What Are the Trends Toward Serving the Disabled?

Disability Awareness Sunday—Leaders like Carol understand that their toughest job is getting their message out.

"Accessibility begins in the heart," says Carol. That sounds like a great theme for Disability Awareness Sunday.[3] Every church can conduct a special service to build awareness and focus on the sovereignty of God. Adults and children must be taught compassion for those with disabilities.

During VBS last summer at Stonebriar Community Church in Frisco, Texas, boys and girls cheered when they raised $1,600 for Wheels for the

---

2. Joni and Friends Ministry, PO Box 3333, Agoura Hills, CA 91301, www.joniandfriends.org.
3. A Disability Awareness Sunday packet of materials is available from Joni and Friends.

World.[4] Wheels for the World is a recycling program which collects, restores, and distributes wheelchairs to needy people around the world. Special needs coordinator Sue Lindahl decorated two wheelchairs with pink and blue streamers and balloons. On the first day of VBS, children saw a video about children and adults who do not have the gifts of mobility. "God touched their hearts," says Sue. "They began bringing piggy banks, soda bottles, and envelopes of money."

The Golden Hills Community Church of Brentwood, California, builds awareness with a powerful purpose statement for their disability ministry: "To make disciples within the disabled community by demonstrating Christ's love, and to equip the congregation to minister to the special needs of the disabled so that they might fellowship, worship, and serve."[5]

Another way to build awareness is to build friendships. Many children and adults with disabilities prefer to be in a regular class. When that is not possible Cheri Fuller in her book *Extraordinary Kids* suggests reverse mainstreaming.[6] Simply invite a couple of students from an age-appropriate class to join the child in his or her special needs class. This can be a positive exchange and build great friendships.

Bay Presbyterian Church of Bay Village, Ohio, offers a special needs support group. "This group is open to mothers of children with hidden disabilities," says Libby Peterson, director of Family Life Ministries. "Parents of children with hidden disabilities face some unique challenges. Many people, who observe a child with hidden disabilities (no wheelchair), assume that bad behavior is the result of bad parenting."

Family retreats and camps—Since many churches fail to build awareness, families with disabilities cling to one another at retreats and camps. "Parents described our family retreat as a bit of heaven," says Margaret Matasic, director of Joni and Friends in North Ohio.

"Unless you have someone close to you affected by disabilities, it may be difficult to imagine the enormity of the additional strain this puts families under." Margaret is quick to admit that the success of this retreat is due to

---

4. Contact Joni and Friends Ministries for more information, www.joniandfriends.org.
5. Wes and Sheryl Haystead, *How to Have a Great Sunday School* (Ventura, CA: Gospel Light, 2000), 101.
6. Cheri Fuller and Louise Tucker Jones, *Extraordinary Kids* (Colorado Springs: Focus on the Family, 1997), 230.

many people from area churches giving back to God their time, talents, and treasures. Her team plans campfire sing-alongs, inner tubing, ladies and men's groups, youth concerts, ropes courses, and wonderful worship times.

One thing that struck Sue Lindahl during the week she spent at the family camp in Texas was the number of single adult caregivers. "Many of these young single professionals take their vacation time to serve," says Sue. "That says a lot about their walk with God and depth of commitment to these deserving families."

How Does a Church Get Started?

Encourage church prayer groups to include those with disabilities as part of their weekly prayer requests. Pray for a compassionate director who feels called to lead the ministry. Recruit a special needs council to research and set policies, set an annual calendar, and plan a budget.

"We do pretty good with including those with special needs in Sunday school, but that's it," says Dr. Jim Pierson, director of the Christian Church Foundation for the Handicapped in Knoxville, Tennessee. "We don't integrate them into the life of the church." Dr. Pierson suggests five ways to train caregivers to serve the disabled.

1. Inspire them to talk to people about their disability. It won't offend them, and it will break down the wall of fear.

2. Teach proper etiquette. For example, when guiding a blind child to a chair, direct them to the side and simply tell them that the chair is on their left. They'll feel for it with their leg and slide into the seat. You don't need to be trained in all the many kinds of disabilities, just the ones that exist in your church.

3. Provide a way for caregivers to observe other qualified teachers at other churches or community centers.

4. Give them a case study. Let them get to know one child and his or her family. Encourage them to follow their student through a daily routine. This will give marvelous insights into the needs of the child.

5. Set up practice teaching events. Team caregivers together, and let one pretend to be the one with a special need. After they spend time in a wheelchair or blindfolded, ask them to critique their experience.

What's the Return on Investing in Disability Ministries?

When special needs families are treated like typical families, they draw near to, not away from, God. Sometimes they need a hug. Never grow tired of listening to or praying for these brave kids and parents. Involve the whole congregation in serving those with disabilities "as good stewards of the manifold grace of God ... that in all things God may be glorified through Jesus Christ" (1 Pet. 4:10, 11 NKJV).

"We started JOY ministry six short years ago," says director Denise Briley of Graceview Baptist Church in Tomball, Texas. "As the mom of a child with severe disabilities, I was glad that God used me and the training my son gave me. It has changed my life and the life of my family." Currently Graceview serves forty-eight families with children, youth, and adults who have disabilities. "We started with my son Clayton, a borrowed basket of toys, and a cassette player," says Denise. "God brought each family one by one. They have been able to worship together, some for the first time in years. Marriages have been saved; brothers and sisters have been involved in ministry. Moms and dads now sing in the choir and teach Sunday school. But the best thing is that people are being saved and building a relationship with Christ. I wouldn't have missed what I call the 'joy journey' for the world."

David and Mary Russell of Plano, Texas, share Denise's enthusiasm. Their daughter, Angela, is a charming three-year-old regular at Stonebriar Community Church. With undiagnosed white matter disorder, Angela can't walk, sit up alone, speak, or eat, but she is a constant joy. She's progressed in ways they never anticipated. "Our child is from God," says David. "Angela has taught us true sacrificial love, and we trust God to fulfill His plan in her life in her current state."

Investment Guide Summary
The cost of special need resources—reasonable!
The cost of special needs training—minimal!
The cost of special needs facilities—affordable!
The cost of reaching Joe, Jerry, Jessica, Clayton, and Angela—priceless!

What's Hot? What's Not?

By Gordon & Becki West

What do Furbies™, bell bottoms, Sketchers™, bleached hair, Nintendo 64™, face sparkles, carpenter's pants, "hanging" at the mall, AOL™ chat rooms, "breakaways," scrunchies, DVD machines, yo-yos, snowboarding, and Beanie Babies™ have in common? They're all fads you are probably hearing about in your preteen class.

Are these trends something we should be worried about? Or are they tools we can use to reach the older child?

Good, Bad or Neutral?

Although some fads are clearly illegal or immoral, others are simply cultural. They may annoy us, but how do we know if they're truly right or wrong? Ask yourself these questions:

- Does the fad encourage the child to pursue a worldly affluence, desiring "stuff" rather than God and His people?
- Is the child engaging in this fad in order to defy authority (especially his parents)?
- Is there anything about the fad that has anti-Christian values?

If the answer to any of these questions is yes, then the fad is getting in the way of the child's relationship with God, and, as teachers, we want to discourage involvement, rather than use it as a teaching tool.

Should Teachers Join In?

If the answer is no to all three questions, should the junior teacher join in with the fad? Should he allow Furbies™ in class? Should he talk about the latest music group?

Kids don't want a big buddy for a teacher. Always maintain your role as a discipler and role model. The older child wants a mature adult upon whom he can lean to make sense of the world. If joining in makes you one of the kids, the answer is don't.

Kids want to be understood and respected. Tolerance of amoral fads, even if they aren't your taste, can be an expression of love. Interest in what the kids like can be an expression of friendship. Becki has connected with one of her students at church by talking about the girl's collection of Beanie Babies™.

The more Becki shows interest in Susan's collection, the more Susan shows interest in the spiritual concepts that Becki is presenting in class.

Use Fads to Teach Preteens

How can fads become useful teaching tools? Here are some tips to improve your teaching of these fad-conscious kids:

To learn about fads, flip through a teen magazine or watch children's TV like *One Saturday Morning* or *TGIF* (both on ABC™), paying special attention to the commercials. Take note of inexpensive fads like yo-yos and scrunchies that you can use in your classroom for incentives.

Use acceptable fads to give you ideas for fun activities for your students.
- Have a collector's party with all the kids bringing in their collectibles.
- Use a Furbie™ to prerecord the keyword or point of your lesson and have it repeat the point for you frequently. The kids will love it!

Choose a specific fad for your class to discuss. Have preteens work together to find biblical principles to support or warn against the fad. This will liven up any classroom!
- Ask your preteens to discuss AOL™ chat rooms (where the language can get rough) or Nintendo 64™ games (many of which are very violent). Both activities could also launch a discussion on stewardship of our time or obedience to parents.
- Help your preteens learn to think biblically. Ask them open-ended questions like, "What does the Bible say about violence?" or, "Can you show me from the Bible whether there is anything wrong with Internet chat rooms?"

The issues closest to your students' hearts and consciences will quickly emerge. Be ready with several key verses to help your preteens see that the Bible does address their everyday issues.

The Most Powerful Trend of All

Finally, love your preteens in spite of their current fad obsessions. The power of love is far more attractive to juniors than any fad.

Evangelizing Today's Child May/June 2000, Junior Child.

Greasing the Wheel of Harmony:
Helping Boys and Girls Get Along in Class

By Pat Verbal

Public school districts across the country are piloting programs to create gender-based schools. Their reasoning is that both boys and girls can learn better without the tension and distraction of the opposite sex. This theory is prevalent in some church programs.

"Our junior girls enjoy their own Sunday school class," said one children's pastor. "The girls love writing in their prayer journals and doing crafts. The boys class plays more physical games and does less paper-pencil activities, but recruiting teachers for an all-boys class is harder."

Separating boys and girls is one way to address their differences, but it doesn't answer the bigger question: How can we create a sense of harmony that will prepare them to serve together in the church?

A Bumpy Ride

Gender issues have been a bumpy ride, especially since the late 1970s. The unisex movement, along with the feminists, tried to minimize male and female differences. Psychologist James Dobson makes clear that gender identity is God-given in his book, *Bring Up Boys* (Tyndale House Publishers).

"God created man in his own image, in the image of God he created him; male and female he created them" (Gen. 1:27 NIV). "For this reason a man will leave his father and mother and be united to his wife, and the two will become one flesh" (Matt. 19:4, 5 NIV). "That is the divine plan. It leaves no doubt that the Creator made not one sex but two, each beautifully created to fit with and meet the needs of the other. Any effort to teach children differently is certain to produce turmoil in the soul of a child" (p. 17).

While modern science reveals hormonal differences that affect men and women's brain activities, it's enough for children to understand that boys and girls were fearfully and wonderfully made by God (Ps. 139:14).

Today's children are busy creatures. Like mice racing around on plastic wheels, they rush to soccer, ballet, music, gymnastics, school, and church. Tension is a part of their lives, and gender conflicts that arise simply add to the friction.

As a teacher who sees these children once a week, do you wonder if you can make a difference? Yes, you can! God places in your hand a "grease can"

(OK, the Scripture calls it "oil," Ps. 23:5; 45:7) to anoint boys and girls in Jesus' name to find their uniqueness and live in harmony.

GREASE the Wheel of Harmony

G—Give children *graceful* role models.

Grace does not describe relationships between the sexes portrayed in today's media. Children need teachers who model graceful attitudes as men and woman co-teach in classrooms. When that isn't possible, invite guests speakers to bring needed balance. Don't let boys think Christianity is "sissy stuff" because all their teachers are women.

- Host career days where men and women talk about how God helps them reflect His grace on the job.
- Build your lessons around stories of godly men and women who worked together to accomplish God's mission such as Moses' brother Aaron and sister Miriam.
- Provide a lending library of biographies showing how God uses men and women throughout history such as Young Readers' Christian Library or Heroes of the Faith Series by Barbour Publishers (Christianbooks.com).

R—Help children *relate* to one another's feelings.

Children need boy friends and girl friends, but it doesn't take children long to realize that friendships can be painful. Jesus understood that when He asked us to "love each other as I have loved you" (John 15:12 NIV). Make your class a place where children develop skills that help them relate to others. Explain that being a good friend means speaking to one another with respect, keeping confidences, and admitting when you've hurt someone.

Hang a mirror in your classroom. At the bottom of the mirror tape a sign that reminds students of the Golden Rule: "Mirror, Mirror on the Wall … Am I treating others the way I want to be treated?"

Children enjoy the story of David and Goliath because most of them know a bully. Bullies are out for power. Bullying behavior by girls as well as boys—not just physical aggression but threats, teasing, name-calling, and social ridicule—must not be tolerated. The best way to "bully-proof" children is to build their self-confidence and help them make good friends. With a friend, a child can laugh about an insult and shrug it off. Without a friend, a child carries it around all day.

When boys and girls fight, help them learn to solve their own problems.

Girl: Make him stop kicking me.

Boy: Oh, stop being such a baby. I'm not doing anything to you.

Teacher: How do you think I feel when I'm trying to teach and you two keep fighting?

Girl: Upset.

Teacher: What might happen if I give the two of you all my attention.

Boy: The other children might feel left out.

Teacher: How would you feel if that happened?

Girl: Bad.

Teacher: What can you do so I won't feel upset and the other children won't feel left out?

E—Provide children with an *exciting* schedule of activities.

Boys and girls enter class excited to see one another, but avoid too much "hang out" time. Children need a structured schedule that quickly focuses on the lesson aim. If they come to class with tensions, free time may cause more distraction.

"Kim told me she liked Jeff. I promised not to tell anyone, but then Brenda came in today with a button that said Jeff + Brenda, so I told Cody to tell Jeff what Kim told me" (and on it goes).

Children love games, but too much competition pits the boys against the girls. Boos and cheers get out of hand, and class ends with name-calling: "Girls are a bunch of losers," or, "Boys are cheaters." Mix the teams up often.

"Our kids enjoy doing group projects such as a drama," says Marthe Moseley, a children's leader in Texas. "I put them in groups of two boys and two girls. I start a story and challenge them to create the ending with a skit. They learn that it takes a male and a female viewpoint to give the story dimension, and each story turns out different."

A—Teach children to *appreciate* their differences.

Boys say girls are a pain when …

- They gang up to tease you.
- They borrow things without asking.
- They get angry at you.
- They ignore you.
- They act bossy.

Girls say boys are a pain when …

- They butt into your privacy.
- They mess things up.
- They fight with you.
- They bug you to play a boring game.
- They blab your secrets.
- They play with creepy creatures.

Help children turn negative attitudes into positives ones. Make two color-ful poster collages from old pictures, magazines, cartoons, and cards. Write "Boys Are Terrific!" in the center of one and "Girls Are Amazing!" on the other. Let children cut and paste pictures that reflect interests, hobbies, sports, fashions, and the fun of being a boy or girl.

S—Encourage children to *serve* one another.

Girls are nurturing. Boys like to fix things. Use these tendencies to teach service.

One summer our church set up a Bible times village. Girls made biblical costumes and mothered the little goat we bought, naming him Gabrielle. A retired contractor helped the boys build small stools. The boys and girls worked together pitching tents. They were sad when the unit ended, but they enjoyed taking home gifts they had made for one another.

In the early church Paul and Lydia served each other as they shared the good news about God's Son, Jesus. Lydia owned her own business; she sold purple cloth, which was valuable. Lydia had heard about God and started a prayer group. When Paul met them, he told them about Jesus. Lydia believed and was baptized. She invited Paul and his friends to stay at her home while in Philippi. Because Lydia gave them her house and food, they had more time to tell others about Jesus (Acts 16:6–15,40; 17:4, 12).

Help boys and girls make a list of thing they can do to help one another tell their friends about Jesus.

E—*Equip* children to live victoriously.

"Girls in class call me names." Don't base your opinion of yourself on what others say about you. Don't overreact to a compliment or a putdown. Kids like kids who like themselves (1 Pet. 3:3, 4).

"Everyone but me has a boyfriend or girlfriend." "There is a right time for everything" (Eccl. 3:1 ICB). The time for a boyfriend or a girlfriend is not ele-mentary school. Your friends are imitating what they see on TV. Someday God will bring a special person into your life.

"A boy in my class uses bad words, and I don't know what to say." Be friendly but firm. Let him know you don't like what he is doing. Pray for him. If you are tempted to use bad words, memorize Psalm 19:14.

A Smoother Ride

What could you do in your class that would be more important than helping boys and girls minister hand in hand? While society talks about unity between the sexes, it continues to dig potholes that promise an even bumpier ride. Harmony can only be found in Jesus Christ. In him, children find *grace* to *relate* to one another in *exciting* ways and *appreciate* their differences. As boys and girls *serve* Jesus using gifts he has *equipped* them with, the church need not fear for the future of its mission.

Who You Calling a Dummy?

By Mark Thompson with Pat Verbal

As a musical ventriloquist, I'm often asked, "How do you carry on a lively conversation with puppets on each hand and not get confused?"

I tell them, "It's just the way my mind operates. I function best when I'm focused and going full speed ahead." This is a skill I treasure; however, it came with a price.

As a child, I was easily distracted, hyperactive, loud, and often annoying. I wanted to learn, but it seemed I spent more time in the principal's office than in class. I was made to write thousands of times, "I will not talk out in class." Twice a week in fifth grade I visited the district psychologist. She gave me a clicker to wear. When I disrupted my class, I had to click it. That added to my frustration! I tried hard to control myself and stop talking, but I had so much to say. In spite of my behavior, my teachers somehow managed to make me feel loved and accepted. This could only have been because of God's intervention.

One of my happiest days in childhood was when my older brother got a ventriloquist dummy and instructional record. I quickly discovered ventriloquism refocused my energies and sparked my imagination. In first grade I won a talent show and began performing at church. Pulling my dummy in my red wagon, I offered neighborhood puppet shows. Once I got a whole five dollars, which was a lot of money for a kid in the 60s. When I was nine, my picture appeared in the newspaper telling about my talents. My father was so proud, he ordered my first business cards.

I always took my dummy, Danny O'Day, to summer camp and kids' crusades. Because leaders and evangelists often invited me to share, I began to understand that my talents were gifts from God. By age eleven I played trumpet in the church orchestra. When I begged for a spinet piano for my birthday, my parents sacrificed to buy one. Within one year I was playing for the church choir. Combining all of these skills, I led my first kids' crusade by age fourteen.

Whatever I did, I attacked with 100 percent determination. Why? Because I'd learned that focusing helped me cope with what I later discovered was Attention Deficit Disorder (ADD). Not only did I cope; I excelled. In seventh grade my IQ tested high enough to accelerate me past eighth grade into ninth. I realized I wasn't a dummy after all.

Throughout my teen years I performed weekly on the Trinity Broadcasting Network. This opened doors for me to serve as a pastor for fourteen years in music and children's ministry. Since 1995, I've annually visited more than a hundred churches performing family concerts and leadership training.

My lifelong passion grew out of my disability because of the encouragement of godly parents, teachers, and friends. My father wasn't so fortunate.

My father also had problems in school. People called him a dummy because he couldn't read. Instead of finishing high school, he worked in a garden while others received a quality education. Later, when he did read, the only book I ever saw him with was the Bible. My father was bright, witty, and hard-working. He taught me great lessons about determination while living with a painful learning disability.

I'm thankful for my mentors who never gave up on a high-strung boy. Their loving guidance enabled me to serve as an ambassador for God. Today I entertain thousands and help lead people of all ages to Christ. Looking out across my audiences, I pray for children with ADD, knowing God has a special plan for their lives. In training seminars I remind teachers that students like me need classrooms with lots of interaction. When we give these kids structure and responsibility, they shine.

If you have a special child in your life, don't get discouraged. Don't dismiss him as some did my father. Help him or her search for talents and develop them for God's glory. Show them love, forgiveness, and acceptance. Believe in them and trust God to do the rest.

I'm having the time of my life. I love every aspect of this traveling ministry. I never forget the heroes who believed in me and gave me opportunities to turn my weaknesses into strengths.

Mark Thompson travels the country bringing his upbeat "Yes to Life" message to audiences of all ages. His music and video resources are used weekly by hundreds of churches. Find out more about his ministry at www.markarts.net.

I Can Do Anything?

By Gordon and Becki West

A few years ago a Hollywood movie made popular a dangerous game for early adolescents. Following the example of one of the teen stars, youth across America began lying down in the middle of busy streets while cars whizzed by on each side—all for the thrill of it!

Early adolescents experience what educational psychologists call the "personal fable." This is the condition we observe in kids who believe, "I can do anything! Nothing can hurt me."

Youth have an inadequate understanding of their personal limitations. That's why teenagers think they can take risks, like driving too fast or drinking too much, without anything bad ever happening to them. It's a normal attribute of preteens, too, but it can be a dangerous phase in their development.

Safe Adventures for Preteens

Recognize and use the older child's desire for risk and adventure. Offer controlled, safe, risk-taking opportunities in your ministries. These will attract preteens and advance their faith in the Lord while still keeping them safe. Controlled risk adventures make up one of the most quickly growing segments of the recreation industry in America, especially for adolescents.

Use these popular activities with preteens:

- *Laser tag*—Today most larger communities have local businesses that offer this fun, space-age version of tag. Large groups can rent out the whole building; smaller groups can pay per person in open sessions. Kids run through an indoor maze in the dark wearing a vest and helmet each containing laser receptors. Others attempt to hit them with laser beams, thus scoring points.
- *River rafting*—Depending on your location, rafting can be either a lazy afternoon or a white-knuckled thriller. One provides time to talk; the other, a memorable bonding experience. Either way, preteens love the water, fun, and relationships built!
- *Indoor rock climbing*—Trained safety experts at licensed gyms help your kids hook into safety harnesses and helmets before attempting to scale a manmade cliff complete with artificial rocks for finger and toeholds.

No Longer Kids, Not Quite Teens

Not all safe-risk activities need to be high-tech or expensive. Taking simple games to a new environment, even just to a nearby park, can transform a familiar activity into one that appeals to preteens, who want to maintain the security of the familiar games of childhood while enjoying the respect and freedom of the approaching teenage years.

We first discovered this while taking a group of ninety preteens to a park near our church during an evening VBS program. The make-your-own-banana-splits-in-a-rain-trough race was a dismal failure. Fifteen to twenty preteens simply could not work together to scoop out ice cream, spray on canned whipped cream, and open jars of maraschino cherries. The pressure of the race exceeded their abilities.

However, the old-fashioned childhood games (like running up and putting your head on a bat, turning around 10 times, and running back) were wonderfully successful. The kids were comfortable (safe) with the familiar games within the context of a recreational environment (the park, away from classrooms).

A Discipleship Moment

While planning these safe adventures may bring the kids in, involvement in the activities opens their hearts. Use verses like these to launch a devotional at an adventure event:

- *Matthew 18:12–14, the Lost Sheep*—This can serve as a wonderful evangelism tool for kids who just experienced a bit of lostness.
- *Mark 4:35–41, Stilling the Storm*—If Jesus could take care of the threats of nature in the lives of the disciples, can't He take care of our lives, too?

While at a camp in Southern Arizona, we found a cave at a nearby national park. The challenge of a one-mile hike, followed by scaling a few rocks and being helped down into a dark cave, proved to be a thrilling (but safe) challenge for our preteens.

Year after year, with hundreds of kids, it has also proven to be an ideal setting for a faith-building discipleship moment. Once we're inside the cave's belly, we ask the kids to turn off their flashlights. The cave is pitch black. Our city kids discover how dark the world really can be.

We read Psalm 119:105, "Your word is a lamp to my feet and a light for my path" (NIV), and we sing "Thy Word" by Amy Grant and Michael W. Smith

(Meadowgreen Music Company/Bug and Bear Music, 1984). The resulting discussion is life-changing. The kids truly understand how risky the dark world is without a faithful light to guide our steps.

Our kids are living in the midst of that dark world. Use their God-given need to take risk as a drawing card for your ministry. Allow your preteens to experience safely controlled risk to prepare their hearts. Then tell them about the God who protects us while leading us through the most exciting adventure of all—being a Christian!

Books, Baseball Bats, Ballet Slippers, Bowling Balls, and Assorted Other Extracurricular Items

By Michael Bonner

This may be stepping up on the proverbial soapbox again. You can make that call when (and if) you finish reading this article. Currently, my mind is flooded with the thoughts that come with summer—a new season, vacations, warmer weather, and changes in our schedules. At the same time it strikes me that summer does not really look like it used to when we were kids.

I remember summer time as a relaxed, fun time. We usually enjoyed a break from the hectic schedule we pursued during the school year. We were not on the go constantly, running from one camp to another, one scheduled event to the next. Now that I am "all grown up" and have kids of my own, I find that their schedule does not look like mine did as a kid. It seems so much busier and in reality probably is. I wonder, which lifestyle is better? Were those "the good old days" I experienced, or will my kids look back and recall their youthful summers in the same way I recall mine?

Our family has gone from schoolbooks, ballet lessons, and piano lessons to baseball bats, swimming lessons, and planned vacations. How about your family? Has there been a slowdown in the pace of summer, or has the frenetic pace just shifted to new things? In the book *The Hurried Child* (Perseus Publishing, 2001), David Elkind states, "The concept of childhood, so vital to the traditional American way of life, is threatened with extinction in the society we have created. Today's child has become the unwilling, unintended victim of overwhelming stress—the stress borne of rapid, bewildering social change and constantly rising expectations." I'm not sure yet, but I may be the parent of three "hurried" children!

A few weeks back my oldest daughter and I went for our annual birthday date together. We had a picnic and then went bowling. We went home, baked cookies together, and played checkers. It was perfect. Five hours of simple, unhurried, unplanned joy! We talked. We listened. We noticed birds, flowers—things there but never seen. After the evening was over, I realized the refreshing feeling of true quality time spent with my little girl. But those opportunities pass quickly. One weekend later I went to a graduation party for someone else's little girl who is going away to college in two months. That will be my little girl soon.

OK, we can now agree I'm on the soapbox! But it's worth it. Let's check our schedules. Are we parenting or chaperoning our kids through life? Are we making memories or making deadlines? Are we investing quality and quantity time in our families? We must reassess our priorities, our time commitments, and what gets the most of our attention. Where is God in the process? Books, baseball bats, ballet slippers, bowling balls—none of these are bad things. The question is, are we being overtaken by the *extra* in *extracurricular*?

Play Doh®!

By Michael Bonner

How long has it been since you've taken time to play with some good old-fashioned Play Doh? If you haven't rolled a ball of Play Doh in a while, you should try it soon. It really can be a lot of fun. Experts say it could relieve stress in your life. (Actually, experts didn't say that as far as I know, but it sure seems to work with two-year-olds!)

Play Doh comes in many colors and can be made into a number of different objects. You can squash it, smash it, splat it, turn it into pretend people, make pretend food—the options are limitless! But there is one thing about Play Doh that isn't so much fun. It is only moldable for a certain period of time and only under specific conditions. When left out for a while, it becomes dry and crusty. It can no longer be used to make fun shapes.

In many ways kids are like Play Doh. They are moldable and bendable. Their spirits can be squashed, and they can be pressed through molds and forced to become objects they really don't want to be. However, it doesn't have to be that way. The Bible says in Proverbs 22:6 NIV, "Train up a child in the way *he should go*, and when he is old he will not turn from it." If you are a parent, you have been given the supreme opportunity to assist God in shaping the life of another person. Further, as part of God's church, we have all been given the supreme opportunity to assist God in shaping lives of others as we are "the church" to all folks with whom we come in contact.

The question for us is this: How is our Play Doh? Have we let it sit too long so that it is getting dry and losing its tenderness? Life can be brief. We have no idea when the Play Doh will "dry up." Let us all be encouraged to make the most of every moment with our kids, our spouse, our families, and one another. Adults and kids alike are much like Play Doh. After all, God is still training and molding each of us in certain areas, isn't he? May we all retain his tenderness and continue to be moldable so we can be used to mold others!

Children's Ministries List

National and International Conferences and Conventions

APCE Conference
Sponsored by: Association of Presbyterian Church Educators
Contact:
> Pat Murphy, Registrar
> 100 Witherspoon St.
> Louisville, KY 40202-1396
> 1-888-728, ext. 5460
> www.apcenet.org
> Email: pmurphy@ctr.pcusa.org

Bilingual Children's Ministries University
Sponsored by: One Way Street, Inc.
Contact:
> Susan Schmidt
> One Way Street, Inc.
> P.O. Box 5077
> Engelewood, CO 80155-5077
> 303-799-2159
> www.onewaystreet.com
> Email: events@onewaystreet.com

BTI Children's Ministry Conference
Sponsored by: Bring Them In
Contact:
> Larry Hipps
> 11323 Hughes Rd.
> Houston, TX 77089
> 281-481-8770
> www.bringthemin.com
> Email: lhipps@sagemontchurch.org

Children's Pastors' Conference
Sponsored by: International Network of Children's Ministry
Contact:

    International Network of Children's Ministry
    P.O. Box 190
    Castle Rock, CO 80104

The Fellowship of Christian Magicians International Convention
Sponsored by: The Fellowship of Christian Magicians
Contact:

    Jim and Kris Austin
    435 Oak St.
    Des Plains, IL 60016
    847-296-7573
    www.fcm.org
    Email: jim@jimages.org

The International Festival of Christian Puppetry and Ventriloquism
Sponsored by: One Way Street, Inc.
Contact:

    Susan Schmidt
    One Way Street, Inc.
    P.O. Box 5077
    Engelewood, CO 80155-5077
    303-799-2159
    www.onewaystreet.com
    Email: events@onewaystreet.com

MOPS International Leadership Convention
(MOPS stands for M.others O.f P.reschoolerS.)
Contact:

    Marcy Decker, Events Manager
    MOPS International
    P.O. Box 102200
    Denver, CO 80250
    303-733-5353
    fax: 303-733-5770
    www.mops.org
    Email: info@mops.org

Promiseland Conference
Sponsored by: The Willow Creek Association
Contact:
> Nancy Gruben
> The Willow Creek Association
> 67 E. Algonquin Rd.
> South Barrington, IL 60011
> 847-765-0070
> fax: 847-765-5046
> www.promiselandonline.com

Online Networks

Childrensministry.com
> www.childrensministry.com

Children's Ministry Magazine
> www.cmmag.com

Children's Ministry Today
> 8469 Seton Ct.
> Jacksonville, FL 32244
> 909-777-3339
> www.childrensministry.org
> Email: info@childrensministry.org

Children's Pastors' Network
> 8469 Seton Ct.
> Jacksonville, FL 32244
> 909-777-3339
> www.childrensministry.org/the_network/index.htm
> Email: info@childrensministry.org

Kidology, Inc.
> 535 Andrew Lane
> Lake Zurich, IL 60047
> 847-726-9860
> www.kidology.org
> Email: tim@kidology.org

Sunday School Teachers' Network
www.christiancrafters.com

National Organizations and Associations

Association of Christian Schools International (ACSI)
P.O. Box 35097
Colorado Springs, CO 80935
1-800-367-0798, ext. 115
fax: 719-531-0716
www.acsi.org
Email: david_smitherman@acsi.org

Child Evangelism Fellowship
P.O. Box 348
Warrenton, MO 63383-0348
1-800-300-4033
www.gospelcom.net/cef

Children's Ministries of America
P.O. Box 4974
Oak Brook, IL 60522
1-888-922-0702
fax: 630-916-1140
www.childrensministries.org

Christian Educators Association International
P.O. Box 41300
Pasadena, CA 91114
626-798-1124
fax: 626-798-2346
Email: info@ceai.org
www.ceai.org

Christian Juggler's Association
    1709 West Seminary Dr.
    Fort Worth, TX 76115
    Contact: Nathan Dorrell
    1-800- 363-4410
    fax: 980-754-2750
    www.juggling.org
    Email: cja@juggling.org

The Fellowship of Christian Magicians
    7739 Everest Ct. N.
    Maple Grove, MN 55311
    763-494-5655
    www.fcm.org

The Fellowship of Christian Puppeteers
    FCP Mail Center
    107 Moore Allen St.
    Dudley, NC 28333
    919-731-2261
    www.fcpfellowship.org

For Kids Only, Inc.
    P.O. Box 10237
    Newport Beach, CA 92658
    1-888-646-9584
    www.fko.org

International Network of Children's Ministry
    P.O. Box 190
    Castle Rock, CO 80104
    1-800-324-4543
    www.incm.org

Performance Artists

Astounding Bruce Carroll
      32695 Cypress Dr.
      Springfield, LA 70462
      www.astoundingbruce.com
      Email: astoundingbruce@yahoo.com

Dean-O and the Dynamos
      BibleBeat Music
      P.O. Box 7407
      Laguna Nigel, CA 92607
      1-866-656-2328
      www.biblebeatmusic.com
      Email: deano@biblebeatmusic.com

The Donut Man and Duncan
      Rob Evans
      P.O. Box 1625
      Beach Haven, NJ 08008
      609-492-2363
      www.donutman.com
      Email: rob@donutman.com

Dr. Kaos
      311 S. Fourth Street
      St. Charles, IL 60174
      405-314-3484
      www.drkaos.com
      Email: booking@drkaos.com

Evelyn James, Storyteller
      P.O. Box 133233
      Tyler, TX 75713
      903-939-9039
      www.itellstories.com
      Email: espjames@tyler.net

For HIS Kidz
    P.O. Box 292
    Zelienople, PA 16063
    1-866-774-7469
    www.forhiskidz.com
    Email: info@forhiskidz.com

Geddy the Gecko
    John Mallory
    412 S.E. Fourth Ter.
    Dania Beach, FL 33004
    954-924-0218
    www.geddythegecko.com
    Email: geddy@geddythegecko.com

Mark Thompson, Ventriloquist
    Mark Arts, Inc.
    P.O. Box 2321
    Redmond, WA 98073
    1-800-867-6579
    www.markthompson.org
    www.markarts.com
    Email: mark@markthompson.org

Mary Rice Hopkins and Co.
    P.O. Box 362
    Montrose, CA 91021
    818-790-5805
    www.maryricehopkins.com
    Email: booking@maryricehopkins.com

Miss Pattycake
    Integrity Music Just for Kids
    www.integrity music.com

Mister Bill
    P.O. Box 3677
    Redondo Beach, CA 90277
    310-727-9877
    www.mrbillsworld.org
    Email: info@misterbill.org

Ned and Joan Way
    P.O. Box 19229
    Louisville, KY 40259
    509-361-4267
    www.NoWay.org
    Email: way@aye.net

Jeff Smith
    "God Rods"
    Salt and Light Ministries
    5105 Timbercreek Court
    Richmond, Virginia 23237
    www.saltandlightmin.org

Wendy and the James Gang
    P.O. Box 431
    Granville, OH 43023
    1-888-548-7625
    www.wendyandthejamesgang.com
    Email: david.james@livingrock.com

Products and Services Directory

Bible Games

Bible Games Company
P.O. Box 237
Fredersicktown, OH 43019
1-800-845-7415
www.biblegamescompany.com

Susan Harper "The Game Trunk"
309 Hollyhill Lane
Denton, TX 76205
940-367-4755
www.chministries.com

Child Abuse Prevention Resources

Strang Communication
The Guardian System
600 Rinehart Rd.
Lake Mary, FL 32746
1-800-451-4598
www.charismalife.com

Children's Books

Augsburg Fortress Publishers
100 S. Fifth St., Suite 700
Minneapolis, MN 55402
1-800-328-4648
www.augsburgfortress.org

Barbour Publishing, Inc.
      1810 Barbour Sr.
      Uhrichsville, OH 44683
      1-800-852-8010
      www.barbourpublishing.com

Christianbook.com
      P.O. Box 8000
      140 Summit St.
      Peabody, MA 01961-8000
      978-977-5060
      www.christianbook.com

Cokesbury
      201 Eighth Ave. S.
      Nashville, TN 37203
      1-800-672-1789
      www.cokesbury.com

Eerdmans Books for Young Readers
      255 Jefferson Ave., S.E.
      Grand Rapids, MI 49503
      1-800-253-7521
      www.eerdsman.com/youngreaders

Standard Publishing
      8121 Hamilton Ave.
      Cincinnati, OH 45231
      1-800-543-1353
      www.standardpub.com

Tommy Nelson
      P.O. Box 141000
      Nashville, TN 37214
      615-902-3306
      www.thomasnelson.com

Tyndale House Publishers
    351 Executive Drive
    Carol Stream, IL 60188
    1-800-323-9400
    www.tyndale.com

Warner Press, Inc.
    Church Sales Department
    P.O. Box 2499
    Anderson, IN 46018
    www.warnewpress.com

Children's Church Supplies/Resources

Axtell Expressions, Inc.
    Dept. CM, 230 Glencrest Cir.
    Ventura, CA 93003
    805-642-7282
    www.axtell.com

Betty Lukens, Inc.
    711 Portal Street
    Cotati, CA 94931
    1-800-541-9279
    www.bettylukens.com

Bible Candy
    1028 East Edna Place
    Covina, CA 91724
    1-877-643-8922
    www.biblecandy.com

Bring Them In
    11323 Hughes Rd.
    Houston, TX 77089
    281-481-8770
    www.bringthemin.com

Children's Ministry Today
    8469 Seton Ct.
    Jacksonville, FL 32244
    904-777-3339
    www.childrensministry.org

Group Publishing Company
    P.O. Box 485
    Loveland, CO 80539
    1-800-747-6060
    www.grouppublishing.com

KidMo!
    1113 Murfreesboro Road
    Suite 106-145
    Franklin, TN 37064
    1-877-610-2935
    www.kidmo.com

LifeWay Church Resources
    One Lifeway Plaza
    Nashville, TN 37234
    1-800-458-2772
    www.lifeway.com

One Way Street, Inc.
    P.O. Box 5077
    Engelewood, CO 80155-5077
    303-799-1188
    www.onewaystreet.com

Picture This!
    236 Castilian Ave
    Thousand Oaks, CA 91320
    (805) 499-9305
    www.bibledraw.com

The Train Depot
>3244 Commerce Center Pl.
>Louisville, KY 40211
>1-800-229-KIDS
>www.TrainDepot.org

Warner Press, Inc.
>Church Sales Department
>P.O. Box 2499
>Anderson, IN 46018
>www.warnerpress.com

Children's Music

Christianbook.com
>P.O. Box 8000
>Peabody, MA 01961-8000
>978-977-5060
>www.christianbook.com

Dean-o
>P.O. Box 3955,
>Mission Viejo, CA 92690
>1-866-656-2328
>www.biblebeatmusic.com

Integrity Music
>1000 Cody Rd.
>Mobile, AL 36695
>251-633-9000
>www.integritymusic.com

Mary Rice Hopkins
>1-877-MATILDA
>www.maryricehopkins.com

Tommy Nelson
P.O. Box 141000
Nashville, TN 37214
615-902-3306
www.thomasnelson.com

Children's Themed Environments

KidMo!
1113 Murfreesboro Road
Suite 106-145
Franklin, TN 37064
1-877-610-2935
www.kidmo.com

Wacky World Studios
148 E. Douglas Rd.
Oldsmar, FL 34677-2939
813-818-8277
www.WackyWorld.tv

Children's Videos/DVDs

Mary Rice Hopkins
1-877-MATILDA
www.maryricehopkins.com

Dean-o
P.O. Box 3955,
Mission Viejo, CA 92690
1-866-656-2328
www.biblebeatmusic.com

Integrity Music
1000 Cody Rd.
Mobile, AL 36695
251-633-9000
www.integritymusic.com

Standard Publishing
    8121 Hamilton Ave.
    Cincinnati, OH 45231
    1-800-543-1353
    www.standardpub.com

Tommy Nelson
    P.O. Box 141000
    Nashville, TN 37214
    615-902-3306
    www.thomasnelson.com

Tyndale House Publishers
    351 Executive Drive
    Carol Stream, IL 60188
    1-800-323-9400
    www.tyndale.com

Choir/Choral Resources

Brentwood Benson Music
    741 Cool Springs Blvd.
    Franklin, TN 37067
    1-800-846-7664
    www.brentwoodbenson.com

LifeWay Church Resources
    One Lifeway Plaza
    Nashville, TN 37234
    1-800-436-3869
    www.lifeway.com

Lillenas Publishing Company
    2923 Troost Ave.
    Kansas City, MO 64109
    1-800-877-0700
    www.lillenaskids.com
    www.lillenasdramas.com

Christian Books

Christianbook.com
> P.O. Box 8000
> 140 Summit St.
> Peabody, MA 01961-8000
> 978-977-5060
> www.christianbook.com

Christian Education Resources and Curriculum

Augsburg Fortress Publishers
> 100 S. Fifth St., Suite 700
> Minneapolis, MN 55402
> 1-800-328-4648
> www.augsburgfortress.org

Bible Visuals International
> P.O. Box 153
> Akron, PA 17501
> 717-859-1131
> www.biblevisuals.org

Caring Hands Ministries
> 309 Hollyhill Ln.
> Denton, TX 76205
> 940-367-4755
> www.chministries.com

Children's Bible Activities Online

Communication Resources
> 4150 Belden Village St.
> Fourth Floor
> Canton, OH 44718
> 1-800-992-2144
> www.BibleActivites.com

Christian Ed Publishers
>9230 Trade Pl.
>San Diego, CA 92126
>1-800-854-1531
>www.ChristianEdWarehouse.com

Cokesbury
>201 Eighth Ave. S.
>Nashville, TN 37203
>1-800-672-1789
>www.cokesbury.com

Cook Communications Ministries
>4050 Lee Vance View
>Colorado Springs, CO 80918
>1-800-323-7543
>www.cookministries.com

Creative Teaching Associates
>5629 E. Westower Ave.
>Fresno, CA 93727
>559-291-6626
>www.mastercta.com

Gospel Light
>2300 Knoll Dr.
>Ventura, CA 93003
>805-644-9721
>www.gospellight.com

Great Commission Publications
>3640 Windsor Park Dr.
>Suwanee, GA 30024-3897
>1-800-695-3387
>www.gcp.org

Group Publishing Company
    P.O. Box 485
    Loveland, CO 80539
    1-800-747-6060
    www.grouppublishing.com

Marketplace 29 A.D.
    P.O. Box 29
    Stevensville, MI 49127
    1-800-345-12AD
    www.marketplace29ad.com

Microframe Corporation
    P.O. Box 1700
    Broken Arrow, OK 74013
    1-800-635-3811
    www.nurserycall.com

Regular Baptist Press
    1300 N. Meacham Rd.
    Schaumburg, IL 60173
    1-800-727-4400
    www.rbpstore.org

Standard Publishing
    8121 Hamilton Ave.
    Cincinnati, OH 45231
    1-800-543-1353
    www.standardpub.com

Strang Communications
    Kids Church
    600 Rinehart Rd.
    Lake Mary, FL 32746
    1-800-451-4598
    www.charismalife.com

Upper Room Ministries
    1908 Grand Ave.
    Nashville, TN 37212
    1-800-972-0433
    www.pockets.org

Christian School/Daycare Programs

Betty Lukens, Inc.
    711 Portal Street
    Cotati, CA 94931
    1-800-541-9279
    www.bettylukens.com

Cokesbury
    201 Eighth Ave. S.
    Nashville, TN 37203
    1-800-672-1789
    www.cokesbury.com

Jtech Communications, Inc.
    6413 Congress Ave., Ate. 150
    Boca Raton, FL 33487
    1-800-321-6221
    www.jtech.com

Christian School Resources

Augsburg Fortress Publishers
    100 S. Fifth St., Suite 700
    Minneapolis, MN 55402
    1-800-328-4648
    www.augsburgfortress.org

Classroom Supplies

Christian Ed Publishers
    9230 Trade Pl.
    San Diego, CA 92126
    1-800-854-1531
    www.ChristianEdWarehouse.com

Church Ministries Distribution
    1-866-746-4263
    churchministriesdistribution.com

Regular Baptist Press
    1300 N. Meacham Rd.
    Schaumburg, IL 60173
    1-800-727-4440
    www.rbpstore.org

Communication Systems

Jtech Communications, Inc.
    6413 Congress Ave., Ate. 150
    Boca Raton, FL 33487
    1-800-321-6221
    www.jtech.com

Long Range Systems, Inc.
    9855 Chartwell Dr.
    Dallas, TX 75243
    1-877-416-4050
    www.pager.net

Microframe Corporation
    P.O. Box 1700
    Broken Arrow, OK 74013
    1-800-635-3811
    www.nurserycall.com

Seeker Nursery Paging Systems
3860 Canterbury Walk Dr.
Duluth, GA 30097
1-866-575-3713
www.seekercommunication.com

Craft Resources

Guildcraft Arts & Crafts
100 Fire Tower Dr.
Tonawanda, NY 14150
1-800-345-5563
www.vbscrafts.com

S and S Worldwide
75 Mil Street
Colchester, CT 06415
1-800-243-9232
www.ssww.com

Curriculum

Big Idea Productions
206 Yorktown Center
Lombard, IL 60148
630-652-6000
www.bigidea.com

Bring Them In
11323 Hughes Rd.
Houston, TX 77089
281-481-8770
www.bringthemin.com

Caring Hands Ministries
309 Hollyhill Ln.
Denton, TX 76205
940-367-4755
www.chministries.com

CharismaLife
600 Rinehart Rd.
Lake Mary, FL 32746
1-800-451-4598
www.charismalife.com

Christian Ed Publishers
9230 Trade Pl.
San Diego, CA 92126
1-800-854-1531
www.ChristianEdWarehouse.com

Cokesbury
201 Eighth Ave. S.
Nashville, TN 37203
1-800-672-1789
www.cokesbury.com

Cook Communications Ministries
4050 Lee Vance View
Colorado Springs, CO 80918
1-800-323-7543
www.cookministries.com

Gospel Light
2300 Knoll Dr.
Ventura, CA 93003
805-644-9721
www.gospellight.com

Great Commission Publications
    3640 Windsor Park Dr.
    Suwanee, GA 30024
    1-800-695-3387
    www.gcp.org

Group Publishing Company
    P.O. Box 485
    Loveland, CO 80539
    1-800-747-6060
    www.grouppublishing.com

Lay Renewal Ministries
    3101 Bartold Ave.
    St. Louis, MO 63143
    1-800-747-0815
    www.layrenewal.com

LifeWay Church Resources
    One Lifeway Plaza
    Nashville, TN 37234
    1-800-458-2772
    www.lifeway.com

Majesty Music
    P.O. Box 6524
    Greenville, SC 29606
    1-800-334-1071
    www.majestymusic.com

Marketplace 29 A.D.
    P.O. Box 29
    Stevensville, MI 49127
    1-800-345-12AD
    www.marketplace29ad.com

Radiant Light/Gospel Publishing House
    1445 N. Boonville Ave.
    Springfield, MO 65802
    1-800-641-4310
    www.GospelPublishing.com

Randall House Publications
    P.O. Box 17306
    Nashville, TN 37217
    1-800-877-7030
    www.randallhouse.com

Regular Baptist Press
    1300 N. Meacham Rd.
    Schaumburg, IL 60173
    1-800-727-4400
    www.rbpstore.org

Standard Publishing
    8121 Hamilton Ave.
    Cincinnati, OH 45231
    1-800-543-1353
    www.standardpub.com

The Train Depot
    3244 Commerce Center Pl.
    Louisville, KY 40211
    1-800-229-KIDS
    www.TrainDepot.org

WordAction Publishing Company
    2923 Troost Ave.
    Kansas City, MO 64109
    1-800-877-0700
    www.wordaction.com

Employment Resources/Services

Group Publishing's Available Church Positions Postings
        P.O. Box 485
        Loveland, CO 80539-0485
        1-800-635-0404 ext.4479
        www.cmmag.com

International Network of Children's Ministry
        P.O. Box 190
        Castle Rock, CO 80104
        1-800-324-4543
        www.incm.org

Event Planning Resources

Jtech Communications, Inc.
        6413 Congress Ave., Ate. 150
        Boca Raton, FL 33487
        1-800-321-6221
        www.jtech.com

Events for Children

Champions of Light
        6801 John F. Kennedy Blvd.
        North Little Rock, AR 72116
        501-835-2838
        www.championsoflight.org

Family Ministries Resources

Group Publishing Company
        P.O. Box 485
        Loveland, CO 80539
        1-800-747-6060
        www.grouppublishing.com

Flannelgraph

Betty Lukens, Inc.
        711 Portal Street
        Cotati, CA 94931
        1-800-541-9279
        www.bettylukens.com

Something Special for Kids
        Sam and Sandy Sprott
        1-800-Us 4 Kids

Gospel Magic and Performers

Dave and Jody
        Shine Like Stars, Inc.
        10945 Colorado Ct.
        Orland Park, IL 60467
        1-877-215-5933
        www.shinelikestars.org

Dock Haley Gospel Magic
        P.O. Box 915
        Hermitage, TN 37076
        615-885-4800
        www.Gospelmagic.com

Jeff Smith
        Salt and Light Ministries
        5105 Timbercreek Court
        Richmond, VA 23237
        804-743-8700
        www.salkandlightmin.org

Mark Thompson
        P.O. Box 2321
        Redmond, WA 98073
        800-867-6579
        www.markthompson.org

Ned and Joan Way
P.O. Box 19229
Louisville, Ky 40259
1-800-229-KIDS
www.NoWay.org

One Way Street, Inc.
P.O. Box 5077
Engelewood, CO 80155-5077
303-799-1188
www.onewaystreet.com

Steve Taylor
P.O. Box 822002
Vancouver, WA 98682
1-888-473-7869
www.stevetaylorpro.com

Internet Resources

Children's Bible Activities Online
Communication Resources
4150 Belden Village St.
Fourth Floor
Canton, OH 44718
1-800-992-2144
www.BibleActivites.com

Childrensministry.com
1-800-447-1070 www.childrensministry.com

Children's Ministry Today
8469 Seton Ct.
Jacksonville, FL 32244
909-777-3339
www.childrensministry.org

Christianbook.com
> P.O. Box 8000
> 140 Summit St.
> Peabody, MA 01961-8000
> 978-977-5060
> www.christianbook.com

For Kids Only, Inc.
> P.O. Box 10237
> Newport Beach, CA 92658
> 1-888-646-9584
> www.fko.org

Group Publishing Company
> P.O. Box 485
> Loveland, CO 80539
> 1-800-747-6060
> www.grouppublishing.com

Leadership Training

Kidology.org
> Karl Bastian
> 830 West Main Street #137
> Lake Zurich, IL 60047
> 847-620-2930
> www.kidology.org

Children's Ministry Magazine
> 6840 Meadowridge Ct.
> Alpharetta, GA 30005
> 1-800-704-6562
> www.cmmag.com/cmml2003

For Kids Only, Inc.
> P.O. Box 10237
> Newport Beach, CA 92658
> 1-888-646-9584
> www.fko.org

International Network of Children's Ministry
   Children's Pastors' Conference
   P.O. Box 190
   Castle Rock, CO 80104
   1-800-324-4543
   www.incm.org

Kids in Focus
   P.O. Box 1225
   Jamul, CA 91935
   Fax: 619-342-4474
   www.kidsinfocus.org

Magazines & Periodicals

Children's Ministry Magazine
   P.O. Box 481
   Loveland, CO 80539-0481
   760-738-0086
   www.cmmag.com

Group Publishing Company
   P.O. Box 481
   Loveland, CO 80539-0481
   760-738-0086
   www.groupmag.com

LifeWay Church Resources
   One Lifeway Plaza
   Nashville, TN 37234
   1-800-458-2772
   www.lifeway.com

The Children's Pastor
   P.O. Box 190
   Castle Rock, CO 80104
   1-800-324-4543
   www.incm.com

Ministry Consultants

Kids in Focus
P.O. Box 1225
Jamul, CA 91935
Fax: 619-342-4474
www.kidsinfocus.org

LifeWay Church Resources
One Lifeway Plaza
Nashville, TN 37234
1-800-458-2772
www.lifeway.com

Ministry to Today's Child
Pat Verbal
8415 Pioneer Dr.
Frisco, TX 75034
1-800-406-1011
www.ministrytotodayschild.com

Preschool Resources

Churchnursery.com
24 H.E. Wilson Ln.
Seabrooke, SC 29940
843-846-6339
www.churchnursery.com

Eerdmans Books for Young Readers
255 Jefferson Ave., S.E.
Grand Rapids, MI 49503
1-800-253-7521
www.eedermans.com/youngreaders

Group Publishing Company
    P.O. Box 481
    Loveland, CO 80539-0481
    760-738-0086
    www.grouppublishing.com

LifeWay Church Resources
    One Lifeway Plaza
    Nashville, TN 37234
    1-800-458-2772
    www.lifeway.com

Lillenas Publishing Company
    2923 Troost Ave.
    Kansas City, MO 64109
    1-800-877-0700
    www.lillenaskids.com
    www.lillenasdramas.com

Randall House Publications
    P.O. Box 17306
    Nashville, TN 37217
    1-800-877-7030
    www.randallhouse.com

WordAction Publishing Company
    2923 Troost Ave.
    Kansas City, MO 64109
    1-800-877-0700
    www.wordaction.com

Puppet Resources

Amaze Healing Wings
    Puppets with a Heart
    16804 Palm St.
    Hesperia, CA 92345
    760-244-8111
    www.amazehealingwings.com

Axtell Expressions, Inc.
Dept. CM, 230 Glencrest Cir.
Ventura, CA 93003
805-642-7282
www.axtell.com

Children's Ministry Today
8469 Seton Ct.
Jacksonville, FL 32244
904-777-3339
www.childrensministry.org

Maher Ventriloquist Studios
P.O. Box 420
Littleton, CO 80160
303-346-6819
www.maherstudios.com

One Way Street, Inc.
P.O. Box 5077
Engelewood, CO 80155-5077
303-799-1188
www.onewaystreet.com

Plushpups – MT&B Corporation
249 Homestead Rd.
Hillsborough, NJ 08844
1-800-682-1665
www.plushpups.com

The Puppet Factory, Inc.
P.O. Box 314
Goodland, KS 67735
785-899-7143
www.thepuppetfactory.com

Puppet Partners, Inc.
    1343 W. Flint Meadow Dr., #2
    Kaysville, UT 84037
    1-877-262-4117
    www.puppetpartners.com

The Train Depot
    3244 Commerce Center Pl.
    Louisville, KY 40211
    1-800-229-KIDS
    www.TrainDepot.org

Vacation Bible School Publishers

Augsburg Fortress Publishers
    100 S. Fifth St., Suite 700
    Minneapolis, MN 55402
    1-800-328-4648
    www.augsburgfortress.org

Big Idea Productions
    206 Yorktown Center
    Lombard, IL 60148
    630-652-6000
    www.bigidea.com

Caring Hands Ministries
    309 Hollyhill Ln.
    Denton, TX 76205
    940-367-4755
    www.chministries.com

CharismaLife
    600 Rinehart Rd.
    Lake Mary, FL 32746
    1-800-451-4598
    www.charismalife.com

Christian Ed Publishers
    9230 Trade Pl.
    San Diego, CA 92126
    1-800-854-1531
    www.ChristianEdWarehouse.com

Cokesbury
    201 Eighth Ave. S.
    Nashville, TN 37203
    1-800-672-1789
    www.cokesbury.com

Cook Communications Ministries
    4050 Lee Vance View
    Colorado Springs, CO 80918
    1-800-323-7543
    www.cookministries.com

Gospel Light
    2300 Knoll Dr.
    Ventura, CA 93003
    805-644-9721
    www.gospellight.com

Great Commission Publications
    3640 Windsor Park Dr.
    Suwanee, GA 30024
    1-800-695-3387
    www.gcp.org

Group Publishing Company
    P.O. Box 485
    Loveland, CO 80539
    1-800-747-6060
    www.grouppublishing.com

LifeWay Church Resources
    One Lifeway Plaza
    Nashville, TN 37234
    1-800-458-2772
    www.lifeway.com

Regular Baptist Press
    1300 N. Meacham Rd.
    Schaumburg, IL 60173
    1-800-727-4400
    www.rbpstore.org

Standard Publishing
    8121 Hamilton Ave.
    Cincinnati, OH 45231
    1-800-543-1353
    www.standardpub.com

Subject Index

Scripture Index

1. Minimum System Requirements

Computer/Processor
- o   Intel Pentium III or AMD Athlon with CD-ROM Drive

Operating System
- o   Windows 98 SE, Window ME, Windows 2000, or Windows XP including all Windows Updates

Memory
- o   128MB RAM

Hard Drive Space
- o   250 MB Minimum

Screen Resolution
- o   800x600 or Higher

2. Contact Information

Technical Support
Email: nelsoncdtech@thomasnelson.com
Web: www.nelsonreference.com
Phone: (615) 902-2440
Fax: (615) 902-2450

SOFTWARE LICENSE AGREEMENT

CAREFULLY READ THE FOLLOWING TERMS AND CONDITIONS BEFORE USING THIS SOFTWARE. Using this SOFTWARE indicates your acceptance of these terms and conditions. If you are not in agreement, promptly return the SOFTWARE package unused with your receipt and your money will be refunded.

LICENSE

The SOFTWARE may be used on a single machine at a time. This is a copyrighted software program and may not be copied, duplicated, or distributed except for the purpose of backup by the licensed owner.

The SOFTWARE may be copied into any machine-readable or printed form for backup, modification, or normal usage in support of the SOFTWARE on the single machine.

You may transfer the SOFTWARE and license to another party if the other party agrees to accept the terms and conditions of this Agreement. If you transfer the SOFTWARE, you must either transfer all copies, whether in printed or machine-readable form, to the same party or destroy any copies not transferred; this includes all modifications and portions of the SOFTWARE contained or merged into other software and/or software programs.

You may not use, copy, alter, or otherwise modify or transfer the SOFTWARE or database(s) or any add-on product's text except as expressly provided for in this LICENSE.

If you transfer possession of any copy or modifications of the SOFTWARE to another party, except as expressly provided for in the LICENSE, your license thereupon is automatically terminated.

LIMITED SOFTWARE `WARRANTY

LIMITED WARRANTY. *Nelson Electronic Publishing* warrants that, for ninety (90) days from the date of receipt, the computer programs contained in the SOFTWARE will perform substantially. Any implied warranties on the SOFTWARE are limited to ninety (90) days. Some jurisdictions do not allow limitations on the duration of an implied warranty, so the above limitation may not apply to you.

CUSTOMER REMEDIES. *Nelson Electronic Publishing's* entire liability and your exclusive remedy shall be, at our option, either (a) return of the price paid or (b) repair or replacement of SOFTWARE that does not meet *Nelson Electronic Publishing* Limited Warranty and that is returned to us with a copy of your receipt. This Limited Warranty is void if failure of the SOFTWARE has resulted from accident, abuse, or misapplication. Any replacement SOFTWARE will be warranted for the remainder of the original warranty period or thirty (30) days, whichever is longer. Outside the United States, neither these remedies nor any product support services are available without proof of purchase from an authorized non-U.S. source.

NO OTHER WARRANTIES. To the maximum extent permitted by applicable law, *Nelson Electronic Publishing* and its suppliers disclaim all other warranties, either expressed or implied, including, but not limited to, implied warranties of merchantability and fitness for a particular purpose, with regard to the SOFTWARE and the accompanying written materials. This Limited Warranty gives you specific legal rights. You may have others, which vary from state to state.

NO LIABILITY FOR CONSEQUENTIAL DAMAGES. To the maximum extent permitted by applicable law, in no event shall *Nelson Electronic Publishing* or its suppliers be liable for any damages whatsoever (including, without limitations, damages for lost business profits, business interruption, loss of business information, or any other pecuniary loss) arising out of the use of inability to use this product, even if *Nelson Electronic Publishing* has been advised of the possibility of such damages. Because some states do not allow the exclusion of liability for consequential or accidental damages, the above limitation may not apply to you.